GROUP PARENT EDUCATION

This book is dedicated to Minnesota's Early Childhood Family Education (ECFE) programs and especially to Betty Cooke and Lois Engstrom, Department of Children, Families, and Learning. They and all of the dedicated and committed ECFE staff across the state have pioneered and persevered in the development of this remarkable universal access system that supports all families through parent and family education throughout the state of Minnesota.

GROUP PARENT EDUCATION

Promoting Parent Learning and Support

Deborah Campbell
*Early Childhood Family Education,
Sauk Rapids – Rice School District*

Glen F. Palm
St. Cloud State University

SAGE Publications
International Educational and Professional Publisher
Thousand Oaks ▪ London ▪ New Delhi

For information:

Sage Publications, Inc.
2455 Teller Road
Thousand Oaks, California 91320
E-mail: order@sagepub.com

Sage Publications Ltd.
6 Bonhill Street
London EC2A 4PU
United Kingdom

Sage Publications India Pvt. Ltd.
B-42, Panchsheel Enclave
Post Box 4109
New Delhi 110 017 India

Printed in the United States of America

Library of Congress Cataloging-in-Publication Data

Library of Congress Cataloging-in-Publication Data
Campbell, Deborah, 1952-
Group parent education : promoting parent learning and support /
Deborah Campbell, Glen F. Palm.
      p. cm.
Includes bibliographical references (p.) and index.
ISBN 0-7619-2767-0
    1. Parenting—Study and teaching. 2. Group guidance in education.
I. Palm, Glen. II. Title.
HQ755.7.C348 2003
649′.1′071—dc21

                                         2003007166

03   04   05   06   10   9   8   7   6   5   4   3   2   1

Acquiring Editor:	Jim Brace-Thompson
Editorial Assistant:	Karen Ehrmann
Production Editor:	Sanford Robinson
Typesetter:	C&M Digitals (P) Ltd.
Copy Editor:	Elisabeth Magnus
Indexer:	Teri Greenberg
Cover Designer:	Michelle Lee

Contents

Preface

As teacher educators of graduate students preparing to become licensed parent educators, we have struggled to find an appropriate textbook for a class on working with parents in groups. This textbook has evolved out of that need and draws from our work as parent educators in Early Childhood Family Education (ECFE) programs in Minnesota, as well as from our roles as educators of future teachers.

Clearly, we are aware of the larger national parent education movement and have attended conferences and served in leadership positions for several different organizations, including Family Support America (formerly Family Resource Coalition), the National Council on Family Relations, the National Parenting Education Network, and the National Practitioners' Network for Fathers and Families. Working with colleagues in different parts of the country has given us a broader view of parent education nationally, as well as a deep appreciation for the unique value of ECFE in Minnesota.

We began teaching graduate classes that address parent and family education methods, group process, and adult education content by drawing on a number of books that had been published in the mid-1980s in addition to other more current articles. However, these resources were limited in their scope and tended to focus more on content and curriculum and less on group process, support, and facilitation. After designing most of our own materials and drawing on various other sources, we decided that a book was needed for our profession with more in-depth concentration on group process and facilitation. This text, therefore, focuses on the competencies and skills of effective parent educators and provides historical background and theoretical frameworks for understanding group parent education. In addition, information is presented on specific teaching methods, parent-child interaction experiences, and guided observation of children's behavior as important components of parent education groups. The book also explores reflective practice as the path to professional development for parent educators.

Although we understand the need for additional literature that addresses the practice of parent education, we have purposely avoided creating a generic parent education book that addresses all the skills and specific knowledge bases required. Areas such as curriculum development, adult education principles, evaluation, and assessment of parent education are not addressed. We recognize the need for knowledge of child and parent development, family relationships, and adult learning theory, and we assume that this will be presented in other areas of training. Understanding group process and dynamics and developing group facilitation skills are essential to effective parent education practice. They stand alone as an area of study and practice but also need to be combined with the other areas identified above to form a solid foundation for professional practice.

Many curricula provide brief introductions to group process strategies and adult education principles as preparation for teaching the curriculum content. Our experience and expertise within ECFE programs have provided us a very different approach to curriculum development and parent educator preparation. We prepare licensed parent educators to develop curriculum materials with and for groups of parents. Parents choose topics of interest, and skilled parent educators design individual sessions that address the topic, meet the needs of individual group members, and reflect current research and strategies, all within an approach of education and support. The art of group facilitation is a key ingredient in this process. In this book, we present group parent education as artistry rather than a collection of skills needed to implement a curriculum. We have learned a great deal from observing, mentoring, and working with experienced and gifted parent educators. Writing this book has pushed us to articulate some of the most important lessons from our experiences as educators, our professional involvement within the field, and our study of existing parent education literature.

Although our experience has been predominantly with parents of young children, ages birth through kindergarten, the information presented in this book is universal to all group parent education settings. Unlike other earlier parent education materials that tend to focus more on content, this book addresses the process and dynamics of group parent education. We encourage the reader to recognize the applicability of the material to any parent group setting.

One of the issues we considered was the need to consistently use either the term *group parent education* or the term *parent group education*. We saw the merit of using *group parent education* to acknowledge that there are many different formats for delivering parent education and that our major focus will be on parent education in groups, not on groups that are involved in parent education. This supports our decision to discuss parent education in a more general manner in Chapters 1 and 2 before moving into theories and practice.

Parent education research has tended to focus on short-term outcomes for different programs (Dembo, Sweitzer, & Lauritzen, 1985; Medway, 1989; Todres & Bunston, 1993). There has also been some research on different approaches to parent education (Hills & Knowles, 1987; Thomas, 1996). Parent education research has tended to concentrate more on intervention than prevention (Todres & Bunston, 1993). Some of the most rigorous studies have focused on parent training with clinical populations (Webster-Stratton, 2000). The research base for the effectiveness of parent education expanded during the 1990s and suggests that parent education as an intervention can be effective in changing parenting attitudes, parenting skills, and child behavior. Most parents in the past have enrolled in parent education classes because of perceived problems with their children (Long, 1997; Todres & Bunston, 1993). The emergence of universal-access parent education and support programs in states like Missouri, Minnesota, and Kentucky (Carter, 1996) has led to some initial study of programs that are more prevention oriented. These initial studies suggest positive changes in parent attitudes and knowledge in prevention-oriented programs (Cooke, 1992; Pfannenstiel, Lambson, & Yarnell, 1996).

Research in parent education has not addressed specific practice issues in group parent education. The content of our book is derived primarily from our clinical practice, observations, and theory interpretations from related fields. The field of parent education, and specifically group parent education, is fertile ground for research on such topics as group dynamics, parent educator characteristics, group composition, and implications of length of classes. The lack of a strong research base is a limitation, but the clinical practice base that has evolved over the last 20 to 25 years provides a rich source of information for the group parent education strategies that are presented in our book.

The issue of diversity is a challenge for the field of parent education. Diversity of family structure, family socioeconomic status levels, and culture are all important factors that influence parent education practice. Carter (1996) described two different approaches to addressing the issue of cultural diversity in parent education. The first is to create culturally specific curricula that promote the unique values, perspectives, and traditions of a group (Cheng Gorman & Balter, 1997). The second, and the approach we have chosen, is to prepare "culturally sensitive" practitioners who are aware of the differences in child-rearing practices and beliefs related to culture. There is limited evidence and discussion to support which approach may be most effective. Some contemporary authors (Hildebrand, Phenice, Gray, & Hines, 2000) attempt to identify culturally specific family beliefs and behaviors as a step toward cultural sensitivity through cultural knowledge and awareness. We struggled, as well, with the question of how to address diversity in the context of group parent education. We have chosen to stress sensitivity to diversity in a general sense through specific examples and by emphasizing the importance of working with all parent groups to define topics, issues, and values. We have intentionally chosen not to identify specific cultural and family structure characteristics that influence group parent education. We believe this approach tends to create stereotypes of cultural groups that may not be accurate or may even discount diversity within groups. We recognize the importance of diversity issues and the need to conduct further research and understand family and cultural diversity.

Audience

The primary audiences that will benefit from this book include both upper-level undergraduate and graduate students who are preparing to work with parents and families, providing group parent education and support services. This may include students in programs of family studies, social work, early childhood education, psychology, marriage and family counseling, or other helping professions. Professionals who currently provide parent education services in groups, such as nurses, educators, school counselors, social workers, family support workers, and marriage and family therapists, will also find the book useful as a specific guide for working with parents.

Unique Features

This textbook has a number of unique features.

- Theories and conceptual frameworks that provide multiple perspectives on understanding group process and dynamics and the role of the leader
- Examples and case studies to illustrate practical application of theories and strategies
- Practical strategies, language, and processes to use for intervention and referral
- Integrated approaches to teaching and facilitating parent groups
- Focus on parent-child interaction time as an important component of parent education and suggestions on how to integrate this format with parent group discussion
- In-depth analysis of parent group dynamics and practice approaches to difficult situations
- Description of reflective practice as a useful approach for promoting professional development and the framing of group parent education practice as artistry that combines intuition and technical skills

Acknowledgements

The authors wish to acknowledge the following people who supported us in writing and completing this book:

- The many parents and children in Early Childhood Family Education programs who have given us the opportunity to learn and grow as parent educators
- The parents and children in the Sauk Rapids–Rice (MN), Bobbinsdale (MN), and District 742 (St. Cloud, MN) Early Childhood Family Education program whose photographs appear in the text
- The parent education students who have participated in our classes and given feedback on early drafts of the book
- The professional parent educators we have observed, mentored, and learned from in our work as teacher educators and supervisors
- Jane Ellison, Karen Kurz-Riemer, Betty Cooke, and Ted Bowman for reading drafts of our work and giving constructive and helpful feedback
- Bill Doherty, at the University of Minnesota, whose levels of involvement model provided us with an important framework for encouraging parent educators to move beyond disseminating information to developing more meaningful relationships and involvement with families
- Nancy Kristensen for her experiences and insight about families with complex issues.
- Aline Auerbach, Delores Curran, Jean Illsley Clarke, Linda Braun, Jennifer Coplon, Phyllis Sonnenschein, and Ted Bowman, whose works we have used as a foundation for teaching about group process in the field of parent education
- Our spouses, Larry Campbell and Jane Ellison, and families, whose encouragement, support, and patience helped us complete this project
- Our children, who have taught us about the joys and challenges of parenting and the value of parent education and support for all parents

1

Group Parent Education

Rationale and Assumptions

Group parent education is alive and flourishing in thousands of programs across the United States and in other parts of the world (Bennett & Grimley, 2001; Carter, 1996; Long, 1997). A group of mothers of toddlers meets one morning a week in Chicago at a Family Resource Center to discuss some of the challenges of managing the energy and emerging independence of 2-year-olds. A group of fathers of Head Start children in California meet once a month to play with their children and talk about how to be involved in their children's lives in positive ways. A group of first-time parents of infants meet weekly in the evening for 8 weeks at a hospital in Washington, D.C., to learn more about infant development and the changing dynamics of family life. Parents of preteens meet for four evenings at a middle school in North Carolina to learn about puberty and the physical changes that 10- to 12-year-olds experience and how to support their children's learning and social development. A group of fathers in a state prison meet once a week for 3 months in Minnesota to learn how to create and maintain a supportive relationship with their children. In each of these programs, a parent educator is responsible for organizing the sessions and guiding parent learning in a group context.

This book is written to examine group dynamics in parent education groups where emotions are intense and the diversity of parent experiences creates a powerful and complex learning environment. Parent educators must understand group dynamics as well as individual needs and personalities as they guide parents in learning to trust each other, to listen to each other, and to understand typical child development and family changes while addressing

1

Photo 1.1   Parents of young children often attend parent and family education
                programs together.

immediate concerns. Facilitating parent groups is challenging work that demands parent educators who are skilled in working with diverse groups and individuals while facilitating group learning and maintaining a positive and supportive group environment.

This chapter will describe reasons that group parent education continues to be an effective format for supporting parent growth and development in contemporary society. The chapter's second section articulates basic assumptions about parents and group parent education that form the foundation for effective practice. The final section describes the major goals of the book and outlines the content.

Rationales for Group Parent Education

Why is group parent education an important and effective format for parent learning? This question will be addressed by looking at the changing social context for parenting and the changing needs of parents. Those participating in parent education groups range from middle-income fathers of infants in Florida to low-income single mothers in South Carolina, mothers of toddlers in a suburb in Minnesota, parents of children with disabilities in Washington, and parents of young children in family literacy classes in rural South Carolina (Carter, 1996). Group parent education programs are located in schools, community centers, prisons, and hospitals (Carter, 1996). These classes are sponsored by a variety of social agencies and address a complex array of parent needs (Smith, Cudaback, Goddard, & Myers-Walls, 1994). Parents come to parent education groups for many different reasons:

- To learn about child development
- To learn how to manage toddler tantrums
- To learn how to support child self-esteem through effective communication
- To learn how to keep their children safe
- To learn how to support and enhance child learning
- To understand new information about brain development
- To learn new strategies for discipline
- To discuss how to share child-rearing responsibilities with a partner

Parents come to parent education with many different goals and beliefs about parenting. They are looking for ideas and support to be good parents. Some people still believe that parents come to parent education classes only because they have problems managing their children's behavior. Many parent education programs are targeted toward parents who have children with behavior problems (Webster-Stratton, 2000). There are also parent education programs for parents who are going through divorce (McKenry, Clarke, & Stone, 1999) and for parents who are at risk for child abuse (Bavelok & Bavelok, 1988). The emergence of universal-access programs for parents of young children in Missouri and Minnesota during the last 25 years has begun to shift this view of parent education as a solution to problems toward a more inclusive view that parent education is a service that can be beneficial for all parents (Carter, 1996). Parent education can support individual growth and development as parents face typical challenges in the family life cycle as well as assist families who may be facing specific problems or stressors.

Parents today are more aware of the diverse resources available to them (e.g., classes, videos, books, magazines, and Web sites) to learn about parenting. They may also be confused by the conflicting advice of parenting experts (Simpson, 1997). Parents realize that the way that their own parents raised them may not be the most effective way to meet their own children's needs in a changing society. For example, the use of physical punishment as a discipline tool is now limited by child abuse laws that have changed standards for parent behavior. Many parents are acutely aware of the perceived faults and failings of their own parents and how these have influenced their own lives. Most parents today also face the task of balancing a career or work and family life in a fast-paced, information-rich society. Parents worry about their children growing up too soon and the dangers they may face as they move into a world where the media depict violence and explicit sexuality (Walsh, 2001). Many parents are having fewer children and don't want to or don't have the time to learn by trial and error, so they look to parent education and the support of other parents in parent groups as a guide to how to best raise their children. They realize that parent education can be a practical educational investment with long-term benefits for their children and family.

Group parent education remains a viable and powerful educational format to meet parent needs for support, information, a sense of community, and direct contact with other parents (Carter, 1996). The proliferation of parenting books, magazines, educational videotapes, and Internet sites has given parents greater access to information and a variety of perspectives on how to raise children (Simpson, 1997). Though these resources have made information readily available, they have also created a new set of issues for parents. Which sources are the most credible and useful? What happens when parents receive contradictory information from books and from their own parents, friends, and family doctors? Should parents put their babies to bed and let them cry for 5 minutes before they comfort them? Should they allow their child to sleep in the same room with them? Should they "train" babies to comfort themselves so they can put themselves to sleep? What happens when their baby gets an ear infection and is up most of the night after they have been trying for the last 2 weeks to get the baby to learn how to sleep on his or her own? Parents find groups of other parents a practical place to learn about what has worked for someone else, find out what is normal, and get support for making the right decision for themselves and their family. Parent groups can be a valuable source of both information and support for parents, especially when a knowledgeable, sensitive, and competent parent educator can help groups address important issues in a safe and supportive environment. Though parents may not always have the time to commit to group parent education, it is a place where many parents are able to form new networks of support and friendships as they face the perennial and contemporary challenges of parenthood.

Some parent education programs also provide the opportunity for parents to bring their young child to a class and spend part of the time together in an environment with other children of the same age engaging in fun and educational activities (Kurz-Riemer, 2001). In Minnesota, where both of the authors have worked in Early Childhood Family Education (ECFE) programs for the last 20 years, parents bring their children ages 0 through 5 to programs on a weekly basis for 2-hour sessions that include both parent-child time and parent discussion time. One advantage of this type of program is that parents are able to observe their children interacting with other, same-age children. They also are able to observe other parents and educators and how they interact with young children. Parents in this context are able to see and understand

Photo 1.2   Parents and infants enjoy an informal setting with floor time
                 activities.

typical child behavior and have a better understanding of their own children. They see that all 2-year-olds struggle with sharing toys. The parent educator also has an opportunity to observe both parent and child behavior and to better understand the dynamics and issues that a parent brings to a parent education session. A parent of a 2½-year-old son who is not interested in toilet training is given specific information about signs of readiness from the parent educator, and other parents in the group empathize about the frustration of trying to be patient and wait for a child to be "ready" when the parent is eager to be finished with diapers.

Parent education in groups has been an effective method for giving parents information and support for over 80 years (Auerbach, 1968; Braun, Coplon, & Sonnenschein, 1984; Brim, 1959; Carter, 1996). It continues to be an important service to parents and meets the needs of parents today by giving them information in a supportive context with face-to-face interaction with other parents. Parent education practice has evolved to include a variety of theories and perspectives on child rearing (Cowan, Powell, & Cowan, 1998). A new integration of these perspectives can guide parent educators toward skillful and reflective practice. Our understanding of parent growth, group process, family dynamics, parenting strategies, and child development has made the practice of parent education in groups more sophisticated and complex (Powell & Cassidy, 2001). The multiple perspectives that provide a foundation of content for parent education and the diverse family and community settings demand new ideas for integrating and matching of content to family and community needs (Powell, 1986). This book will integrate these perspectives to better illustrate how one can be an effective group leader with a variety of parent groups.

Parent education in groups can be very powerful as parents learn to trust each other and to share honest feelings about parenting. Parents are exposed to a variety of different ideas about discipline. A good parent educator helps parents to explore their own goals and values as well as individual child needs in considering how to select and use discipline strategies. Parents begin to appreciate that parenting is an important and complex set of responsibilities that deserves their best energy and efforts. Parent groups will often encounter emotional land mines when participants are trying to sort through their own emerging ideas about parenting from the legacy of their own experiences as children (Gadsden & Hall, 1995). The certainty of one parent about how to handle an eating issue with a 4-year-old can make two other parents in the group doubt their own effectiveness or competence as a parent. Parents may hear or observe other 3-year-olds who seem to be very well behaved while their own 3-year-old child is demanding, is always active, and never seems to listen to them. These represent special challenges that need to be handled effectively if the group experience is to help, not harm or undermine, parents' sense of competence.

Learning child development information and learning parenting strategies are initial steps in becoming effective parents. Parents must also decide what they value in terms of child behavior (Crary, 1993). Do they want their child to be a leader, to be obedient, to be sensitive to the feelings of others, to have good manners? They must consider all of the options for guiding a child's behavior while understanding their child as an individual with unique temperamental and personality characteristics (Kurcinka, 1989). Group parent educators come into contact with strong beliefs about parenting goals and strategies as well as raw, intense emotions related to childhood experiences and current feelings of success and failure. A parent educator must be prepared to guide parent learning and decision making where parents are deeply invested in doing the best they can because they love their children.

This book is designed to build on a long tradition of group parent education as a practical way to inform and support parents. Through effective group facilitation, parents can become more confident with new skills and understanding to experience the joys and manage the challenges of parenting. The next section outlines important assumptions about group parent education that guide current practice.

Assumptions About Parents and Parent Education

The practice of group parent education as described in this book rests upon a number of important assumptions about parents and the process of group parent education. The following assumptions provide a description of the beliefs and values that guide our perspective of group parent education.

1. *Parents care deeply about their children and want to be good parents.* The emotional bond between parent and child is intense, deep, and complex. The literature on attachment research provides some insight into the dynamics of this bond, primarily from a child's perspective (Karen, 1998). This assumption is also based on our observations and experiences with multiple parents in different settings over the last 20 years. Parents care deeply about their children and are motivated to be good parents and do what they think is best for their child (National Center on Fathers and Families, 1995). At the same time, many parents struggle with knowing how to express this caring and are often uncertain about which parenting approaches and strategies will be the most effective and appropriate for their child.

2. *All parents grow and learn through the challenges of parenting.* Parenthood is an important impetus for learning (Cowan & Cowan, 1988; Galinsky, 1987; McBride, 1973; Newman & Newman, 1988; Palm, 1993; Snarey, 1993). Most parents have developed some capacity for caring for their child before the child is born, and others learn it through the experience of parenting. Parenting is a challenge to most new parents. It also provides a unique opportunity for growth and development of cognitive and emotional skills in parents (Newman & Newman, 1988). Parent education in groups presents parents with information about child development and the typical issues that parents face. This provides some normalization of parent concerns and feelings. It also provides parents with new ideas about typical developmental issues. Group parent education provides a safe space to talk about parent-child relationships and honors the emotional depth of this bond. Parents as individuals have the potential to grow into more caring, other-directed, and empathic adults as they take on the responsibilities for child nurturance and guidance (Palkovitz & Palm, 1998). Group parent education can facilitate this growth by supporting parents through typical developmental transitions, as well as through periods of stress and crisis. Parent growth is acknowledged and affirmed in a supportive group context.

3. *Parents bring a unique combination of experiences and strengths to parenting.* Parents do not come as blank slates to group parent education (McGillicuddy-DeLisi, 1990). They come with their own experiences of growing up in different family settings. They have the imprints of the beliefs and practices

that their parents used in raising them. They bring their own images of good parenting. These ideas may coincide with how they were raised or may be in sharp contrast to their own parents' beliefs (Galinsky, 1987). All parents bring some understanding of parenting to a group parent education experience. They also bring unique strengths that can benefit the group in exploring effective parenting practices. Parent groups can be enriched by the diverse experiences and strengths of parents. The parent educator must tap into these resources by providing a safe space to explore these experiences and affirming the latent strengths that parents bring to a group (Curran, 1983; Family Resource Coalition, 1996).

4. *Parenting is shaped by parent beliefs, knowledge, and skills.* In working with parents in groups, it is important to address parent beliefs, parent knowledge, and parenting behavior. For example, parents may believe that children are born as innocent, blank slates to be inscribed with the values that parents hold most dear. Other parents may believe that children will have a natural tendency to try to manipulate parents and must be controlled in a strict and consistent manner so that they will not become spoiled and demanding children and adults. Parent beliefs are not always easy to understand, and parents may not hold a logically consistent set of beliefs. The parent educator must assist parents in clarifying and articulating their beliefs through thoughtful questions and sometimes gentle confrontation. The knowledge that a parent brings to a parent group may consist primarily of his or her own limited experience growing up in a small family with one or two siblings. It may also be based on formal education in child development or work experience with many different children in different circumstances. In this type of context, parents may have developed fairly sophisticated understandings and skills for managing a child's behavior. All of these experiences must be honored in a group parent education setting, for they all make up the rich resources that group members bring to the process of group parent education (Curran, 1989).

5. *Group parent education has a unique and enduring role to play in the evolving field of parent education.* Today there are numerous ways for parents to receive and process new information on child rearing. Printed information in books, parenting magazines, and newspaper columns has been a common source of information during the past 100 years and has continued to become ever more popular and accessible (Simpson, 1997). The introduction of video resources (i.e., TV programs about parenting, educational videos) and Internet resources has brought the advice of the experts into the privacy of parents' homes, where they can access this information at their convenience. Despite the increasing amount and accessibility of information and advice on parenting, the role of the parent group still plays an important function for many families. The group may replace some of the informal support systems that parents had in previous generations. Many new parents do not live close to

their own parents, who may also be less accessible as grandparents continue to work and pursue their own careers and interests. Many parents are also eager to hear about the challenges of parenting from peers facing similar issues unfamiliar to their own parents, who raised children in a different generation with different expectations and demands.

6. *Parents learn from each other and help define and understand norms while adjusting their own ideals with current realities.* Group parent education provides a unique social context for helping parents to define their own ideals and to compare these ideals with group norms. Galinsky (1987) described a model of parent growth and development that is based upon comparing ideal images of what children and parent-child relations should be like with the realities of parenting that they experience. The group context of parent education can give a parent of a toddler new understanding of the toddler's typical push for independence when the group discusses tantrums. Parents may also raise their expectations for their child if they see that other 2-year-olds are able to sit still during a snack time. Parents often use their observations of other children as a way to adjust their own expectations and behavior toward their children (Galinsky, 1987). The parent group provides an opportunity for parents to do this in a direct and interactive manner by discussing expectations, individual differences, and the most effective ways to guide their child toward acceptable behavior. Guided observation is a regular part of some parent education groups. Good parent educators are able to guide parent discussion and thinking toward a clear understanding of developmental norms and the application of these norms to individual children.

7. *Parents represent diverse family and community contexts, beliefs about parenting, and cultural values.* Parent educators must be able to understand and accept this diversity in parents and adapt their skills for different types of groups. Family diversity manifests itself in a variety of different ways that characterize family life in America today (Fine & Lee, 2000). First, family structure has been changing to include more single-parent families, more cohabiting couples, more gay and lesbian families, and more remarried families in addition to the two-parent married family (Demo, Allen, & Fine, 2000). Another area of family diversity that has a major impact on family life is employment. There are dual-career families, the more traditional breadwinner and stay-at-home parent family, and families where one parent works full time and the other parent works part time. In single-parent and extended family structures, employment patterns may also vary. The tension in our culture between working and stay-at-home mothers continues to be an issue that frequently emerges in parent education groups. Cultural diversity has been another important area of diversity that influences family life and must be considered in group parent education (Fine & Lee, 2000). The increasing numbers of children of color and the dramatic increase of new immigrants from all parts of the world present additional challenges to parent educators. Parent educators who work with

parents in groups must be able to understand the potential impacts of family diversity upon parent groups. It is often easier to facilitate a group that is more homogeneous. There may even be limits to group heterogeneity that parent groups can accommodate and still function effectively. The parent educator must bring parent differences out into the open in a respectful manner that helps parents to better understand both their own views and those of other parents. Diversity can be a powerful stimulant for new ways of thinking and acting as a parent. Diversity within parent groups can also be a powerful resource for learning and new understanding.

8. *Facilitating group parent education is an art that blends a parent educator's dispositions, skills, and knowledge to meet the needs of a specific parent group.* This artistry is honed through experience and reflective practice to increase the effectiveness of group parent leaders. Parent education has been provided by different professionals and paraprofessionals in a variety of contexts (Cowan et al., 1998). An underlying premise of this book is that group parent education is a complex task that requires specific preparation and development of competencies that lead to effective practice. The development of certification and licensure programs for parent educators has provided some of the important dimensions of preparation for this work. The National Council on Family Relations (NCFR) has created a framework for content areas for family life educators through the Certified Family Life Educator (CFLE) program (Powell & Cassidy, 2001). The Minnesota Board of Teaching has defined a specific set of teacher competencies for licensure in parent education. Parent group education as an art still needs to be more carefully explored to identify the boundaries and dimensions of this artistry. This book attempts to articulate the unique features of group parent education and to advance this artistry through a deeper understanding of parent group dynamics and effective group facilitation skills.

This book is written for parent educators who work with groups—both current practitioners and students at the undergraduate and graduate levels who are preparing to work with parents in groups. These students may be in parent and family life education, social work, early childhood education, or marriage and family therapy classes. It is written to apply to a variety of different parent groups, with the major emphasis on education versus therapy or peer support groups (Braun et al., 1984).

Goals for the Book

The book will address a number of important goals in attempting to move the practice of group parent education to a new integrated level of understanding that incorporates family diversity, a variety of theoretical perspectives, and best practices derived from the literature and our own clinical experiences. These goals include

1. *Understanding how parents learn and grow through group parent education.* It is important to understand how parents learn in the context of parent education groups and how they adopt new ideas and behaviors to use as they interact with their child. The sharing and processing of new ideas and feelings with a parent group provides multiple pathways to new learning.

2. *Understanding the various perspectives/theories that guide practice.* Parent education in groups has become more complex and sophisticated. It currently incorporates a number of different frameworks that must be understood at a basic level to see the benefits of each perspective. Multiple conceptual frameworks provide a unique blend of insights into the complex dynamics of parent group education.

3. *Understanding and managing diversity in parent groups.* The increase in diversity of family structures, cultural beliefs, and parenting practices makes the facilitation of parent groups more complex and challenging. This complexity can lead not only to more opportunities for learning but also to more potential hazards for parents who are trying to develop parenting beliefs and practices consistent with their values and goals for their children. Cultural beliefs and values about parenting are also evolving as families adapt to social changes. Many immigrant families, for example, face the challenge of adapting to U.S. values and laws about child-rearing and discipline practices.

4. *Understanding and managing the dynamic balance between education and support in parent groups.* Most parent education tends to include information for parents, as well as emotional support for the difficult choices that parents make and the stressful issues that today's parents face. Education and support are approached as dynamics that can be carefully blended and balanced. Some parents are looking for new ideas about child rearing, whereas others are seeking support for the challenges they are facing in raising an active toddler or a challenging older child.

5. *Understanding the important skills educators need to effectively facilitate parent groups.* We are learning more about group process as it applies to parent groups and the emotional content that parents bring to parent education sessions. This book articulates the specific skills that parent educators need to manage group dynamics and individual learning. This focus on skills is offered to help individuals examine their current facilitation skills to assess their strengths and to identify areas for improvement.

6. *Exploring common problems/challenges in group parent education and possible strategies for addressing these problems.* The book will address specific

problems that are common in parent groups today. It is helpful for group leaders to gain insight into these behaviors, to understand their possible origin and meaning. These situations will be examined along with a range of possible strategies to apply.

7. *Examining parent education services for families with complex needs and providing some guidelines and boundaries for practice.* Parent education has been seen as an important service for families with many different needs, including families with literacy needs, families with children with disabilities, and families with parents who have been neglectful or abusive. Parent group leaders need to understand the unique challenges of this work and to develop strategies that address some of the unique issues that they will face.

Summary

The continued importance of group parent education and the evolution and improvement of parent group education practice are the reasons for pursuing the goals in this book. Our understanding of parent group dynamics and effective practices has continued to grow through increasing knowledge about family, parent-child relationships, and adult education. The artistry that Auerbach described in her 1968 book provides a useful perspective for contemporary parent educators. This book is presented as an integration of our growing understanding of both theory and practice of group parent education. Reflective practice is described as an effective approach to supporting practice and moving the field toward a better understanding of promising practices.

Discussion Questions

1. Why are group parent education programs an appropriate and effective format for contemporary parents in the United States?

2. Do you agree with the statement that all parents care deeply about their children? Why or why not?

3. What does parent education as artistry mean to you?

2

The History and Evolution of Group Parent Education

We have seen that the leader in parent group education is part of a fascinating interplay of people and events in which he plays a decisive role. In taking on this role, he assumes responsibility to see that the group sessions become the learning experience for which the program is set up. The description of the procedures that facilitate this learning have naturally included what the leader does at various steps to help the parents achieve the group's goal. Obviously, his performance is not static or fixed. He acts in certain ways at certain times, as different stages of group development are reached and specific episodes occur. He acts as the particular moment requires and fits the immediate moment into the overall plan.

—A. Auerbach,
Parents Learn Through Discussion

The leader in a parent education group plays a dynamic role in the complex process of group parent education. This is a role that has evolved over time as our understanding of children, parenting, adult education, and group process has changed. This chapter will provide a brief historical review of the evolution of parent education in groups. The changing nature of parent education and the role of the group leader will be traced from the 1880s through the present. An integrative model of competencies for group leaders in parent education will be presented to reflect our current understanding of this role. This model also serves as a guide for self-evaluation and reflection on developing parent group facilitation knowledge and skills. An assessment tool is presented in Appendix A as a way to identify current strengths and limitations around competencies for parent group leadership.

Historical Overview of Group Parent Education

Parent education in groups has been traced back to the early 19th century, when groups of mothers in New England formed maternal associations (Berger, 2000). These groups, composed primarily of middle-class mothers, met and discussed issues such as discipline and moral training. They might be comparable to our contemporary parent support groups where parents share knowledge, experiences, and feelings as part of a mutual support and learning process. Early forms of mass media such as books and magazines about parenting followed from the 1820s through the 1840s (Sunley, 1955). Parenting was becoming a more specific area of study, as seen in the thoughtful reflections and writings that were being produced during this time. The information and support that parents (mothers) can share in a group setting about the joys and challenges of child rearing were experienced by parents at least 200 years ago. Though little is known about the early years of parent education in the United States, we have more extensive information about the evolution of parent group education over the past 100 years (e.g., Auerbach, 1968; Brim, 1959).

Auerbach (1968) described the early evolution of parent group education as carried on by the Child Study Association, which began in 1888. "At that time a small group of mothers came together to get the best information they could find to help them understand and deal with their children" (p. 14). The fields of academic psychology, child development, and psychoanalysis began to develop a knowledge base that was shared with parents to improve their understanding of child development and to suggest effective parenting techniques. This information was shared with parents through public meetings, conferences, and written materials. Parents were eager to learn about child psychology and to use this information generated by research and clinical practice to guide and improve their child rearing and family lives. The small discussion groups for parents that emerged in the 1920s were often led by professionals in child psychology and parent education who shared knowledge about child development and parenting techniques with parents in a lecture and discussion format (Anderson, 1930).

Parent education as a unique field of study began developing important roots during the 1910s in several different areas. Public health nurses, social workers, early childhood educators, psychologists, and home economics educators all used the emerging knowledge base about child development and effective parenting to provide parent education services to different populations of parents. Public health nurses provided information on child rearing and health-related issues through home visits to low-income families. Health-related information about issues like feeding infants was important to infant well-being during this time, when the infant mortality rate was very high. Social workers provided information on parenting to poor immigrant families through settlement house programs in urban areas to help parents adjust to life in the United States. Psychologists and early childhood educators were more likely to work with middle-class parents in study groups or nursery school settings, sharing the latest research and theory about child development. The 1920s was a particularly active time for parent education, which was connected to progressive education and the recognition of the importance of parents in children's early learning (Arlitt, 1932). The development of parent education services through different formats and the development of academic training for parent educators took place during this time (Anderson, 1930).

Discussion groups led by trained parent educators were popular in the 1920s and 1930s (Arlitt, 1932). The first groups were conducted in a didactic manner as lectures, with the leader playing the role of a teacher. Auerbach (1968) described the evolution from the 1920s to the 1950s of different approaches to parent group education:

> At first, groups were conducted didactically, with the leader acting as the teacher in the traditional, academic sense. They then became lecture-discussions, with the leader acting as a speaker and answering questions in a discussion period. Subsequently, they took the form of discussion groups, in which parents learn through participation in the group process. (p. 14)

In this last approach to group parent education, the increasing knowledge about group dynamics and effective group facilitation skills emerged as important competencies for guiding parent learning. The study of small-group behavior in the 1940s and 1950s influenced the changes in our approaches to group parent education and recommended a more active role for parents in defining and discussing parenting issues (Auerbach, 1968).

The continued development of group parent education during the 1950s and 1960s built on this new understanding of group process and how learning could be facilitated in groups rather than taught in a more traditional lecture format. Auerbach (1968) described various trainings for parent group facilitators, from social work students and early childhood educators to public health nurses and church leaders, that she conducted during the 1960s. These trainings were directed at different groups of professionals who were parent education practitioners. Each group came to parent education training with a different set of skills and a unique knowledge base that was developed in their professional discipline and related preparation. A generic set of skills for parent group leaders emerged from these training efforts and was applied to each group in different ways to build upon their already acquired knowledge and skill base. For example, social workers might have experience with group therapy and understand group dynamics around emotional issues but might have limited information about child development and use of the group to stimulate learning new knowledge and skills. A variety of institutions continued to sponsor group parent education during this time. The mental health of children rather than their physical health was the primary focus of parent education during these two decades, as the knowledge base about child social and emotional development became a primary focus (Brim, 1959).

New parent education initiatives continued to emerge during the late 1960s and 1970s. These were often organized around targeted populations of parents who "needed" parent education. The Head Start program as a part of the War on Poverty focused on low-income children and their parents. Though initially the program was an early education intervention for young children, it soon became obvious that parents were essential partners in this intervention process (Bronfenbrenner, 1978). Parent education was one way to teach parents effective ways to support and reinforce early education lessons at home. Parent education services were often delivered on an individual basis through home visits. The group parent education model was included and fit well with the Head Start philosophy of working collaboratively with parents. Parents of children with disabilities were another target population who participated in group parent education (Auerbach, 1968; Braun et al., 1984). Parent education was also developed as a primary prevention strategy to combat child abuse and neglect during the1970s and 1980s (Bavelok & Bavelok, 1988).

A renewed interest in parent education for parents of young children occurred in the 1980s and 1990s in response to dramatic family changes and a renewed focus on the importance of parent-child relationships. Both Missouri and Minnesota initiated state-level, universal-access programs that used group parent education as the primary format for educating parents. There were also numerous targeted initiatives for parent and family education in other states during this time (Family Resource Coalition, 1996). Parent education for parents of young children continued to flourish in a variety of contexts such as community family resource programs, early childhood programs, early childhood special education programs, and health care programs.

Thomas and Cooke (1986) examined parent education services in Minnesota during the early 1980s. They discovered that parent education services were offered in a variety of settings, such as hospitals, schools, early childhood programs, mental health agencies, churches, and social service agencies. This study introduced the word *embeddedness* to describe the role of parent educator in these different institutional settings. This concept acknowledges that most people who deliver parent education services do so as part of a larger professional identity such as social worker, psychologist, public health nurse, pediatrician, or early educator. Parent educator is not their primary role or identity, but it is one of the important functions that they fulfill in their role as helping professionals. The diversity of parent education services in different settings in the 1980s and 1990s reflects the deep roots that have continued to grow from the early part of the 20th century and that have sprouted numerous new branches over the past 25 years. This diversity has also made it difficult to develop a common understanding about what parent education is or whether it should develop its own professional identity (Carter, 1996). Consequently, parent education groups are facilitated by a wide variety of lay and professional leaders with different levels of preparation and different approaches to educating parents. The knowledge base that supports parent education practice (i.e., child development, adult education, group process and dynamics) has continued to expand, yet the development of parent education as a unique profession has been stymied by the lack of consensus on who should facilitate parent education groups and what level of preparation is needed to work with different groups of parents and families.

Defining Parent Education

Some of the current confusion about parent education can be traced to both changing definitions and different contexts for defining parent education. Initially, parent education had the specific focus of improving parent knowledge of child development and introducing effective techniques for child rearing. Some of the confusion about the purpose and scope of parent education has come from conceptual models that define parent education as one approach to parent involvement in education programs or see it as one aspect of parent support services in the community (Epstein, 1995; Family Resource Coalition, 1996). Family support is defined by Dunst (1995, quoted in Carter 1996) as "a broad array of services and activities that are designed to enable and empower by enhancing and promoting individual and family capabilities that support and strengthen family functioning in general and parenting capabilities specifically" (p. 8). The specific meaning and role of group parent education can get lost in these broader contexts of parent involvement in education settings and community family support.

The National Parenting Education Network (NPEN) has developed the definition of parent education that will be used in this book. Carter (1996) described NPEN as a group of parenting education leaders who are working together to strengthen the field of parenting education. NPEN (1999) defined parent education as "a process that involves the expansion of insights, understanding, and

Photo 2.1   School settings provide a comfortable atmosphere for parent groups.

attitudes and the acquisition of knowledge and skills about the development of both parents and their children and the relationship between them."

This definition provides a clear focus on important goals and the process for parent growth and changes. It is a good fit for understanding group parent education. The parent group provides fertile ground for the growth described by this definition. It also provides the flexibility to address the multiple goals and needs of contemporary parents. The focus is on the educational process, which takes advantage of the strong affective component of parenting to support parent growth.

The development of specific curriculum materials (e.g., Systematic Training for Effective Parenting [STEP], Parent Effectiveness Training [PET], Active Parenting, the Nurturing Program), coupled with some skepticism about professionals and experts on parenting, led to the development of more parent education support groups and peer-led parent education groups (Hamner & Turner, 1996). The idea that the genuineness and practical knowledge of experienced parents make them the most effective parent educators has a wide appeal. This is especially true given that parenting experts don't agree about the best ways to rear children and parents are sometimes confused about which advice to follow. Minnesota Early Learning Design (MELD, 2002) is a good example of peer-led parent education. The MELD program recruits parents who have participated in a parent group, providing them with some training on group facilitation skills and supplying curriculum materials to conduct parent education/support groups. This approach has been adopted as a model by many programs in the United States, and MELD provides excellent training and support for these groups. There are also professionals from a variety of disciplines (social work, nursing, psychology, and early childhood) who continue to function as parent group leaders. There have also been some efforts to create a more defined professional role for parent educators and family life educators through focused preparation programs that lead to a license or certificate in parent or family life education (Powell & Cassidy, 2000).

Minnesota is one state that has developed a Parent Educator teaching license. The license has attracted people from a variety of different disciplines and built upon previous college course work and work experiences. The initial license in the mid-1970s identified a specific set of course requirements that were necessary to complete a parent educator licensure program. The development of the Early Childhood Family Education (ECFE) program in Minnesota created a new impetus and need for more specific training for parent educators. A new license was created in the 1980s that required a bachelor's-level degree and course work in child development, parent education, family relations, adult education, group process, and parent education methods. A student teaching experience was also required to gain practical experience leading parent groups under the supervision of a licensed parent educator. These requirements replicated teacher-training programs for K-12 teachers during this time. This specific licensure program went through further revisions in the mid-1990s as all teaching licenses moved to a competency-based model, where students were required to demonstrate the general competencies of effective teaching and the specific competencies of parent education. Other examples of this movement toward specific professional preparation are the Certified Family Life Educator (CFLE), created by the NCFR, and Family Support credential, created for family support workers in New York through a program at Cornell University (Powell & Cassidy, 2001).

Braun et al. (1984) attempted to draw some important distinctions about group services for parents. They described three distinct types of parent groups: the support or self-help group, the education group, and the therapy group. These distinctions are helpful in defining some boundaries for the practice of group parent education. There is still some uncertainty about the boundaries between therapy and education, with the broadening of goals for parent education and new, more challenging populations of parents that are often served by parent education programs (e.g., family literacy programs, incarcerated parents). The National Extension model of parent education (Smith et al., 1994) carefully articulates a set of interconnected goals for parent education that includes a variety of "critical parenting practices" such as guidance, nurturance, care for self, understanding, teaching, and advocacy. These goals match a more diverse and holistic set of needs of parents in the late 1990s and reflect the complexity of parenting today. With regard to goals, methods, and providers, group parent education does differ in some important ways from parent support or self-help groups and from therapy groups (Braun et al., 1984). Each of these services can play an important role in supporting good parenting.

The focus on parent education as a unique professional field begins to define some boundaries that allow the field to grow in depth, not just breadth. This growth can lead to more thoughtful and more effective practice. The Braun et al. (1984) book on group parent education described practice at a very concrete level. It made a strong case for the importance of parent education as a unique category and defined a specific knowledge base, personal characteristics, and skills that parent educators should acquire. These are very similar to the descriptions that Auerbach (1968) presented 15 years earlier. The addition of more specific educational methods by Braun et al. (1984) provided a more balanced view of the parent educator role that blends both group facilitator and educator roles and skills. Auerbach's description of parent education practice and the need for balance in a number of areas also reflected a deep understanding and appreciation for the artistry of parent education. Both Auerbach (1968) and Braun et al. (1984) understood the importance of the role of the parent group leader and contributed to our current knowledge of effective practices in group parent education. Kumpfer and Alvarado (1998) also placed a strong value on the role of parent educator in their description of factors that influence the quality of parent education programs.

Lessons From History

The evolution of group parent education over the past 100 years illustrates a shift from an emphasis on didactic teaching about children and child-rearing techniques to a complex interplay of sharing information, employing interactive teaching methods, and facilitating parent discussion. The art and science of group parent education have both become more sophisticated. The scientific gains are reflected in the growing knowledge base about child development, family life, and parent-child relations. Advances in artistry are seen in the growing appreciation of family diversity, where family culture and values, family structure, and socioeconomic status are all perceived as important factors in understanding families and designing engaging and effective educational methods. The development of preparation programs for parent educators has helped to more clearly define a baseline of knowledge, dispositions, and skills that support effective parent education. Research on the efficacy of parent education has focused primarily on parenting programs as defined by a specific curriculum. There has been limited research on the parent educator as a variable in the effectiveness of parent education programs. Kumpfer and Alvarado (1998) estimated that the "quality of the trainer" accounts for between 50% and 80% of the quality of the program. The preparation of parent group leaders may be the most important factor in improving program quality, yet this has not been the focus of parent education research and evaluation studies (Kumpfer & Alvarado, 1998; Medway, 1989; Todres & Bunston, 1993).

Several important lessons can be gleaned from this brief overview of the history and evolution of group parent education:

1. *Parent education has deep roots related to a variety of disciplines and professional roles.* Parent education is often embedded in and one of the functions of a larger professional role such as nursing or social work. No one discipline has focused on parent education in any depth. It is clearly a multidisciplinary field. There have been a couple of attempts to create a separate identity for parent educators. The late 1920s and the early 1930s literature indicate a strong effort to create a professional identity through the definition of specific educational requirements and the development of a professional organization with a journal (Anderson, 1930). This early initiative faltered after the Laura Spellman Rockefeller Foundation withdrew funds during the mid-1930s (Brim, 1959). More recent attempts have come during the last 20 years through the development of licensure and credential programs in parent and family education (Powell & Cassidy, 2000). It is likely that the field will continue to exist in a variety of institutions and that professionals will remain embedded in other disciplines. The development of a unique profession for parent educators remains uncertain despite the growing knowledge and skill base that has been identified.

2. *The goals of group parent education will continue to expand and to reflect the multiple roles of parents and the complexity of parenting today* (Smith et al., 1994). Groups for parents continue to expand and become more focused on age of child, level of child ability, family culture, and family structure (Carter, 1996). This movement challenges parent group leaders to be better prepared to address the diversity of parent needs and to work closely with parents in identifying their needs and developing effective group parent education programs.

3. *The practice of group parent education will continue to evolve as the art of balancing education and support, group and individual needs, factual information and feelings, needs of parents and needs of children, and needs of mothers and needs of fathers* (Auerbach, 1968). Facilitating parent education groups effectively is a real art requiring both sensitivity and skill. Parent group leaders must contend with a growing body of factual knowledge as well as the increasing

awareness of family diversity. Practice of group parent education will benefit from clearer boundaries, more research on the quality of parent educators, and more carefully defined preparation programs. The identification of promising practices through increased research and reflective practice will also help to improve the art of group parent education.

This historical overview provides some background for understanding the current state of the art of group parent education. The final section of this chapter provides a detailed description of important competencies for parent group leaders. These competencies represent an integration of different ideas about effective group leaders that are organized into three categories. The set of competencies also serves as a framework for self-assessment and reflection for parent group leaders.

Competencies for Parent Group Leaders

The competencies for parent educators are presented in three different categories: knowledge, dispositions, and skills. These three areas are borrowed from teacher preparation models. This list of competencies is presented as a specific description of knowledge, skills, and dispositions that have emerged from the literature on group parent education (Auerbach, 1968; Braun et al., 1984; Powell & Cassidy, 2000). The competencies that have been identified as general areas of knowledge for parent education include child development, family dynamics, parent-child relationships, adult learning, community resources, diverse family systems, and group dynamics and group facilitation skills (Auerbach, 1968; Braun et al., 1984; Kurz-Riemer, 2001). In the section that follows, the focus is specifically on group dynamics and group facilitation skills, which are the primary focus of this book.

KNOWLEDGE

The following are areas of knowledge that are specifically related to understanding group dynamics and facilitating parent learning in a group context:

1. Understanding the developmental stages of group process as applied to parent groups

2. Understanding theories of group dynamics that can be applied to parent groups

3. Understanding the roles and boundaries of the parent group leader

4. Understanding the emotional aspects of parenting issues and how these influence parent group learning

Photo 2.2   Parents gain support from sharing ideas and issues.

5. Understanding different leadership styles and their effects on parent group behavior

6. Understanding a variety of ways to assess parent and family strengths and limitations in the context of parent groups

7. Understanding a variety of active learning methods to assist parents in solving problems and making decisions

8. Understanding and being aware of various community resources for parents and families and how to connect parents to these resources

9. Understanding family and community diversity and how diverse values and beliefs influence parenting behavior as well as parent group dynamics

DISPOSITIONS

The category of dispositions refers to character traits and emotional attitudes that have been identified as important for parent educators (Auerbach, 1968; Braun et al., 1984; Clarke, 1984). These are different from general personality traits or types such as introvert and extrovert. Each individual will have his or her own unique blend of these dispositions:

1. *Maturity:* Parent group leader is clear about his or her own identity and able to clearly focus on the needs and issues of parents in the group.

2. *Caring:* Parent group leader is able to focus on the needs of parents and demonstrate understanding, compassion, and support for parents.

3. *Nonjudgmentalness:* Parent group leader appreciates the complexities of parenting and accepts parents without blaming them for their problems or mistakes. The focus is on helping parents and understanding that there are no easy answers.

4. *Sensitivity:* Parent group leader is able to perceive and respond to individual parents' needs and feelings.

5. *Organization:* Parent group leader is able to express goals clearly and provide direction toward parent learning.

6. *Flexibility:* Parent group leader is able to change direction as needed and balance between individual and group needs of parents.

7. *Creativity:* Parent group leader is able to design interesting and engaging parent sessions.

8. *Enthusiasm/Optimism:* Parent group leader has a positive attitude about people and the subject matter and is able to excite parents about learning.

9. *Honesty:* Parent group leader is clear about his or her own knowledge and limitations.

10. *Genuineness:* Parent group leader is honest and open in his or her relationships with parents

11. *Humor:* Parent group leader is able to appreciate and express what is humorous without ridiculing people or their problems.

SKILLS

Below are general skill areas followed by specific behavioral indicators to assist parent educators in assessing their group skills.

1. Creates a warm and welcoming environment
   a. Greets each parent or family member in a welcoming manner
   b. Demonstrates a genuine interest in parent and child well-being
   c. Uses effective openings for a session and involves parents in an engaging and nonthreatening manner

2. Creates a safe environment for parents to share ideas and feelings
   a. Helps group establish and implement ground rules
   b. Elicits a variety of opinions, values, and philosophies from parents
   c. Affirms parents in a genuine and supportive manner

3. Guides a discussion, giving it form and structure
   a. Informs parents of agenda and goals for the session

   b. Helps parents identify needs and concerns
   c. Keeps the group focused on the group goals and the topic of discussion
   d. Asks clarifying questions to better understand parent issues
   e. Restates and clarifies parent ideas/issues
   f. Summarizes important ideas/issues

4. Models acceptance of each individual as someone to be listened to and respected
   a. Listens carefully to parents
   b. Gives nonverbal messages of acceptance
   c. Accepts and acknowledges negative feelings and distress
   d. Restates and/or acknowledges parent contributions to the discussion
   e. Addresses diversity and facilitates discussion around differences in values, culture, and family structure

5. Takes responsibility for establishing a positive and supportive learning environment
   a. Helps parent to identify and set their own goals
   b. Invites parent participation, using a variety of methods
   c. Challenges parents to evaluate and reconsider their ideas
   d. Uses concrete examples to bring abstract concepts to life
   e. Adapts information to meet different parent capabilities

6. Fosters relationships and interaction among group members
   a. Encourages participation of all of the group members
   b. Connects parent comments and experiences to point out common themes
   c. Engages the group in problem solving for individual group members
   d. Addresses conflicts in direct and respectful manner

The self-assessment tool in Appendix A, which is based on the knowledge-disposition-skills categorization of parent group leader competencies, should be used to identify current strengths and possible areas for improvement. When using this tool for self-assessment, it is important to remember that the tool was not developed to present the profile for an ideal or perfect group parent educator. No one should expect to develop all of these competencies to their highest levels. The unique profile that is obtained from completing the tool will reflect your personality, previous preparation, and experience. Your reflection on this profile should help you as a practitioner to feel more comfortable with and appreciate your strengths as well as identify potential areas for professional development. Use it as a guide for self-understanding and improvement, not as a report card of your competencies.

Summary

Chapter 2 provides an overview of the history and development of group parent education with a specific focus on the last 100 years. Examining these historical roots elucidates some of the issues that continue to challenge parent education today, including the meaning of parent education, the practice of parent education in many different contexts, and the complexity of the role of parent group leader. This complexity is demonstrated through the integration and description of competencies that parent group leaders need to acquire to become effective in their work with parents. This careful description of the knowledge and skill base for parent group leaders forms the foundation for the information presented in the remaining chapters.

Discussion Questions

1. What are the major changes in the approach of professionals to group parent education over the past 100 years?

2. Why is the role of the group parent educator more complex today than it might have been in 1930?

3. How has embeddedness of parent education shaped our current practice? What are the advantages and disadvantages of this characteristic of the field?

3

Conceptual Frameworks, Part I

Models for Understanding Group Dynamics

Parent education groups represent a variety of different purposes that range from teaching parents specific behavioral techniques to sharing stories and support about the trials of being new parents to challenging traditional attitudes about discipline. To provide a better understanding of the complex dynamics in different parent education programs, key conceptual frameworks will be outlined. A conceptual framework is composed of a set of concepts and assumptions related to practice that are woven together to elucidate important dynamics of parent learning and support in group parent education. These perspectives mirror the different theoretical frameworks that have been used for understanding families. The first two frameworks have been applied to group dynamics in very specific ways and parallel family processes of development and instrumental and expressive family functions. The systems theory and feminist frameworks offer additional insights into parent group dynamics based on concepts used to understand family dynamics. This chapter will provide an introduction to four frameworks that will be used throughout this book. It will also describe the primary contributions of each framework for understanding parent learning and parent group dynamics. Each framework or perspective makes a unique contribution to our understanding of group parent education.

These frameworks are not fully articulated and tested theories about parent groups. They are carefully constructed sets of concepts based on family theories and group practice that have been applied to parent education practice. The research emphasis in parent education has been on curriculum format, content,

Photo 3.1   Parents of infants in parent education groups often form new
friendships as they share common experiences.

and program outcomes, not on group dynamics. The purpose of describing
different conceptual frameworks here is to acknowledge different ways of thinking about parent groups. They reflect different assumptions, goals, and strategies for facilitating parent groups. Together they represent a patchwork
understanding of groups and group dynamics that can be integrated into
useful guidelines for practice.

The first framework, the developmental perspective, describes how a group
changes over time in predictable ways (stages). The functional approach, a second
framework, examines the two basic functions of groups and how these apply to
group parent education. A third, a systems perspective, utilizes systems theory
concepts such as open and closed systems, goal-generating systems, and synergy
to describe salient aspects of group dynamics in parent education. A fourth
perspective, a feminist framework of gender-responsible leadership (Van
Nostrand, 1993), uses gender as a critical concept for understanding parent group
dynamics, parent roles, and power. Chapter 4 will outline three additional conceptual frameworks that focus on different perspectives for understanding the
role of parent group leader. These two chapters introduce the theoretical founda-
tions for group parent education. They help to describe and explain different
ideas about parent group dynamics and the role of parent group leader.

Framework 1: The Developmental Perspective—Stages of Group Development

The life cycle of a group tends to progress through several predictable stages, following patterns typical of other developmental stage theories for children, adults, and families. Parent groups, like other groups, are dynamic; they possess an energy that moves them through a variety of experiences that encourage learning. The developmental perspective of groups indicates that they, like other living things, have a cyclical pattern of growth and development. This section will examine stages of group development and how these stages apply to parent group dynamics.

A commonly accepted theory of group development identifies five separate stages: forming, norming, storming, performing, and adjourning (Curran, 1989). Each stage has specific characteristics and goals that require careful attention from the group leader. Group members have particular needs, as well as tasks to accomplish during each stage toward the common purpose of group learning and support in group parent education. It is helpful for the parent educator to be aware of the dynamics and behaviors during each stage so that he or she can respond to them and assist the group in moving to the next stage.

There are, however, some limitations in applying the stages of development framework to all parent groups. Groups must be ongoing and of sufficient duration for these stages to occur. Parent groups that meet a limited number of times (fewer than four times) may exhibit some of the characteristics of individual stages; however, an ideal representation of group development will typically occur in groups that meet for longer periods of time. Additionally, there is generally overlap between the stages (Corey, 2000). Groups may move back and forth between stages or may move quickly through one and perhaps become stuck in another. The stages, therefore, should not be seen as absolute or as following a preordained time frame. Finally, group membership and characteristics can greatly influence the stages of development. For example, if established groups are open to new members, the developmental progress may be affected when new parents join. Members who enter an existing group have not experienced the previous stages and will need to proceed from a different point. Their presence also changes the structure of the group, and this variation may interfere with the group's progress. Past experiences of parent participants may also change the development of groups. Members who have had other experiences in groups, who know each other or the parent educator, or whose personalities make them comfortable or uncomfortable with the group experience can influence group development. Group development theory helps parent educators to understand typical stages, but each group is unique and will experience its own version of the group life cycle.

STAGE 1: FORMING

Groups begin with the forming stage. In this initial stage, the group is coming together as members get to know each other and the leader. The forming stage should feel safe as parents begin the group experience, perhaps with some uncertainty about what it will be like. Parents may "be on their best behavior," and the overall atmosphere can be described as polite. Time is spent on practical matters, as well as sharing information regarding the purpose of the group and discovering common interests of the group members. There may be some small talk, with guarded self-disclosure, as members begin to make informal connections to other individuals in the group.

During the forming stage, parents may have questions such as

- "Will I be accepted in this group?"
- "Do I belong here?"
- "Can I be myself?"
- "What will this experience be like? Will it be what I expected?"
- "Are there other members with whom I feel comfortable?"
- "Will I get my needs met here?"

Goals for the parent educator are to share the necessary basic information about the group, to set a positive, welcoming tone, and to help parents feel comfortable and get acquainted with each other. Activities such as asking parents to share "one thing they like best about their child" encourages them to actively participate early on in the group and may provide more safety than asking members to share information about themselves. The parent educator typically provides more structure during the forming stage of the group, for the purpose of ensuring safety for members. However, maintaining too much structure early on may set a pattern for the duration of the group experience in which the group expects the leader to do all the work, thus stifling discussion. This can inhibit participation, spontaneity, and ownership.

STAGE 2: NORMING

The second stage in development is the norming stage. This stage occurs early in the life cycle of a group and is often intertwined with the forming stage. Goals are stated, expectations shared, and group rules set. The parent educator may ask the parents to spend time identifying what they want from this experience, choose particular topics or issues they want to explore, and share some of their own expectations for the group.

Parents ask:

- "What are the rules here?"
- "How should I behave?"

- "What will I get from this experience?"
- "What role will I play in this group?"

It is beneficial for ongoing groups to develop ground rules. This can be done in a variety of ways, including parent educators presenting a prepared list of suggested ground rules and asking for additions or the group designing their own. Either way, it is important for group members to have some input into the development of ground rules because shared ownership of the group is an important task of early group development.

Ground rules are agreed-upon rules or guidelines for the group. Group members, along with the leader, adopt the rules using a consensus model. Ideally, ground rules should be written and then posted on the wall at each session so they can be referred to if needed. If a ground rule is broken, the leader may need to remind the group what has been agreed upon. For example, a ground rule may have been set that members avoid talking about others who are not present. If the group begins to discuss an absent parent, the leader has a responsibility to protect that person and can refer to the ground rule: "When we designed our ground rules, we agreed that we would avoid talking about members who aren't present. Let's make sure we follow that rule in our discussion."

If the group accepts new members after the group has begun, they also need to be aware of the ground rules, so posting them and reviewing them occasionally may be helpful. Couples who share attendance, where one parent attends one week and another the next, may provide a challenge for the parent educator. In this case, it is recommended that the facilitator remind parents to share information with the absent co-parent so that they will be aware of what has been discussed or decided.

Group norms are also developed during this stage. Norms tend to be subtler and are often not stated. They are standards that indicate what behaviors are expected of group members. Group norms are similar to social skills that each of us learns in order to function in society. They are a guide to behavior and offer a sense of consistency and predictability for members so that they know what to expect.

All groups have norms. There are norms for parties, parent-teacher conferences, church meetings, standing in line in the grocery store, and eating in a restaurant. People follow these social norms to conform and to fit in. Group behaviors or norms are typically modeled and often unstated. Group norms may be that parents openly share their feelings, that parents feel comfortable disagreeing with each other and/or the leader, that humor is accepted in the group, that food can be brought into the session, or that parents speak freely without waiting to be asked a question. Members quickly internalize these norms. This happens quietly and may not be verbally noted, but members quickly learn what is acceptable and what is not. Parents with limited social skills

Box 3.1   Sample Ground Rules

1. Everyone participates.
2. Everyone has the right to pass.
3. All opinions are honored.
4. All disclosures made in the group are confidential.
5. Leader stays in a position of respect for self and others.

Set 2

1. We are here to share our feelings and experiences about parenting, but this is not a therapy group.
2. We will respect and maintain confidentiality.
3. We will avoid interrupting each other.
4. We will all participate and avoid side conversations.
5. We will try not to discuss persons who are not present.
6. Our goal is to accept people and avoid making judgments.

may miss or incorrectly interpret the cues from the leader and other members that identify norms. They may behave in ways that do not match the norms of the group and may therefore not be accepted by others. The group leader plays a role in modeling acceptable behavior and may even need to gently confront behaviors that do not match the group norms. For example, a parent who swears in the group may offend others. Although most parent educators may ignore a few inappropriate words, a constant infusion of them needs to be addressed. Speaking with the parent privately after group to point out that others seem offended and asking his or her cooperation may be necessary to bring this member's behavior back into the accepted range of group norms.

The norms governing communication within a group are established quickly in the initial stages. Parents watch carefully to learn the "rules" of communication. If the parent educator speaks first and members wait until they are questioned, this will probably develop as a pattern or norm. Ideally, communication in a group will flow between members, as well as from the leader. A leader who speaks after each parent offers a thought or opinion establishes this as a norm and inhibits free discussion between members. When observing parent education groups, it is interesting to track the flow of conversation. If every statement made by a parent is followed by a comment from the parent educator, it is likely that this pattern was established early on as a group norm.

Parent educators have the initial responsibility to model appropriate norms in a group. Members carefully observe the leader as he or she sets an informal or formal atmosphere, welcomes or discourages questions, offers ample opportunities for parents to talk, or dominates the discussion. Parents observe the leader's use of humor, language, and behavior to set the standards of their own behavior. Although the parent educator plays a predominant role in setting the group norms, group members also observe the behavioral cues of other parents to make decisions about their own behavior in this setting.

During the norming stage, members are beginning to feel comfortable, or perhaps uncomfortable, about the group experience. They are carefully listening to each other with a spirit of cooperation and respect. There is beginning to be an open exchange of ideas, and members tend to feel safe staying on neutral topics. Some groups may become stagnant in this stage and be reluctant to move on.

During this stage, the parent educator encourages connections between members, listens carefully to learn more about each individual, and takes advantage of members' willingness to participate in this safe environment by choosing topics and issues that encourage discussion. Though any topic can elicit controversy in a group, topics such as common characteristics of children this age, communicating with children, and fostering healthy self-esteem tend to offer enough safety for parents to participate without fear of high levels of self-disclosure or conflict.

The parent educator also can use this stage to find similarities between members and build on common interests and issues. Parents have a need for inclusion and a feeling of belonging in their group. Activities that offer opportunities for noting commonalities and facilitation strategies that build on and connect parents' issues will help to lay a foundation during the norming stage where connections are made and a comfortable and safe atmosphere develops. Because the next stage of development challenges this safety, parent educators can mention that "groups typically go through stages, and there will be times when we disagree. This keeps things interesting, and as long as we are respectful to each other, it is good to have a variety of opinions and ideas." This sets the tone that things may change and also gives parents permission to be honest when sharing their views

STAGE 3: STORMING

Groups now move into the storming stage, where an established sense of trust allows members to disagree with each other or the leader. Conflicts between members may arise as different values and ideas emerge. Until now the group has operated at a fairly safe level, where most issues were met with agreement from the group. Perhaps there were differences of opinions, but they were not generally expressed. Tension may now result from diverse opinions or from personal or relational issues. Parents may feel judged because of responses to self-disclosure and therefore not accepted by certain members. Or they may feel a need to defend their viewpoints, which may differ drastically from those of others. Members ask themselves:

- "Do I agree or disagree with this idea?"
- "What can I contribute as a group member?"
- "To whom do I feel most connected?"
- "How comfortable am I with conflict?"

The response to the storming stage is unique to each parent. Common reactions may be those of either "fight or flight." Individuals who come from families where conflict and disagreement were not allowed may have a strong negative reaction to any controversy. They may attempt to mediate the conflict and bring the group back into a safer state, or they may withdraw emotionally from the group through lack of participation. Others may have family or other life experiences where conflict was common and intense and may act out aggressively in their interactions. Ideally, parents will be able to handle some conflict by respectfully agreeing to disagree and will accept the guidance and modeling of the facilitator who sets this as an acceptable norm.

During the storming stage, the parent educator acts as a moderator of conflict. The term *conflict* may arouse a negative reaction. It is the role of the facilitator to assure the group that conflict is not always negative and can be a positive way for adults to learn from each other. It can also be stressed that the parent educator's role is to ensure a sense of acceptance for all members and that the expectation for discussion is that everyone will be treated respectfully. The leader's attitude about conflict is quickly interpreted by the group. If conflict is avoided at all cost and immediately stopped by the facilitator, members will soon learn that there is no room for divergent thinking in this group. If the leader, how-ever, models an acceptance of different ideas and at the same time maintains an expectation of respect for all members, parents will learn not only that conflict is allowed but also how to approach it. Learning how to constructively challenge the ideas of others will assist in moving the group into the next stage of development.

It is during the storming stage that the group either breaks down or moves through the tension into the next and most productive stage of development. If the storming stage is accepted by the parent educator as an expected aspect of development and as a means of moving into a more productive level, parents will be more accepting. Parent educators benefit from taking a reflective approach to understand how they personally react to conflict. Family-of-origin issues have a powerful impact on group leaders' responses to conflict. Although the setting and the participants are different, the presence of conflict can elicit an emotional reaction from a group leader who remembers conflict issues within his or her own family. Examining experiences of conflict in other areas of the group leader's life will give a broader understanding of these dynamics. The parent educator who can consciously avoid personalizing conflict will be able to work with this dynamic as a means of group development, rather than struggling to eliminate it. The presence of conflict and disagreement can be challenging for parent educators, especially those who are unaccustomed to it, but when managed appropriately, it becomes a positive growth experience for a parent group.

STAGE 4: PERFORMING

Ideally, all groups will reach this stage in their developmental process. It is here that the group becomes solid; group morale and loyalty are high. Members feel an appreciation for each other and the experience. Collaborative problem solving brings support to individual members, and the focus of the group is working on issues and reaching goals. There is usually a high level of honesty in the performing stage, where members are free to share ideas, opinions, and feelings. As members solidify their relationships with each other and the leader, a connection develops that is built on mutual respect and reciprocal care. The group is now characterized as having fun and working hard together. During this stage, parents are actively involved and focusing on the work of the group. There is less uncertainty than in other stages, less focus on questions of purpose or needs, and more intentional problem solving and support. It is during this stage that parents become more aware of the group identity that has evolved and the needs of individual members, rather than focusing on their own participation. A balance between relationships and tasks has been achieved, and there is shared ownership and responsibility to the group by all members.

The topics addressed during this stage can have more depth, and the level of self-disclosure increases. Family-of-origin issues, stresses of families, and co-parenting issues have now become safe topics. Parents trust they will be able to disclose feelings and experiences to the group and the leader without judgment.

The performing stage of the group is the most productive and satisfying for both the members and leader. The parent leaves a session armed with new knowledge and a sense of accomplishment for having participated with other group members. The parent educator has accomplished a major goal of assisting members to solve problems, address issues, and collaboratively support each other in their journey of parenting.

STAGE 5: ADJOURNING

The final stage of group development is the adjourning stage, where the focus is on the termination of the group. There is a sense of accomplishment that goals have been achieved and that real learning has occurred. There may also be some apprehension or sadness in anticipation of the end. Members may have become close to each other and now wonder what is next. This is an important stage in the life cycle of a group, and the parent educator will need to pay close attention to the needs of members.

Parents may ask:

- "Will I miss this experience?"
- "What will happen to the relationships that have developed?"
- "How can I express my feelings about ending?"
- "What comes next?"

Just as parent educators plan for closure of each session, final closure to the group must also be planned. Depending on the depth of involvement, parents may need an opportunity to express their feelings about the experience. They may be asked, "What is the best thing you have gotten from this experience?" They may need an informal opportunity to plan for some kind of continuation of the experience. Although the formal group is finished, parents may choose to continue to meet informally for support or socializing. The parent educator can assist in empowering members to make these arrangements but needs to be willing to abandon the role of facilitator. He or she will not be involved in this process of continuation.

Typically, agency-sponsored parent education groups ask parents to evaluate their experience in this group. This is most likely done with a written evaluation, giving feedback to both the program and the parent educator. Although adult educators may feel their performance is being judged, it is important to carefully consider the feedback from parents and adjust future groups accordingly. Table 3.1 is one example of a program evaluation form that addresses program satisfaction and assessment of different program components.

A second type of program evaluation might focus on parent self-assessment. The purpose of this type of evaluation is to better understand program outcomes for parents. Table 3.2 is an example of a program impact questionnaire. This type of assessment asks parents to reflect on different program goal areas and report on changes that they may have experienced as a result of participation in the program. Program outcomes may also be measured in a more formal and objective manner with pre- and posttests using self-report measures on parent attitudes to assess parent changes.

The stages-of-development theory provides a framework for parent educators to understand and respond to the needs of the group over time. Although each group is unique and will progress in a different way, this model provides a typical and perhaps ideal guide for understanding the life cycle of a group. Table 3.3 summarizes the different stages with challenges and possible strategies to address these challenges. By viewing the group process through a developmental perspective, the parent educator realizes his or her responsibility to both the parent and the group.

Table 3.1   Parenting Program Evaluation

We would like to know how you feel about this program and how it has helped you. This information will be helpful for improving the program. All of the information will be confidential and will be shared only as group information.

Program Components

    Write down what you like or dislike about each part of the program and then rate it, using the numbers 5 = Excellent, 4 = Very Good, 3 = Good, 2 = Fair, and 1 = Poor to describe how you feel about each component. Put the rating in the space before each item.

_____1. Individual interviews before program began

_____2. Small-group exercises

_____3. Discussion

_____4. Video clips and discussion

_____5. Handouts/articles

Additional Comments

1. What did you like best about the parenting program?

2. What are the three most important ideas about parenting that you are taking away with you?

3. What specific ideas would you offer the teacher about how to change this program next time around?

    a) Length of time
    b) Content to add or delete
    c) Methods
    d) Size of group
    e) Other comments

4. How would you describe the program to a parent who was thinking about taking the class?

Table 3.2   Early Head Start Program Impacts on Child, Parenting, and Family

The purpose of this survey is to find out from parents how the Early Head Start program has changed you and your child during the past year.

Answer these questions about your child (the youngest if you have more than one child).

Child's age_____

Mark an X at the point on the line that best describes the amount of change you have seen in your child that you feel comes from being in the Early Head Start program.

Comment after each item on how the program helped with this change.

A. Child Changes

1. My child is comfortable separating from me and staying with the teachers.
   ____ I _____ I _____ I _____ I _____ I _____
   No Change   Some Positive Change   Great Positive Change

2. My child is beginning to explore the environment at Head Start and play by him/herself.
   ____ I _____ I _____ I _____ I _____ I _____
   No Change   Some Positive Change   Great Positive Change

3. My child enjoys the parent-child time activities with me.
   ____ I _____ I _____ I _____ I _____ I _____
   No Change   Some Positive Change   Great Positive Change

4. My child likes Early Head Start and trusts the teachers.
   ____ I _____ I _____ I _____ I _____ I _____
   No Change   Some Positive Change   Great Positive Change

5. My child is beginning to do more on his/her own.
   ____ I _____ I _____ I _____ I _____ I _____
   No Change   Some Positive Change   Great Positive Change

6. My child is beginning to express his/her needs with words.
   ____ I _____ I _____ I _____ I _____ I _____
   No Change   Some Positive Change   Great Positive Change

7. My child likes books and having books read to him/her.

____ I _____ I _____ I _____ I _____ I _____
No Change   Some Positive Change   Great Positive Change

Describe other changes that you see in your child from participating in Early Head Start.

B. Parent Changes

Mark the changes that you have seen in yourself from the Early Head Start Program this year. Please comment after each item how the program had helped or not helped you.

1. I understand more about how children grow and learn.

____ I _____ I _____ I _____ I _____ I _____
No Change   Some Positive Change   Great Positive Change

2. I am more aware of how my child communicates his/her needs.

____ I _____ I _____ I _____ I _____ I _____
No Change   Some Positive Change   Great Positive Change

3. I have learned new fun activities to do with my child.

____ I _____ I _____ I _____ I _____ I _____
No Change   Some Positive Change   Great Positive Change

4. I am better able to set clear limits for my child.

____ I _____ I _____ I _____ I _____ I _____
No Change   Some Positive Change   Great Positive Change

5. I am more patient with my child.

____ I _____ I _____ I _____ I _____ I _____
No Change   Some Positive Change   Great Positive Change

6. I enjoy playing games with my child.

____ I _____ I _____ I _____ I _____ I _____
No Change   Some Positive Change   Great Positive Change

7. I am more confident in making decisions about my child.

____ I _____ I _____ I _____ I _____ I _____
No Change   Some Positive Change   Great Positive Change

8. I have developed predictable routines with my child.

____ I _____ I _____ I _____ I _____ I _____
No Change   Some Positive Change   Great Positive Change

Are there other areas where parenting has changed in positive or negative ways because of the Early Head Start Program?

(Continued)

Table 3.2   Continued

C. Family Life Changes

How has the program changed your family life? For example, better communication among family members, closer as a family, more stress, less time as a family. List the most important positive and negative changes that you have experienced related to your participation in Early Head Start.

Positive Changes in Family Life

Negative Changes in Family Life

Framework 2: The Functional Approach—Task and Maintenance Functions

Education and support in a parent group are in many ways analogous to the task and maintenance functions described in cooperative group learning literature (Johnson & Johnson, 1975). The word *function* in this context refers to the basic goal orientation for parent groups in terms of accomplishing specific educational outcomes and creating and maintaining a healthy group environment. These two sets of functions complement each other in parent groups. The leader is responsible for monitoring how these functions operate and for maintaining a balance between goal orientation and group maintenance activities. Each group member, as well as the leader, brings personal characteristics, ideas about learning, and specific skills to the group context. For example, Susan may be very good at asking clarifying questions to keep the group focused on the goal of understanding child emotions. Derek may bring a good sense of humor that helps relieve tension and creates a group atmosphere of fun. Janine knows how to support and affirm a parent who is struggling with toddler tantrum behavior. The role of the parent educator is to be aware of the different functions that support building a sense of group cohesion and those functions that support the learning of new ideas, new ways of thinking, and new skills. The professional parent educator has the primary responsibility to understand how the two functions work in a parent group setting. The leader must be able to identify and model specific behaviors that support each function.

Table 3.3   Stages of Group Development: The Role of the Parent Educator

Stage	Goal	Challenges	Parent Educator Strategies
Forming	Setting warm, welcoming tone Addressing specifics of group Encouraging connections between members	Addressing apprehensiveness of parents Addressing limited self-disclosure Addressing uncertainty about group experience	Building relationships Connecting parents' experiences and ideas Providing welcoming atmosphere
Norming	Setting group ground rules Discussing goals Determining group norms	Providing meaningful discussion within safe setting Setting appropriate behavioral norms	Modeling norm expectations Listening carefully to learn Encouraging and modeling disclosure
Storming	Encouraging divergent thinking Acknowledging and accepting disagreement in the group	Monitoring conflict Maintaining respect	Utilizing conflict positively Modeling acceptance of diversity
Performing	Achieving goals Achieving honest/ open atmosphere Sharing group ownership Addressing in-depth topics	Keeping parents focused Fostering shared decision making	Maintaining group momentum Providing meaningful topics and discussion Facilitating shared ownership
Adjourning	Realizing accomplishment Providing positive ending Evaluating experience	Approaching end of group Dealing with unmet needs	Providing closure activity Sharing possible resources Providing evaluation tool

Box 3.2 lists some of the critical behaviors that support the maintenance function for cooperative group learning (Johnson & Johnson, 1975). These were modified to illustrate how they would create a sense of support in a parent education group. The parent educator is responsible for both modeling these behaviors and affirming or encouraging parents when they exhibit them.

Box 3.2 Maintenance Functions in Group Parent
Education

1. Encouraging participation by all members
2. Keeping harmony and willingness to compromise
3. Helping to reduce stress/relieve tension
4. Translating messages for the group when something is confusing
5. Monitoring emotional climate of the group
6. Observing and describing group process and dynamics
7. Articulating standards of behavior for the group
8. Listening to and reflecting concerns of different members
9. Helping create a feeling of group trust
10. Helping resolve interpersonal problems in the group

Awareness of the importance of maintaining a healthy group atmosphere is essential for parent group leaders. In a group that is functioning in a positive manner, many of the behaviors that support group maintenance are shared among members. The parent educator has both more responsibility and greater investment in creating a supportive group environment. An effective group parent educator has created a positive group atmosphere when the maintenance behaviors are shared among group members according to their individual characteristics, skills, and strengths.

The particular mix of parent personalities and characteristics will influence the sense of cohesion in a group. Also, the length of the group is an important factor influencing group cohesion and the potential sharing of behaviors to maintain a positive group environment. If the group has more time to grow and develop, it will exhibit more sharing of group maintenance behaviors as people define their roles and feel successful at contributing to a positive group atmosphere. For example, in an evening parent group of 14 mothers and fathers, Georgia has taken on the role of asking questions of a quiet group member to invite her participation in discussion. Paul is frequently an observer of group process, noting the energy level of the group and how the group solves problems when there is a conflict. Sometimes a group will share bringing a snack for the parent group time. This could also be seen as a way to build group cohesion: Besides providing refreshment, it can create a sense of caring for each other that comes from sharing a snack prepared by one of the group members.

Box 3.3 outlines some of the important task orientation functions. Though having fun and sharing support during challenging times is important, most parents also want to feel a sense of accomplishment through learning new ideas and strategies for effective parenting.

Box 3.3   Task Functions in Parent Education Groups

1. Providing new ideas and opinions for the group
2. Asking others for their ideas and opinions
3. Getting a discussion started
4. Providing directions to the group to complete a task or exercise
5. Summarizing major points in a discussion
6. Clearly defining a problem
7. Bringing positive energy to get a task completed
8. Evaluating what the group has done and what remains to be completed
9. Checking in with group members about pragmatic details of ideas
10. Coordinating different tasks and goals to ensure completion on time

---

The parent educator takes responsibility for guiding a group toward their goals of learning, processing new ideas, and practicing new strategies. As the group evolves, these tasks also begin to be shared among parents. A parent who attended a recent workshop on car seats for infants may share this information with the group. The parent educator may know that Angela is always ready to start a discussion and look to her when the group seems to be bogged down. The parent educator may also engage the entire group in summarizing the major points for the discussion of the day. The goal of shared leadership has a very delicate balance when a paid professional parent educator is leading a group. The more a skilled leader engages the strengths of the group, the more resources can be accessed for the whole group. Parents come to most groups with an abundance of information and support resources. The parent educator monitors and orchestrates these resources so that the group experience is a positive learning experience. The functional perspective creates an awareness of the behaviors that support the two major functions in a successful parent education group.

The primary contribution of this model is the principle of balance and how to maintain a healthy group atmosphere while assisting the parent group in defining and achieving their goals. The functional framework assists the group leader in discovering and utilizing the strengths that different group members bring to the group. Some members bring a sense of caring and concern for other group members that enhances the relationships between group members. Others may bring a good sense of humor that allows the group to laugh at some of the perils of parenthood. The group leader must recognize the contributions of each member and strive to maintain a sense of balance between education and support.

Framework 3: A Systems Perspective for Understanding Group Process

Family systems theory is used by therapists to understand family relationship patterns, to strengthen functional behaviors of families, and to change those behaviors that are dysfunctional (Broderick, 1993). In this framework, a family is seen as a system that is made up of individuals who interact with each other as information and energy are exchanged between members and also with the outside environment. Internal family dynamics and relationships between the family and outside systems are both examined. Family members are connected to each other, but they still maintain their individuality; they function as members of the system and also as independent people. Some of the important concepts in family systems theory focus on relationship and communication patterns and include

- Open and closed systems
- Rules, roles, and communication
- Dynamic equilibrium
- Synergy
- Diversity

These concepts from family systems theory can also be applied to understanding parent group dynamics. This section will examine how systems concepts can provide important insights into relationships and communication patterns that can assist parent educators in understanding and managing internal group dynamics.

Two general goals for parent groups as systems are (a) to create supportive relationship patterns and (b) to develop open and healthy patterns of communication. Each group builds and expands on these goals by generating its own unique goals that meet the needs and interests of parents in the group. The concept of open and closed systems is used in a variety of contexts. For example, Satir (1972) described an open family system as one in which members have a high sense of self-esteem; communication is direct, clear, specific, and congruent; and rules are overt, current, and open to change. In a parent group, educators also attempt to create an open system of communication to provide a healthy space for the development of caring and supportive relationships and openness to individual parent growth and learning.

Groups, just like families, develop and maintain patterns of rules, roles, and communication that keep their structure open and flexible or closed and rigid. Every group has particular rules that govern behavior and add predictability and stability for members. Rules may be explicit in that they are clearly stated, as in the case of ground rules. These rules are often negotiable and can be changed through discussion and consensus. Others may be implicit; typically defined as norms, they are modeled and often unspoken. The existence of group rules is imperative for healthy functioning. Without the structure and safety that rules offer, a group could not function effectively.

Group members also have roles within the system, just as each family member has a particular role. In families, birth order, gender, and temperament often determine what role a member plays. In a group, these factors may also influence members' roles. For example, members with more parenting experience may take on a leadership role, offering advice or suggestions founded on their own knowledge base. Group members whose temperament encourages the use of humor, mediation, support, or other influential behaviors may take on a particular role in the group to provide this aspect of group dynamics. Roles can be positive in helping to establish a cohesive and caring group or disruptive to the group by going off on a tangent and distracting the group from the main topic.

Just like families, groups develop patterns of communication, both verbal and nonverbal. Members in parent groups may communicate openly and honestly as they share their views, feelings, and experiences. In other groups where the level of trust is underdeveloped, members may communicate only what they think is expected of them. For example, groups may develop patterns where the parent educator initiates most of the talking by asking questions of specific group members. Another group may share only comments that show agreement with the views of the parent educator. These patterns typically develop very early as the group is establishing norms and members unconsciously learn what patterns of communication are expected and acceptable.

Modeling by the parent educator is crucial in developing an environment of open communication. The parent educator listens carefully, uses nonverbal communication that is affirming and accepting, encourages different views, and gives clear and direct verbal messages. The process of creating an open parent group is described in detail in Chapter 5, where the focus is on developing relationships within the group. The open system concept also stresses the importance of connecting with outside resources to meet the needs of parents in groups. This may include bringing in a speaker on nutrition for parents who have expressed a need for this information or making a referral to a mental health practitioner to help a parent who is struggling with episodes of depression. Systems theory provides helpful guidelines for monitoring relationship and communication patterns that are open and create a healthy group environment for parent growth and learning to occur.

Family systems theory also examines family behaviors that keep the family's structure open and flexible or closed and rigid. A group may be welcoming to new members, or it may be a closed system that works to keep "outsiders" isolated. Issues of belonging can arise in these groups when new members are added throughout the span of the group. The parent group may also function in ways that are open to new information, ideas, or strategies, or it may respond with resistance to new ideas. Parent groups that meet on a regular basis and are ongoing tend to take on one or the other of these characteristics.

Nonverbal patterns may also emerge in groups that support or exclude certain members. Seating patterns, judgmental or nonjudgmental gestures or facial expressions, use of eye contact that avoids certain members, or looks for approval from the parent educator are all examples of subtle nonverbal behaviors that can easily become ingrained in the behavior patterns of group members and leaders.

Another important concept that can be derived from systems theory is synergy. Synergy is the realization of the unique energy and power that is generated when a group is able to combine the diverse resources and strengths of individual members in a positive manner to achieve group goals. Synergy is group "magic" where the whole is greater than the sum of all of the individual parts. This principle is often experienced in a positive way and is one of the reasons that group parent education remains a unique and powerful learning experience.

For example, synergy is experienced in a group during a discussion on sex role development in children when the group knowledge and experience base comes together to create unique insights and new opportunities for learning. Both mothers and fathers talk about and share their experiences and leave with a greater appreciation for how gender roles are learned and how they as parents can limit and constrain their child's growth and development. Synergy in a parent group explains the powerful learning that goes on within a group that is open and has developed comfortable and trusting relationships.

A parent group, just like a family, may have a desire to keep things in balance. Dynamic equilibrium is another systems concept that can be useful to apply to parent education practice. This concept conveys the importance of both stability and change in a group. The developmental perspective described earlier in this chapter charts different stages of group growth and change. The systems concept of dynamic equilibrium emphasizes the importance in group learning, of creating a sense of stability and trust that allows for critical self-reflection and potential change in individuals and for the group. This allows the group to evolve to the stage of positive "group performing." The parent educator must create the safety and stability to challenge the group to move to the next stage to meet the next set of issues.

If conflict arises, members may also work hard to keep a sense of equilibrium in the group. Often group members bring the feelings and behavior patterns of their family into the parent education group. For example, those who are uncomfortable with conflict or controversy in their families replicate these feelings and responses in the group. If a disagreement occurs, perhaps even respectfully, some members may respond in ways that divert the attention of the group or mediate the difference of opinion. When the atmosphere of the group changes because of conflict, members may feel a sense of being out of balance and may respond by trying to bring things back into a homeostatic balance.

Diversity or differences between members are often dealt with in families by forming subgroups with those who share some similarities or commonalities. In systems theory, these are called subsystems. Similarly, group dynamics may draw parents to form smaller groups or subsystems. They may consist of members who are of similar gender. Mothers or fathers in the group may begin to identify as a subsystem and sit together, agree with each other, and connect on a separate level from other members. Parents who have something in common that is not shared by other members may begin to form a special bond that separates them from others. Subsystems, similar to cliques, may also begin to form when dual relationships exist for group members. Parents who socialize outside the group may feel naturally more drawn to each other in this setting. Though subsystems are typical in families and also in parent groups, ideally members of these groups will identify primarily with the group as a whole and see their main function as working as a member of the larger system or parent group. Each member needs to have a sense of belonging within the group. To be functional, both families and groups need to cherish and respect the individuality of each member, while allowing for the development of subsystems.

The primary contribution of systems theory is to assist the group facilitator in approaching parent groups as complex and dynamic systems that thrive on diversity, positive energy, and a clear set of goals. The concept of reciprocity is also relevant to understanding parent groups. Child development researchers (Bronfenbrenner, 1979) have begun to understand and have articulated parent-child relationships as reciprocal. The extension of reciprocity between the parent group leader and individual members or the whole group provides an indicator of healthy group functioning. Though parent group facilitators are given the responsibility for making the group work, it is much more of a two-way street than is often acknowledged or practiced. The systems perspective helps group leaders to understand the dynamic nature of groups and the importance of developing healthy relationships with balanced, reciprocal communication patterns. Parent groups that can attain peaks of group synergy have tapped into the dynamic power of group parent education.

Framework 4: A Feminist Perspective on Parent Group Dynamics

The feminist perspective brings a different focus and emphasis than the previous three frameworks by directly addressing gender and gender dynamics in groups. There is literature that examines gender as a factor in small-group dynamics and begins to make some predictions about typical behavior patterns that occur in mixed-gender groups (Van Nostrand, 1993). This literature has not been extended to look specifically at parenting groups, but the general patterns of male/female communication behaviors that have been observed (Tannen, 1990) also can be applied to parent groups and should be considered when facilitating mixed-gender groups. The gender mix in groups needs to be considered in examining specific problems that may occur in male-female communication patterns. In many parent groups today, couples attend together or alternate attending sessions, making the gender composition of groups both more equal and ever-changing.

It may be that the predominance of female participants and female parent educators has limited the need to carefully review gender as a factor in parent education. The recent emergence of father-only groups (Johnson & Palm, 1992; McBride, 1990, 1991) and the current focus on responsible fatherhood programs (Levine & Pitt, 1995) have initiated some discussion on mother and father differences in relation to parent education. These are reflected in Palm's (1997) description of different needs, goals, and interests that fathers and mothers may exhibit as they come to parent education groups. Tannen's (1990) discussion of male and female communication differences also provides some food for thought about the influence of gender on parent group dynamics. Descriptions of gender differences in parent education are approached with some skepticism. The move to be more inclusive and talk about generic parents instead of gender stereotypes has stunted our understanding of gender as an important factor in parent education.

The feminist perspective on mixed-gender groups and group dynamics that may be most relevant to parent educators comes from Van Nostrand (1993). She made a strong case for group leaders to increase their sensitivity and awareness of gender bias and sexism in mixed-gender groups and to take steps toward what she labeled "gender responsible leadership." She presented some important concepts that can be applied to parent education groups. Because parent groups may be perceived as an environment with female dominance in terms of numbers of both leaders and participants, the concern over gender bias and male dominance may take on a different twist. In addition, females have been socialized for parenthood more directly and tend to bring both more knowledge and experience to parenthood (Palm & Palkovitz, 1988). These factors tend to lead to more power for women in mixed-gender parent groups, and it cannot be assumed that males will automatically have more privilege or power in the typical mixed-gender group parent education setting. The concepts that will be explored here are gender-responsible leadership and male privilege through male patterns of dominance and detachment combined with female patterns of deference and problem description. The basic assumption with this perspective is that we should strive for a balance of power and involvement between genders in mixed-gender groups.

Gender-responsible leadership (Van Nostrand, 1993) is defined as leadership that recognizes gender bias and sexism in self and others, takes steps toward remediation, and creates a balance of power. The awareness of gender bias in groups that are predominantly female, such as parent education, tends to be attenuated. How can there be bias against women when women appear to have control of the groups both as leaders and as the majority of participants? It becomes clearer how this may occur when one looks at what happens when an individual male joins a parent group. In these cases women are likely to be very welcoming and pleased to see a man taking an interest in his children by attending a parent education class. They may also be likely to listen more carefully and to defer to his interests in group interactions.

How does male privilege, the assumption that male needs, opinions, and interests are more important, fit with parent education? Van Nostrand (1993) identified two common patterns in mixed-gender groups that men display that help them to maintain male privilege: dominance in the group setting and detachment from the group. Two typical female responses that also interact with these male behavior patterns and assist men in maintaining this power privilege are deferring to men in a group setting and describing imbalance problems but not acting to resolve them. Examples of these dynamics are presented in the brief examples of group interaction described in Boxes 3.4 and 3.5.

The two examples in Boxes 3.4 and 3.5 provide some insights into potential gender bias and the concept of male privilege in a parent group setting. Gender dynamics often seem to be avoided or circumvented in mixed-gender parent groups. This could be considered collusion with the members who are exhibiting biased behavior patterns. It may also be that the group has not developed to the point where confrontation is likely to be successful because a trusting relationship has not been established with the fathers in these two situations. There are also more subtle gender-related dynamics that may work to maintain male privilege. For example, some men may use humor or sexual innuendo to distract from and even discount the content issue that is being discussed.

The feminist challenge to be gender-responsible leaders and its application to parent education groups need further study as fathers come more frequently to join mothers in parent education groups. It is clear that some strong socialization patterns continue to influence males and females to think and behave in different ways. These differences can continue to create an imbalance of power in mixed-gender parent groups. The feminist perspective reminds parent educators that gender and gender dynamics are potent factors to consider in understanding parent groups. In a typical parent group, there may be one or more fathers who attend on a regular basis, and even more are likely to come to evening groups. Many men enjoy being part of a mostly female group and quickly adapt to the rules and take on a more cooperative style of participation, which is perceived as the group norm. It is difficult to make broad generalizations

Box 3.4   Example of Male Domination

A group of parents of toddlers meets once a week on Wednesday mornings. The group consists of eight parents—seven mothers and one father. The mothers attend on a regular basis, and the father comes every third or fourth week when he can take time off from his job. When the father, Jeff, does come, he is warmly greeted by the group leader, who goes out of her way to say that she is so glad he made it today and that she wishes that more fathers would take the time to come to classes. Jeff appears very comfortable in the group and doesn't mind talking about his twin 2-year-old daughters. He likes to describe how smart they are and all the new words that they are learning. The leader has noticed that when Jeff does come he tends to dominate a discussion, telling stories and freely giving advice to the other mothers in the group. Some of the mothers, especially Carmen and Celina, who are typically quiet, hardly say a word when Jeff is present. Carol makes a comment 1 week after Jeff has attended a group how the group is different when a dad participates. The group leader, Joyce, lets the comment go this time because she doesn't want the group to talk about a parent who is not present. At the same time, she is aware of the difference in group dynamics and wonders what she should do as a group leader to address this issue in a positive and direct manner.

In this parent group, it appears that Jeff has a privileged position that allows him to be the center of attention and get his needs met. The mothers in the group have deferred to this privilege by not asserting their own needs. Even Carol, who "diagnoses the dysfunction," only describes the problem, hoping someone else will take action. It is especially difficult with a father who does not attend on a regular basis to confront and/or limit this privilege. The fear would be that he might not come back. Joyce, the group leader, must recognize this pattern early on and take steps to intervene to protect the quiet members of the group, who may not be getting their needs met. What would a gender-responsible leader do in this situation?

about negative gender patterns in parent groups, but gender must still be considered an important factor (temperament or individual personality traits may also be a factor) in understanding group dynamics and problems that group leaders of both genders may encounter. The gender of the group leader is another area that needs further examination as more men are involved as both participants and educators (Konen, 1992).

Box 3.5 Example of Male Distancing From the Group

Kerry is the quiet father of 3-year-old Sam. He comes to the Tuesday evening parent group on a regular basis, as his wife Sheila is a nurse who works the evening shift at the local hospital. Kerry is often the only father in the group. Sometimes he sits back from the group with his arms folded and a look of mild boredom. In a parent discussion about discipline and bedtime, the parent educator, Joanne, trying to involve Kerry in the group, asks him how he would get Sam to stay in his room once he was put to bed. Kerry responds, "That would never happen. Once I tell him to go to bed, he knows I mean business and he won't play games with me." The mother who has been struggling with this issue grows silent and embarrassed, and the group pauses to process Kerry's response. The group leader confers with her supervisor the next day about what is going on and asks how she can engage Kerry to participate in a positive manner. They discuss the role of gender and the pattern of maintaining male privilege by withdrawing from the group and discounting others' ideas and feelings about parenting. Men in parent groups sometimes maintain distance from the group and also maintain a mask of competence and control over difficult parenting situations. What would a gender-responsible leader do in this situation?

Discussion Questions

DEVELOPMENTAL PERSPECTIVE

1. Compare and contrast the sample ground rules in Box 3.1. How do you think each might have been developed? What kind of group does each imply to you?

2. How do you typically respond to conflict? How comfortable or uncomfortable are you when conflict affects others or yourself? How might your feelings about conflict affect your performance as a group facilitator?

3. What are the major benefits of parent assessments of program components? How can parent self-assessment of changes assist a program?

FUNCTIONAL PERSPECTIVE

1. Consider your role as a group leader regarding task and maintenance functions. With which do you feel most comfortable? Why?

2. To facilitate a balance of task and maintenance functions, what goal might you set for yourself?

SYSTEMS PERSPECTIVE

1. Consider the following questions about your own family of origin:
   a. What roles did various members play?
   b. What rules did your family have? Which were stated; which were implied?
   c. Would you describe your family of origin as an open or closed system? Why?

2. How aware are you of your own nonverbal behavior? What do you notice about the nonverbal behavior of others?

3. What advantages and challenges could you anticipate as a group begins to form subgroups or subsystems?

FEMINIST PERSPECTIVE

1. How important is the concept of male privilege to understanding group dynamics in mixed-gender parent groups? Why?

2. What are the sources of power that women may bring to a mixed-gender parent group?

3. How important is the gender of the parent group leader to mixed-gender parent education groups? Explain.

4

Conceptual Frameworks, Part II

Models for Understanding the Role of the Group Leader

Whereas the four conceptual models presented in Chapter 3 focus on group development, functioning, and dynamics, this chapter will explore three additional frameworks that address the role of the group leader: (a) the levels of involvement of parent educators in a group setting, depending on the purpose and needs of the group; (b) styles of leadership that influence group process; and (c) moral character of parent educators that affects ethical thinking and behavior related to group leadership.

Framework 5: Levels of Involvement for Parent and Family Educators

The challenge of understanding and maintaining clear boundaries between parent education and therapy is addressed by Doherty's (1995) model of levels of involvement for parent and family educators. Doherty has developed a continuum approach to conceptualizing and defining levels of involvement with parents, based on intensity, necessary knowledge base of the practitioner, and requisite skills for prevention, education, support, and intervention. Having originally designed the model for physicians and later for school psychologists, Doherty has adapted it for parent and family educators as a way of encouraging the inclusion of personal experiences, emotions, and feelings in parent education. Doherty's model provides a structure for parent educators to meet the needs of parents that includes the important affective aspects of learning without crossing into therapy in the group or individual setting.

Uncertainty about how deeply to delve into the feelings and experiences of parents in groups challenges most parent educators. Defining parent education solely as providing information and teaching practical skills, while defining therapy as dealing with personal experiences and feelings of parents, limits both disciplines. Therapy typically involves some educational components, often parent education, that meet the needs of adult learners. It includes the intense feelings, attitudes, and values of parents in therapeutic settings. In this model, parent education is not therapy, yet it can be therapeutic. The inclusion of the learners' personal experiences and feelings distinguishes parent education from standard educational courses in child development. Parent education by its nature has more personal depth than other forms of education. Yet there are limits to the depth that is appropriate to explore. Therapy has depth, often without safety, and basic parent education that focuses only on information has safety without depth. The levels of family involvement model allows parent educators to approach their work through a continuum model that distinguishes differences between therapy and parent education and allows varying levels of involvement to meet the diverse parenting needs of individuals and groups.

The five levels are presented from minimal involvement with families through family therapy, with each level building on skills of the previous level. The model can be used either in group work with parents or in one-to-one interaction. This section will describe each level of involvement, focusing primarily on Levels 2, 3, and 4.

LEVEL 1: MINIMAL EMPHASIS ON FAMILY

Level 1 is included not as a recommended strategy for parent educators but as an example of the least possible involvement with parents. Parents are included in Level 1 experiences only for practical or legal reasons. Policies are created and implemented by professionals with little attention to the needs or input of parents.

Level 1 Example: A school may conduct informational meetings for parents to learn about policies and procedures that have been developed. Parents are not involved in discussion but participate by receiving the necessary information from professionals. In this level, there is no partnership between parent and professional, and the main focus is on the needs of the institution to convey policies to parents.

LEVEL 2: INFORMATION AND ADVICE

Level 2 involves parents in learning particular content regarding child development, parenting, and family life. The parent educator is required to have good teaching and presenting skills because the main focus is on sharing information and advice with parents. The educator engages the parents in the learning process by eliciting questions, making practical recommendations, and providing information about community resources for families. Frequently, one-time presentations regarding a particular aspect of parenting are classified as Level 2 practice. However, many ongoing parent education groups function at this level, with parents as recipients of the knowledge shared by the educator.

Because the skills and knowledge base of Level 2 typically are addressed and emphasized through most training programs for parent educators, this level provides a high level of comfort for group leaders. Parent educators feel confident in utilizing solid teaching skills to present information they understand. However, working exclusively at this level with parents does have limitations. Level 2 provides a safe environment for parents to learn new information and skills, although void of any emotions or references to feelings. This limits the depth for learning. Although parents are receptive to information about child development, without involvement in meaningful and personal discussion of their beliefs and feelings, real change is unlikely to occur in their family life.

Level 2 Example: A 3-week parent education series is offered by a family support agency on the topic of using effective discipline strategies with preschoolers. Registration is open to the public. A parent educator, trained in child development, presents a 1-hour session each week that includes basic developmental information about preschoolers, realistic expectations of parents, and specific techniques that parents can use to guide their children's behavior. The group leader does most of the talking, using handouts, overheads, and short video clips to demonstrate the topic. Parents are encouraged to ask questions, and recommendations are given by the parent educator to address specific discipline challenges of the group. The series ends after 3 weeks with parents learning about appropriate expectations for children and new strategies of discipline.

LEVEL 3: FEELINGS AND SUPPORT

Level 3 builds on the solid knowledge base of child development, family life, and parenting that encompasses Level 2. It is in this next level that parent educators elicit feelings and experiences of the group members and use their personal disclosures as an important part of the learning experience. In addition to being a confident teacher, the Level 3 parent educator must use more involved communication and facilitation skills, such as

- Empathetic listening
- Gentle probing for feelings and personal stories
- Creating an open and supportive climate
- Learning enough about parents' circumstances to be able to offer tailored recommendations
- Identifying family and/or psychological dysfunction
- Being able to conduct a referral for other services

These skills are also foundational to the work that therapists do with clients, but at this level in parent education the focus remains on typical parenting issues and stays within the professional realm of parent education. Whereas most of the Level 3 skills are basic to relationship building and nurturing a trusting learning environment, the ability to "identify family or psychological dysfunction" may evoke concern from some parent educators. Initially, this skill may seem beyond the scope of parent education, a profession that focuses on normal child and family development. It is this very strength of parent education, understanding typical development, that provides a parent educator with the ability to identify what is not within the range of healthy functioning. Understanding typical development of children and family issues provides an immediate guide for parent educators to recognize behaviors or issues that cannot be universalized. Being able to identify family and/or psychological dysfunction does not imply that parent education can or should treat these issues. It does, however, require the parent educator to make a determination that further services may be beneficial and to be able to conduct a referral. Parent education in this context may also provide supportive therapeutic services as an adjunct to individual therapy, with the possibility of parent educator and therapist collaborating to complement each other's involvement.

Typical issues in Level 3 settings deal with normal stresses in family life, rather than more traumatic situations or challenges that stem from painful family-of-origin experiences. The focus remains on parenting issues, and the skillful parent educator keeps the participants grounded in issues as they currently affect parenting. The perspective is generally on the here and now. Although some childhood recollection and understanding of the effect of parents' backgrounds is beneficial, the primary work is done on the challenges of parenting children.

Doherty (1995) stated that "combining as it does the cognitive and affective domains in a non-intrusive manner, Level Three is the optimal level of intensity

Photo 4.1   A parent educator introduces new ideas to a group of parents.

for most ongoing parent and family education activities" (p. 354). Whereas Level 2 provides a comfort zone for both educator and participant, Level 3 challenges both to experience a more meaningful teaching and learning experience.

As with each level, there are limitations to Level 3. Parent educators must feel confident in their abilities to address emotional responses in a group. They must have insight into their own emotions regarding parenting and family issues in order to keep them separate from the emotions of the parents. Common mistakes at Level 3 are to move too quickly back to Level 2 when emotions arise, to cut off a parent by turning the issue back to the group for ideas, or to probe too deeply into the parent's emotions and thus become intrusive in an effort to help.

Level 3 provides a level of involvement with parents toward which all parent educators can work. By allowing and encouraging feelings and experiences of parents, the parent educator becomes both a teacher and a supporter of parents in their learning. Ongoing parent education groups develop through relationship building that creates an atmosphere of trust. It is in this setting that parents learn to trust the leader and each other, allowing a deeper level of disclosure and investment in the learning process.

Level 3 Example: An ongoing parent education group is addressing the issues of discipline of preschoolers. The group has met for 5 out of 15 sessions, and parents feel comfortable with each other and the leader. Time has been spent during the previous weeks getting to know each other and developing an open atmosphere where parents feel free to discuss. The topic content includes strategies for guiding children's behavior but also allows for much open discussion about issues and challenges.

The parent educator encourages members to share some of their experiences by asking questions such as "What are you experiencing with your children around discipline issues?" Several parents express frustration over current challenges with getting children to cooperate. The parent educator gently probes to learn more about the situation with statements such as "Tell us more about what happens" and "How do you feel when he reacts this way?" Supportive comments such as "This can be a challenging stage when children are beginning to assert themselves" reassure parents. Self-disclosure comments such as "I remember dealing with similar issues with my own daughter" can ensure that the parent feels listened to and understood. The leader then moves to the remaining group members for ideas and similar experiences. This not only provides some problem-solving opportunities but also universalizes the issue, thereby assuring the parent that he or she isn't the only one struggling with this concern. The parent educator offers some suggestions based on realistic expectations of children this age and encourages the parent in applying some of the new strategies. Although the parent educator supports and encourages the parent, information about child guidance is also shared. In this format, rather than doing a formal presentation, the group leader teaches within the context of a group discussion and elicits and builds on members' views, feelings, and experiences.

LEVEL 4: BRIEF FOCUSED INTERVENTION

Building on the skills of Levels 2 and 3, Level 4 moves to a more interventive approach to parent education. Parent educators must have more background and training in family systems to make an assessment of the situation and execute a planned brief effort to help the parent address a more challenging parenting or family interaction problem. Typically, the issues benefiting from a Level 4 intervention occur in groups of parents that are in higher-risk situations. These might include parents with multiple stressors, those involved in the child protection system, those who are chemically dependent or are living in abusive relationships, teen parents, or those who are incarcerated. Although these populations generally bring more challenging issues to a group, other more typical parent education groups may move into Level 4 as issues arise. Level 4 situations generally go beyond typical parent-child issues and may involve co-parenting conflicts, interfering family members, or struggles with services from another family support system. Though some of these circumstances may be viewed as mainly affecting the parent, the parent educator intervenes to assist the parent make a change with respect to parenting issues. Although the couple relationship may also be of concern and may even be contributing to the problem, Level 4 parent education does not focus on changing patterns in personal relationships that are unrelated to parenting and/or family issues. If the parent begins to move into couple or relationship concerns, the parent educator may ask, "How does that affect how you are parenting?" or "How is this affecting your family life?" This keeps the focus on parenting and family relations, which is the purpose of the parent education experience. If the group leader sees that the marital or personal relationship may benefit from further services, a referral should be made privately with the parent.

Doherty (1995) considered Level 4 parent education an elective competency level. He acknowledged that "it represents the upper boundary of parent and family education practiced by a minority of professionals who choose to work with special populations of parents and seek special training in family assessment and basic family interventions" (p. 355). Parent educators who work in Level 4 must be self-aware, authentic, and flexible; have good problem-solving skills; and be willing to take risks (Campbell, Kristensen, & Scott, 1997). Furthermore, Level 4 requires a clear contract with the parent or group of parents to engage in more intensive work than regular Level 3 information and support activities. Whereas Level 3 is presented as a level in which all parent educators should easily function, Level 4 is typically the exception in parent education settings. With the growth of parent education programs that serve populations with more complex issues, Level 4 skills will allow meaningful experiences for diverse groups. However, the need for Level 4 intervention in every parent education setting is not warranted.

In addition to understanding family systems theory, the Level 4 parent educator needs to be able to

- Formulate a series of questions that provide a detailed picture of the family's dynamics
- Develop a hypothesis about the problem
- Work with the parent for a brief period of time on the issue either in the group or one to one
- Know when to return to Level 3 support or when to refer the parent to therapy and be able to work with therapists and community support systems in collaborative relationships
- Use communication and facilitation skills that probe, clarify, and help the parent to develop a strategy for change
- Be comfortable with confrontation, interpretation, immediacy, and assisting parents with setting goals

Doherty (1995) believes that programs that provide Level 4 services also require consultation for staff with a therapist who can assist in maintaining healthy boundaries and place firm limits that avoid the therapy role. Providing insight into complex family dynamics and behaviors assists parent educators to work interventively with parents and still stay grounded in the goals of the program.

A Level 4 intervention typically refers to a brief amount of time allocated to an individual parent's concern during a group session. This is a one-time effort that begins only after permission is given by the parent, as well as the other group members. The parent educator responds to cues from the parent that a Level 4 intervention may be appropriate. These include situations where

- The parent keeps returning to a particular concern that goes beyond typical parent-child issues
- The parent dominates group time with the concern
- The parent expresses or implies immediate desire for advice, intervention, or change
- The parent demonstrates a higher level of emotional distress
- The facilitator is concerned about an issue that seems problematic, but the parent has not directly focused on it

Level 4 also has limitations for the parent education setting. Because it is the most intensive level of involvement, parent educators may assume it is the preferred level. They may believe that their groups are not beneficial to parents unless Level 4 intervention occurs. Because these interventions focus primarily on an individual's issue, group time is reallocated, which may be inconsistent with group ground rules that encourage equal participation. It is important to remember that if Level 4 interventions are used, it is to be on a limited basis. Finally, because Level 4 requires more complex and involved skills, ongoing training and support are required for staff. Programs need to be willing to provide consultation with therapists on an ongoing basis.

Additionally, there are characteristics of parents and their circumstances that should make the parent educator cautious about moving to a Level 4 intervention. If any of the following exist, a parent educator should not initiate a Level 4 intervention:

- The problem is not related to parenting.
- A serious mental illness or chronic family dysfunction exists.
- The parent is emotionally unable to engage in the process.
- The parent is unmotivated to change or has rejected Level 3 support.
- The group is not ready for this level of depth.

According to Doherty (1995), the most controversial aspect of this model is its inclusion of Level 4 within the scope of parent education. He recognized the concern that it could be viewed as moving the profession into an area outside the realm of education. However, he stated that "if the field is to adapt to the growing needs of families, then it will have to face the challenge of preparing some of its practitioners for more in-depth work with families who can benefit from the unique blend of information, support, and non-intrusive problem solving that Level Four can offer" (p. 357).

Level 4 Example: A special group has been offered for parents involved in the child protection system. Typically, parents in this group have been referred from social service agencies who work closely with the parent educator. The focus will be on providing discipline and guidance to elementary school–age children. As the parent educator begins the group, parents immediately feel comfortable and begin disclosing information about their own painful and abusive childhood experiences. The parent educator supports them with empathetic comments and keeps the group focused on how these experiences can affect parents' discipline choices for their own children.

One parent becomes quite emotional and describes how she often loses her temper and is verbally aggressive to her child. The parent educator determines that these incidents are probably not reportable as child abuse but realizes that they are of great concern and that this parent has few resources in finding alternative approaches. The parent educator uses the skill of immediacy by reading the parent's emotional cues and says, "I'm concerned about some of the things you are saying. I'm wondering if you would like to spend some time working on this issue right now." The parent agrees and the parent educator asks the group for permission. "It looks like Joan is interested in focusing on this challenge here in the group. It is probably something that many of us could benefit from, but I also realize it takes time away from our agenda. We can either do this now or she and I can talk about it privately after group. How do you feel about working on her concern here tonight?"

Requesting permission from the group helps to minimize other members' negative reactions to spending a larger amount of time than usual on one member. The parent educator uses objective questions to gently probe in order to get a picture of what the circumstances really are. This helps to clarify the issue for the parent educator, the other members of the group, and also the parent. If the parent hasn't already had enough time to express feelings about the situation, the parent educator allows for this. The group leader then makes some interpretive, nonjudgmental comments that summarize what is happening with the parent. A statement such as the following may help to universalize the issue, focus on the behavior, and offer the parent an opportunity to identify:

Something we know about parents is that when they are experiencing stress and their own childhoods were difficult, they may often choose discipline techniques that aren't very effective. They may not have the experiences of being treated respectfully as a child, and it seems natural just to repeat their own experiences. Does this sound like what happens for you?

Next, the parent educator assists the parent in developing a plan of action. This discussion may include opportunities for group members to support and assist. The process begins with asking the parent to consider which strategies he or she would feel comfortable trying. This is followed by getting a commitment to try a few new strategies, facilitating a plan, identifying obstacles and resources, summarizing with a time frame, and empowering the parent to make the change.

This intervention may take 20 minutes of group time; then the parent educator moves back to continue the topic with parents. In this example, the group moves from Level 3 to Level 4 intervention to address a particular issue and back again to Level 3 support.

LEVEL 5: FAMILY THERAPY

Level 5 is clearly outside the boundaries of parent education. Therapy involves a longer process of repeated sessions that focus on treating serious psychological and family problems and encourage significant change in family interaction patterns. Although trends in therapy have changed so that brief focused therapy is becoming more common, the intensity of involvement with a family is still of more depth than is appropriate for parent education. Whereas Level 4 stays focused on parenting issues, Level 5 includes couple relationship issues, complex family-of-origin problems, and mental disorders of individual family members. A Level 5 therapist works comfortably with intense emotions and difficult family issues. A therapist may escalate conflict in the family in order to focus on it and assist with change or work intensively with a family during times of crises. At this level, the mental health professional not only is able to identify family and psychological dysfunction, as in Level 4, but specifically works to address these dysfunctions through intense therapeutic interventions.

Doherty's levels of involvement model provides a useful framework in which parent educators can work. It makes a clear distinction between education and therapy by providing levels of parent education according to intensity of involvement. This boundary can assist parent educators who work with a variety of parents with diverse needs to determine which level is most appropriate for each group. Doherty suggests Level 3 as the ideal degree of intensity for ongoing parent education, Level 2 as appropriate for one-time information presentations, and Level 4 as appropriate for specialized work with parents with more intense needs.

Framework 6: Leadership Style

Each parent educator develops a unique style that is influenced by his or her personality traits and temperament, as well as his or her perspective of the parent educator role. A parent educator whose personality is outgoing and extroverted, who uses humor easily, and is described as a "people person" is likely to create an atmosphere in groups that reflects these qualities. On the other hand, a more quiet, introverted, and reflective facilitator will be likely to set a very different tone. It is important to realize that different styles appeal to different group members. Therefore, there is no one style of leadership that works well with all groups and all individuals.

A parallel can be made between parenting styles and group leadership styles. Both parenting and leading groups have some features in common. Both involve mentoring, guiding, teaching, and supporting. Just as categories of parenting styles help us understand parents' roles and potential impact on their children, group leadership styles can be classified in ways that provide a model to understand how styles influence group process.

THREE STYLES OF GROUP LEADERSHIP

Just as parents can be classified as having permissive, democratic, or authoritative styles with their children, group leaders follow similar patterns. A continuum from nondirective to structured styles delineates varying approaches in leading groups.

The *nondirective* style, which most closely resembles a permissive parenting style, uses a very free-flowing, low-key approach. In this group, the leader plays a role of peer and observer. If the group functions well with this type of leadership, members feel a high level of ownership. Parents choose the direction, and the atmosphere is very informal.

The nondirective style of group leadership, similar to the permissive parenting style, does, however, have drawbacks. Parents may feel unsure of the purpose of the group and wonder about the role of the facilitator. With a nondirective approach, strong personalities tend to dominate, and without intervention and guidance, some members' needs will not be met. For most parents, this type of group experience has more deficits than rewards.

At the other end of the continuum is the *structured* leadership style. This parent educator reflects an image of expert and authority. Following very detailed agendas and structured discussion and activities, the group progresses toward a predetermined goal. Some group members may appreciate a structured experience because they feel a clear sense of accomplishment as they gain new skills and knowledge. Others may feel too controlled and dependent on the leader for their learning experience. In a very rigidly controlled group, there is a high level of safety because spontaneous sharing does not occur. Some group members may feel most comfortable in this setting because the group is predictable and safe. However, safety without depth cannot provide the best experience for adults to learn and grow together.

As with most continuum perspectives, there are positive and negatives for each category. Extremes at either end will probably meet the needs of a very small number of participants. Although there is no one style that is effective with every group, a style that uses differing qualities in a more balanced approach is usually most desirable.

A *facilitative* style balances the positives of both nondirective and structured approaches. This style uses the skills of a parent educator to provide guidance and support without monopolizing and controlling every aspect of group process. A facilitative leader minimizes the traditional teacher role, while presenting options that allow parents to make their own decisions. This style combines the need for some amount of order with flexibility to meet spontaneous and individual needs. For example, a topic and agenda are developed, but flexibility is allowed for modifications as the session progresses.

A facilitative style clearly reflects that the leader accepts overall responsibility for the group but that parents play an active part in the process. It also allows for a comfortable atmosphere and parent ownership without abandoning a purposeful intent. Facilitative leadership combines informality and formality, structure and flexibility, and professional authority with peer influence to create a balanced approach to group process. This blending of characteristics allows for the broadest appeal for a meaningful group learning experience.

Although different parents find that aspects of different styles fit best with their own personality and learning style, the type of group and setting also influence the need for varying styles. For example, a more directive style may be necessary when leading a group of teenage parents. Because of the youth and inexperience of the parents, it is generally not advisable for a parent educator to routinely expect that the parenting decisions will always be in the best interest of the child. A nondirective facilitator in this setting may be encouraging irresponsible parenting choices by allowing too much of a self-help and hands-off approach.

Experienced facilitators typically have developed a style that works well for them. However, in assessing the makeup of the group, the style of the parents, and the purpose of the experience, a facilitator may find it necessary to slightly adjust a predominant style. Group facilitators should not be chameleons who act differently with each group. However, enhancing qualities of particular styles that still allow a genuine approach may enable the facilitator to match a style to the needs of each group.

Nondirective Style Example: Matt is an experienced facilitator who leads parent groups. His style is very nondirective. On the first night of class, Matt states that "this is your group and you can make it whatever you want." Some of the parents look confused, but others jump right in to decide what issues they want to address. Matt has a wealth of knowledge regarding families, parenting issues, and child development. He does very little formal planning for each session and tends to "let the group go their own way." Several parents in the group are very outgoing and immediately take charge of the group. They rely on Matt for specific information and resources, but generally the group time is an open discussion that flows from one topic to another.

- What are some positive aspects of the atmosphere of this group?
- What limitations do you see?
- How might some quieter members feel about this experience?
- At the end of 10 sessions, how do you think parents might feel?

Structured Style Example: Jo is new to her role as a parent educator. This is her first experience leading a parent group, and she is enthusiastic and full of ideas. She plans carefully for each session and makes a detailed agenda with a time line to stay on schedule. Each 10-minute section is structured with activities to teach a particular skill. She drafts detailed questions to determine whether parents are grasping the skills she has chosen to share.

Several parents in the group clearly enjoy the hands-on and group activities and come into each session curious about what is planned for this week. Others seem less involved in the activities but often interrupt to bring up a related issue or idea. Jo listens to these interjections, responds or affirms, and quickly moves back to the agenda.

- Why might Jo plan her sessions as she does?
- What type of parent would benefit from and enjoy this style of parent group?
- What is missing in this experience for others?
- At the end of 10 sessions, how do you think parents might feel?
- How might Jo be as a facilitator 5 years from now?

Facilitative Style Example: Mike is a parent educator who is very comfortable in his role. He enjoys the parents in his groups and feels that he has a solid knowledge of child development as well as group skills that keep parents coming back each week. During the first few weeks of the parent group, Mike spends time getting to know the group members and plans some structured activities for them to learn about each other as well. Additionally, each session includes time for informal sharing of issues parents bring to the group.

Mike encourages parents to share their ideas and support each other. He also guides the group process and clearly offers purpose and direction to this learning experience. Weekly planning results in sessions that address topics chosen by the parents, includes practical information, as well as ample time for discussion. Mike pays close attention to the cues of the group members and modifies the direction of the group as needed.

- What are Mike's strengths as a facilitator?
- How might parents respond to his leadership?
- How does he balance teaching and supporting?
- How might these parents feel after the 10-week session ends?

The leadership style of a parent educator tends to evolve over time, and the three styles identified may be used as a way of thinking about personal tendencies and how to match these to different groups' needs and goals (Table 4.1). It may be appropriate to be more structured and directive at first with a particular group and then to move to a facilitative style as the group and their needs evolve and change.

Framework 7: Moral and Ethical Character of Parent Educators

A parent educator's style of leadership can be complemented by his or her moral character. There have been numerous attempts to list the important characteristics of parent educators (e.g., Braun et al., 1984; Clarke, 1984; Powell & Cassidy, 2000). These lists tend to combine technical skills, dispositions, and character. The focus in this section will be on dispositions and character. *Character* or *virtue* is used to refer to moral and ethical qualities of group leaders. The major emphasis is often on skills that parent educators must develop as group facilitators. The issue of character has been neglected but is critical for guiding ethical practice and defining in moral terms the good parent educator.

Table 4.1   Parent Educator Leadership Style

Nondirective	Facilitative	Structured
	Leadership Role	
Observer	Guide	Authority
Peer	Facilitator	Director
	Model	Teacher
	Supporter	Advisor
	Collaborator	Expert
	Resource	
	Mentor	
	Group Descriptors	
Free-flowing	Relaxed	Information-focused
Low-key	Purposeful	Controlled
Parent-directed	Respectful	Formal
Informal	Individualized	Dependent
Self-help	Interdependent	
Independent		

The Minnesota Council on Family Relations (MCFR) Ethics Committee of the Parent and Family Education Section has been developing an approach to ethical thinking and practice in parent education for the past 10 years. In this process, the group generated a long list of 40 to 50 virtues that were reported as important by parent educators (MCFR, 2000). This list was overwhelming and contained some redundant characteristics. The group, in consultation with Doherty (personal communication, 1994), reviewed the list and selected the three virtues of parent educators that seemed most relevant to ethical practice in contemporary American society. These virtues describe the characteristics of parent educators that are most important to address current parent and family needs. These virtues will be described, and the implications of this model for group parent education practice will be delineated.

The first virtue that was selected was *caring*. Caring in the context of parent education refers to the disposition to "enhance the welfare of family members as agents in their own lives" (MCFR, 2000, p. 3). Caring is an essential place to start with building a relationship that will be supportive without being enabling. Genuine caring provides a safe place for parents to build trust and to feel comfortable in growing as parents. The parent educator must develop this caring to include all parents, especially those who may have very different beliefs and behaviors about child rearing or exhibit behaviors that are potentially harmful to children. Caring is expressed through understanding and support for parents to make thoughtful decisions about parenting.

A second virtue that emerged as important was *prudence or practical wisdom*. This virtue includes the ability to carefully consider different needs and make decisions based on reflection and consultation. Prudence or practical wisdom was selected to counter the tendency to circumvent difficult decisions and accept any beliefs or behaviors around parenting as being as good as or of equal value to any other set of beliefs or behaviors. Relativism sometimes gets confused with acceptance of family and cultural diversity. An ethical parent educator recognizes that there are conflicts in beliefs around issues like gender roles and discipline techniques. It takes both wisdom to see contradictions in values and courage to help parents consider what trade-offs they are making in selecting potentially harmful parenting practices. Practical wisdom can be modeled for parents so they may see how to make difficult decisions about child rearing. For example, a parent educator may believe in the importance of avoiding physical punishment with very young children and may also believe in respecting different cultural beliefs about child rearing. The conflict in principles may paralyze the parent educator who through no response to a parent description of inappropriate physical punishment in a group setting appears to condone this action. Prudence will help parent educators to manage potential conflicts like the one above in a thoughtful and respectful manner.

The final virtue that was selected was *hope* or *optimism*. This is defined as the ability to look at the strengths of different family members and other professionals and to see positive potential even in the most difficult situations. The complexity of family life and the many difficulties that some parents may face (e.g., intergenerational poverty, abuse) can be discouraging to parent educators. Families may also face barriers created by program or public policies that can increase family stress and create a sense of hopelessness. A sense of hope and the ability to see the strengths in parents and children can help maintain a positive energy to help individual families move forward and advocate for families in the public arena. This virtue helps parent educators to acknowledge that parents care about their children and want the best for them. It also is a strong affirmation of the ability of parents to grow and change. A sense of hope and optimism is most important for parent educators working with families in difficult circumstances.

Individuals bring many different strengths and positive characteristics to the practice of parent education. There may also be specific areas, such as being judgmental about certain types of families, that parent educators will have to focus on to change dispositions and develop new ways of thinking. The three virtues that have been described provide a strong moral character foundation for parent educators working with families in contemporary U.S. society. Many other virtues could be added to the list, such as honesty and genuineness. The individual moral character of the parent educator is important and establishes a strong foundation for ethical thinking and practice.

Integration and Summary of the Seven Conceptual Frameworks

The important concepts and applications for the seven different conceptual models are summarized in Table 4.2. Each model highlights important points to consider in the actual practice of group parent education. There are areas of overlap that were not addressed, such as group ground rules, which was discussed as a developmental framework issue. Ground rules also could be considered from a systems theory perspective and from a feminist perspective, which would offer different insights. There is no clear model for integration of the perspectives from these different frameworks. A group leader will benefit from being familiar with each framework and the concepts they present to have a more holistic understanding of group dynamics and access to different strategies for guiding group learning and support. There is great potential for cross-fertilization of different frameworks that the creative and thoughtful parent educator may discover. There also may be other frameworks that could be applied to parent education groups.

This set of frameworks was selected because they clearly provide some deeper understanding about groups, as well as providing a basis for the practical strategies and tips that are often included in parent education material. Tips or practical group strategies by themselves are often taken out of context, and the practitioner has to experiment in a trial-and-error fashion to learn when to apply them. It is important for parent educators to begin with the developmental framework to understand how a group grows and changes over time. The functional perspective can easily be combined with the developmental framework to understand how the balance of group functions evolves over time. The systems framework provides a model for optimal group functioning and some salient indicators of positive or negative group dynamics. Feminist theory alerts parent educators to potential gender imbalance issues in mixed-gender groups and suggests new areas for research to better understand the role gender may play in parent group dynamics. The levels of involvement model identifies both boundaries for parent education practice and the skills needed for effective parent and family education

Table 4.2   Summary of Conceptual Frameworks

Framework	Major Focus	Important Concepts	Applications
Developmental— stages of development	Typical patterns of group development over time	Specific stages – Forming – Storming – Norming – Performing – Adjourning	Responses to manage stages and guide group toward healthy growth. Helping to develop group rules
Functional framework	Basic group functions and balance	Task functions Maintenance functions Balance/equilibrium	Recognizing multiple roles of participants
Systems theory and group process	Group functions as a dynamic system	Goal-generating systems Open/closed systems Dynamic equilibrium Subsystems Synergy	Guidance in understanding needs, values, and goals Monitoring group energy and connecting with outside resources Creating opportunities for synergy and group learning Managing subsystem dynamics
Feminist theory	Gender role socialization and influences on mixed-gender group dynamics	Male privilege – Detachment – Dominance Female dynamics – Deferment – Diagnosing Gender-responsible leadership	Creating power balance in mixed-gender groups Understanding gender role socialization and group patterns
Levels of involvement	Focus on depth of involvement and skills of parent educator	Levels of involvement 1: Minimal involvement 2: Information/ advice 3: Feelings and support 4: Brief focused intervention 5: Family therapy	Creates guidelines for boundaries for practice Clearly delineates skills needed at each level of involvement

Framework	Major Focus	Important Concepts	Applications
Role of leader styles	Role of leader and relationship to parent group	Leadership styles – Nondirective – Facilitative – Structured	Assists parent educator in assessing and monitoring own style
Moral character	Character/virtues of leader	Virtues/character – Caring – Prudence – Hope/optimism	Creates virtues/moral character to guide professional/ ethical behavior

practice. Finally, the focus on group leadership qualities describes styles of leadership and examines the importance of moral character for ethical leadership. This set of frameworks represents a variety of perspectives drawn from family theories and practice to enrich our current understanding about parent education practice in small groups.

Discussion Questions

LEVELS OF INVOLVEMENT MODEL

1. In which of the levels, Level 2, 3, or 4, do you feel most/least comfortable in your work with parents? Why?

2. What skills will you need to function at a higher level of involvement?

LEADERSHIP STYLE

1. Which of the three styles is most appealing to you? Why?

2. Do you tend to like order and structured activities?

3. Are you comfortable not knowing what will happen next?

4. Do you see your role in the group as that of an expert or a peer?

5. How much flexibility would you allow with a planned agenda?

MORAL/ETHICAL CHARACTER

1. Of the three primary virtues described in this section, which do you believe would be most commonly found in a beginning parent educator? Why?

2. Which would take the most time to develop? Why?

5

Relationship Building

The Heart of Group Parent Education

The relationship between parent educator and parent is difficult to define. It is unlike traditional teacher-student relationships involving professionals sharing knowledge with learners. It is not a friendship with reciprocal feelings of closeness and intimate connections. For the educator, it is based on a unique blend of roles within a context of mutual respect, exploration, and affective learning. For the parent, the relationship provides mentoring and guidance from a supportive leader.

To further understand this relationship, an examination of the role of parent educator may be beneficial. The parent educator functions on a cognitive level when teaching skills and sharing information. However, according to Doherty's levels of involvement model, the role, and thus the relationship, expands at deeper levels of interaction. A parent educator who focuses on relationship building enhances the professional role to include support, guidance, advocacy, encouragement, and affirmation. This redefines the relationship in a broader and more meaningful way. Perhaps what makes this relationship unique is that it develops from a learning experience that focuses on one of the most challenging and rewarding aspects of life—parenting and family relations, where the content is not merely learned but lived.

This chapter will examine the importance of building relationships in successful group parent education settings. Strategies that encourage the critical development of trust, caring, rapport, and empathy will be addressed as ways of enhancing the experience for both the parents and leader. Attending skills that convey genuine concern and help to build relationships will also be addressed. Finally, special consideration will be given to issues that arise as the relationship between group leader and member develops, such as managing self-disclosure and maintaining professional boundaries.

The success of ongoing parent education groups depends greatly on the foundation of a strong, supportive relationship between the parent educator and the participants. If the group is to move through the expected stages of development and arrive at a point of genuine learning and new insights, a positive relationship must be nurtured. If we assume that the group experience has the potential to provide parents an opportunity for growth beyond learning new skills and information, attention to this very important connection is vital. The relationships among parents can also be supported by the group leader. These relationships lay the foundation for trust and growth within the group setting.

Trust

Trust in the leader is imperative for healthy group functioning. It is a primary focus for the group leader in the early stages of group development. The parent educator must present him- or herself professionally as someone whose expertise and leadership abilities are trustworthy. The group leader is seen as a guide who is reliable, knowledgeable, and sensitive in directing the group process and group learning. More important, the parents must feel a sense of trust in the group as an environment where it is safe for them to learn, grow, and share a part of themselves. A parent educator needs to focus more on developing a sense of trust within the group experience than a trust in his or her own abilities. A leader who is seen as having a quiet sense of competence in this role sets a foundation for a positive group experience.

How do group leaders provide an atmosphere of trust? Generally, this happens in the same way that trust is developed in any relationship. Group leaders model respect for members and provide an open and accepting atmosphere where parents feel free to share concerns and learn from others. Maintaining a sense of trust is a continual process. Changes in group dynamics, in levels of self-disclosure, and in types of responses from other members or the facilitator can influence the stability of trust. Continual attention to these issues is necessary throughout the life of the group.

Additionally, a variety of methods can be used early on in the development of the group that will promote trust. A beginning activity that allows parents to choose and reflect on statements that speak to what is important to them as group members will promote an atmosphere of trust. For example, the parent educator might post specific statements regarding what group members might

Photo 5.1   Parent educators connect with parents through interactions with their children.

need to feel comfortable in this setting and ask parents to choose those that are most meaningful to them. Statements such as "I need to be able to say what I think without being judged," "I can take the time I need to feel comfortable here," or "I can always choose to 'pass' if I do not want to respond" can generate an open discussion that enhances the level of trust and allows parents to get their needs met early on in the group experience.

Activities that gradually give parents an opportunity to share information about themselves and their children also encourage the development of trust. An icebreaker that asks parents to "share one characteristic they have in common with their child" is a fairly safe way for parents to disclose something about themselves and their children and, at the same time, learn about others in the group.

Caring

Although group leaders can learn and use a variety of facilitation skills and may understand concepts of group process and have expertise in the areas of family and parenting information, if they do not have a genuine sense of caring for members, the group experience will not be successful. Genuine caring is giving genuine attention to someone by using verbal and nonverbal skills that convey attentive concern. When a parent shares his problems or experiences within the group, a caring leader will maintain eye contact, give empathetic responses, and listen intently to demonstrate a genuine sense of caring. Giving adequate time to a parent's concern, holding off on the planned agenda, and focusing on the parent's content as well as feelings demonstrate care.

Parent educators also demonstrate a caring attitude by following through on assisting a parent and following up on progress. If a parent shares a particularly difficult challenge in a group, the parent educator shows caring by checking on the situation at the following session or perhaps through a quick phone call during the week. A comment such as "I've been thinking about your situation and wonder how things are going" shows a parent that he or she has been heard and that someone cares. Paying attention to individual issues and noting details of the parents' stories will assist leaders in demonstrating a genuine concern for each group member. This extra attention is critical in developing a trusting relationship.

Rapport

Rapport is a healthy connection that is based on similarities between people. Rapport seems to occur most quickly between people with more similarities than differences. Through appropriate self-disclosure, a parent educator makes a connection with members that shows they share some qualities and experiences. It is necessary, however, that the parent educator remain genuine in this process and not attempt to "be" like group members. Although there may be many differences between the leader and the parents, time spent focusing on similarities will enhance the level of trust between leader and members. Parent educators and group members may differ in gender, class, or culture, but the most obvious similarity is their interest in the well-being of families and children. Group leaders can focus on more personal similarities that support common experiences, number of children, family-of-origin experiences, hobbies, or other fairly safe examples. Focusing on similarities with particular members that elevate the status of the parent educator should be avoided. For example, noting that the group leader lives in the same neighborhood as one or more of the group members may connect him or her with those parents, but it also identifies a difference from others.

Finding similarities between group members is also an important aspect of developing group member rapport. A skilled facilitator will connect members' ideas and experiences to foster a sense that members have critical issues in common. Universalizing concerns about safety, bedtime, and discipline in a group of parents of toddlers will strengthen connections between members. Forming a general sense of what is similar across all group members is critical for everyone to be able to recognize him- or herself as belonging with this group.

Empathy

Empathy is the ability of the leader to understand others from their frame of reference, rather than from his or her own. An empathetic parent educator is able to think with, rather than for or about, group members. He or she is able to offer empathetic responses that demonstrate genuine listening and understanding.

Each of us sees a separate reality in that we look at the world through our own lens, made up of a variety of experiences, values, attitudes, and personal attributes that shape our views. Parent educators benefit from examining their own lens so they understand why they see things a certain way. An understanding of how family experiences affect their view of parenting and family issues is critical. Group leaders, by carefully examining what makes up their "lens," gain an understanding of the biases and beliefs that they bring to this role. By acknowledging these beliefs and understanding their origin, parent educators can become aware of their influence as they strive to respond objectively to group members' perspectives.

A variety of factors influence our perceptions. Our own family of origin and its dynamics, values, experiences, socioeconomic status, ethnicity, and culture influence our understanding of others. For example, a parent educator whose family background has included an affluent and protected lifestyle will bring assumptions, values, and experiences that may influence perceptions of particular parents in groups. Limited experiences with people living in poverty may inhibit understanding by group members whose life experiences are different from their own. Though it is not possible or recommended to require a match for each parent with a group leader of similar background, it is important for parent educators to realize how these experiences can influence our perception of others.

Additionally, parent educators become empathetic to group members when they can see what composes the lens of each parent. They can then understand why this parent holds particular beliefs and makes specific parenting choices. By incorporating this perspective into their work, they will be able to develop an empathetic and nonjudgmental relationship with each parent and thus create an atmosphere of trust.

Encouraging Healthy Relationships Between Group Members

While parent educators are focusing on being caring and empathetic as they develop a sense of rapport with members, they also need to focus on the relationships between and among parents in the group. It is difficult for parent educators to directly teach group members to be caring and empathetic, but modeling these qualities can create an atmosphere of respectful expectations and reinforce desired behaviors.

Statements that affirm positive supportive behaviors or comments between parents such as the following will assist in nurturing an atmosphere of trust:

"It helps to know others have gone through this."

"Thank you for describing your similar experiences."

"One of the good things about being in a group is that we can support each other."

Linking ideas of one parent to another not only keeps the group process moving but also links members together. By pointing out common themes and issues shared by parents in groups, the facilitator can help make important connections between individual members. Group members may rely on support from each other outside the group experience as their relationships move to another level.

Another method that can assist in building relationships between parents in groups is to structure some dyad or small-group work within a session. Many parents feel more comfortable talking in a smaller group and will freely bring up issues and ideas. Quiet members or those with limited social skills may feel even more comfortable discussing in groups of three, where there is less pressure to speak. In this setting, the responsibility of discussion is divided by one more person and may provide another layer of safety for a quiet group member. In addition to encouraging more discussion, small-group work links parents and strengthens relationships. It encourages personal sharing and helps individual members develop rapport with each other, as well as allowing for more active participation and disclosure.

An astute facilitator will balance dyad, small-group, and large-group work. If a pattern is established where each session relies heavily on opportunities to talk in small groups, parents will quickly learn that they don't need to participate in the large group because they know that time will be provided for small-group discussion. This arrangement may seem safe but can lack depth. Additionally, it limits the group facilitator's opportunity to learn more about individual group members because meaningful discussion happens between two or three parents. To miss the opportunity of learning from a larger number of parents and the facilitator is to miss the power of the group experience. Parent educators who believe in a dual responsibility to each individual member and also to the group can see that this behavioral pattern jeopardizes the potential richness of the group experience.

Strength-Based Approach

In any relationship, people appreciate affirmation of their strengths. Parents learn early on that if they focus on the positive behaviors of their children, those behaviors will typically increase. This same strategy works well for group leaders. Parent educators who look for strengths in each parent, as well as assisting parents in finding their own, will develop more rapport and build a strong connection with each member.

Unlike some other helping professions where a deficit model is used and the professional's role is to fix a problem, parent education encompasses a broader scope. Parent education can be preventive, supportive, educational, and/or interventive. The type of group and the needs of the members will determine which role is necessary. However, in each of these levels, a strength-based approach is desirable.

A major assumption about the strength-based approach is that all parents have strengths and that focusing and building on them provides a positive approach for growth. Parent educators need to believe, with few exceptions, that all parents have some attributes that are positive. Occasionally, when working with parents with multiple needs and risk factors, group leaders may find it difficult to identify a particular parent's strengths. The parent may also feel unable to articulate personal strengths. However, strengths may be identified as simply being willing to participate in a parent group, being able to get one's children dressed and to school each morning, finding services one's child needs, or being a good listener.

Identifying strengths may require both the group leader and parent to reframe a particular skill or quality. For example, a parent who seems to be constantly calling on professionals for assistance may be seen as a parent who puts the needs of his or her child above all else. If we can reframe what may seem like a negative behavior, we are able to see that within that behavior there may be a strength. This parent could be described in a deficit approach as over-involved or demanding. However, in a strength-based approach, this parent could also be seen as a tireless advocate for his or her child. A parent educator who is able to identify strengths, even those that may be hidden, may find it easier to relate to and work with a particularly challenging parent. Additionally, helping parents focus on the positive aspects of their parenting can promote growth in their role with their child. By encouraging these positive aspects, parent educators can help parents appreciate and build on their strengths.

Parents can benefit from learning to identify their own strengths. However, they may be reluctant to verbalize their strengths. They may feel uncomfortable speaking positively about themselves or may truly be able to see only their challenges. Parents may even say, "I don't know" or "I don't have any." Facilitators can remind group members that everyone has strengths and indicate that they will return to them. Typically, parents are more comfortable identifying positive qualities or strengths of their children. Group leaders may need to begin with exercises that provide parents an opportunity to focus on their children before they are able to focus on themselves. A variety of methods can be used to help parents adopt a strengths perspective. With a little assistance, every group member should be able to see him- or herself through a strength-based lens. These questions may facilitate an open discussion on strengths:

- "What do you think you're best at in parenting?"
- "What are your strengths, and where did you get them?"
- "What would your kids say they like about you?"
- "Share one compliment you have received about your parenting."
- "What strength do you see in someone else that you also have?"

If these questions are asked, the parent educator may begin by sharing his or her own strengths. Through this modeling, parents may feel more willing to participate. Parents may appreciate being asked to write their responses first and then share. Finally, as the group progresses, activities that encourage parents to share their impressions of strengths of others in the group may be used. This can also foster a high level of trust in the group and build connections between members. However, it is important to note that issues of gender, culture, and class may affect the appropriateness of using such techniques. Particular group members may not have been socialized to feel comfortable affirming others in face-to-face settings. This seemingly positive experience may not feel genuine to all members. Additionally, not all group facilitators are comfortable using this strategy. For an activity where parents verbally affirm each other to be successful, the parent educator must feel confident modeling this approach within a group that has demonstrated a readiness for this level of genuine interaction.

Being cautious in finding a realistic balance in a strength-based approach is helpful. If parent educators only focus on strengths and ignore parents' challenges, they negate the need for change and discount parents' issues or concerns. This may feel good for a while, but real issues may never be addressed and growth cannot occur. A strength-based approach lays a solid foundation for relationship building and skill development. However, the larger goal is to keep a strengths perspective while addressing challenges and encouraging opportunities for change.

Special Considerations in Building Relationships

NONVERBAL BEHAVIOR

Observers of human behavior and communication are aware that nonverbal behavior plays a significant role in relationships. Typically, we are very aware of others' gestures, facial expressions, and use of body to communicate, but we are often unaware of the impact of our own. Group leaders need to be aware of their own nonverbal expressive and receptive behaviors and also be able to interpret and respond to the verbal expression of group members. Videotaping themselves leading groups can provide a valuable learning opportunity for parent educators. Asking a trusted peer to observe and give constructive feedback may also assist group leaders in learning more about the impact of their own behaviors.

Facial nonverbal expression has a huge influence on our communication. Eye contact, subtle expressions that convey understanding, smiling, or frowning can all influence how our message is received. Each of these behaviors, along with the use of our body, makes up our attending skills. Attending skills, along with our words, tell group members that we are paying attention to them, that we care about them, and that we are nonjudgmental in our responses. Nonverbal behaviors that help connect us to group members are important. Actively listening by leaning in when someone is speaking, focusing on his or her face, and nodding and gesturing in agreement or understanding gives clues to the speaker that he or she is being heard and understood. These nonverbal gestures assist in building a trusting relationship.

Cultural distinctions, however, must also be considered. Each culture has different rules about physical space, gestures, and other behaviors. Although parent educators cannot be experts on the nonverbal norms of each culture, it is beneficial to be aware that differences exist and to learn as much as possible about them. The group leader will benefit from understanding his or her own norms regarding nonverbal behavior and recognizing that they are not universal.

We can also learn to interpret the nonverbal behaviors of group members for insight into their behaviors and level of satisfaction with the group experience. Parents who separate themselves physically from the group by choosing a chair on the edge and moving slightly away from the group may be telling us they don't feel connected or lack a sense of belonging—or they may need more leg room to feel comfortable in this setting. Parents who cross their arms during the entire group session may be shutting everyone else out—or they may be physically cold. Parents who avoid eye contact with others, particularly the leader, may not be paying attention to what is being said or may disagree with the ideas of others—or they may have a cultural influence that teaches that eye contact is disrespectful. Misinterpretation of nonverbal expression may occur if our insight into behavior is not kept tentative. Parent educators can assess nonverbal behavior and speculate on possible interpretations but must be open to the possibility that they may not be accurate.

SELF-DISCLOSURE

For a sense of trust to develop in a parent education group, members and the leader need to feel free to reveal and also not to reveal information about themselves. Appropriate self-disclosure tends to bring the group to another level of healthy development where members openly share parts of themselves with others. Inappropriate self-disclosure can weaken the group and shake the sense of trust that has developed. Self-disclosure issues of both the parent educator and the group member provide areas of consideration for the leader.

It is important for the parent educator to use self-disclosure appropriately in a group. Parents need to understand who the leader is, know something about what experiences he or she has had, and have a sense of what makes this person a trustworthy group leader. This can be accomplished through thoughtful self-disclosure. A parent educator will typically share information about background, experience as a group leader, and personal information that relates to this role. This type of information is important for the parents to hear and also sets the expectation that parents will feel safe sharing some information about themselves. Parent educators also model that sharing personal details of their lives is not appropriate. Although it is typical for group members to self-disclose at a deeper level than the facilitator, this modeling sets the norm for what is acceptable.

The amount of self-disclosure should be monitored carefully by the parent educator. Sharing too many examples of his or her own children may be interesting initially but soon becomes tedious and distracting for group members. Each time a parent educator chooses to use self-disclosure, there should be careful consideration of its purpose, along with a realization that the disclosure is taking time from other members. A moderate amount of self-disclosure by a group leader is more effective than too little or too much (Cormier & Cormier, 1998).

In deciding whether to self-disclose, it is helpful to consider the goals of such a strategy. Self-disclosure may be used to develop rapport. This is accomplished as parent educators set an open atmosphere, demonstrate empathy, encourage trust, enrich communication, and show that they are human. These behaviors build healthy connections with parents.

Self-disclosure by the group leader may also encourage self-understanding by the parent. Sharing a common experience helps to universalize an issue and can be seen as a teaching tool. It may allow a parent to understand his or her own experience by identifying with the experiences of the group leader.

Self-disclosure may occur on several levels. Informational self-disclosure holds more safety for the parent educator. Common experiences and situations are shared to encourage an empathetic response from the group members. This

Photo 5.2   Healthy groups provide an atmosphere that welcomes self-disclosure.

level of self-disclosure represents a lower level of sharing and is most commonly used. Statements like "I went through a similar experience when my child was that age" assist in building a healthy and trusting relationship with parents.

Self-disclosure may also occur on a deeper level through sharing feelings along with information. In addition to sharing a common experience, the facilitator includes reactions, feelings, and responses to this personal sharing. Statements like "I remember struggling with this as a parent and really wondering if I was doing the right thing" move the level of disclosure to more depth. This type of self-disclosure is used less frequently, may have more emotional connotation, and exposes the vulnerability of the facilitator in a more meaningful and human way. Parents, especially those who are experiencing frustration or other emotional reactions to parenting challenges, will appreciate feeling that others truly know what they are going through at an emotional level.

The second and deeper level of disclosure does not come without risk, however. Parent educators need to use this level selectively. Otherwise, they may be seen as too needy or taking too much time from the group for their own issues. Parent educators who have children of similar ages to the group members' children will often be dealing with some of the same issues. Though it is healthy to make this connection through disclosure, it can be unproductive for the group to focus too much on the parent educator's issues. Although this type of disclosure offers an opportunity for empathy, the parent educator's personal emotions and beliefs may interfere with understanding others' perspectives.

Group leaders who, as parents themselves, have already experienced some of the challenges others bring to sessions often are reminded of stories and examples from their own families. Though sharing examples occasionally may help to support parents in the group, they should be used on a limited basis. Parent educators may find that they, like all parents, enjoy recalling a special memory or experience involving their own children. They can allow themselves the pleasure of recalling the example without sharing it verbally with the group. By doing this, the parent educator makes a clear distinction in this relationship between what one would share with friends and what one shares as a group leader. For example, during a discussion on temperament, a parent educator may be reminded of her own children whose temperaments are drastically different. When he or she is visiting with a friend about this topic, it would be appropriate to share a story about these differences in some detail. However, in the role of the parent educator, either a general comment or no comment about having two children whose temperaments are very different would be appropriate choices. This takes self-discipline, is more respectful to the group, and allows for the privacy of the leader's own children, who may not appreciate being discussed.

Another responsibility of the parent educator is to encourage and monitor the self-disclosure of group members. Without some level of self-disclosure from parent participants, the group may feel very safe but will have little depth. It is the role of the facilitator to model and provide a trusting environment where self-disclosure is accepted and also to protect a parent and others from too much or inappropriate self-disclosure.

It may be helpful to consider why parents would under– or over–self-disclose. Parents who are reluctant to disclose information or experiences typically have a lack of trust in this setting. This may be the result of unhealthy dynamics in the group, behaviors of other members, or a lack of connection with the group leader. It may also be related to past negative experiences when they shared information and later felt regret. Negative experiences with other family support agencies may need to be overcome before a parent feels free to self-disclose in this setting. Unwillingness to disclose may also result from a family background that taught members not to trust others, especially those perceived to be authority figures.

The parent educator's responsibility to this group member is to be patient and respectful of his or her choice. Providing a safe and emotionally nurturing environment may eventually allow members to take small risks in self-disclosure. Modeling a respectful and nonjudgmental attitude should provide some assurance of safety.

Conversely, there are parents in groups who will over–self-disclose. They may begin sharing detailed personal information during first sessions. This can make other group members feel uncomfortable and perhaps question if this is the experience they were seeking. They may wonder if this is the norm and if they too will be expected to share on such a personal level. Each group experience has an unwritten contract or expectation of the group leader and also the members as to what this experience will be, what depth of participation is expected, and what norms will be observed. Excessive self-disclosure early on in a group's development may provide uncertainty for other members as they observe the leader's reaction.

Parents who over–self-disclose may do so for a variety of reasons. They may have poor social skills and not realize that this behavior makes others uncomfortable. They may like to dominate or monopolize and enjoy the attention it brings. They may be very needy and looking for sympathy from other members. They may enjoy shocking other people and watching their reactions. They may have had a previous experience in another type of group, perhaps a therapy group, that had different norms for individual sharing. Or they may be testing the trust level, skills, and response of the parent educator to see how he or she will handle this shift in group atmosphere.

The parent educator has a responsibility to keep self-disclosure at an appropriate level. Determining the appropriateness of the self-disclosure will require the parent educator to assess the development stage and expectations of the group. Sharing in a parent education group is different than in a therapy or counseling setting, where individuals may be encouraged to open up deeply and express their emotional responses to particular life experiences. Though parents often self-disclose complex feelings and emotions in parent education settings, the focus remains on parenting issues. The facilitator has a responsibility to keep the member and other parents focused on issues of parenting. Occasionally, a parent may begin to share detailed personal information about family of origin or intimate stresses in their present family. The parent educator can offer a supportive comment and pull the focus back to how this relates to parenting. Comments like "That must have been very difficult for you. How do you think it has affected how you parent your own children?" offer acknowledgment and keep the parent and the group focused on the purpose of the group experience.

A parent may also share information that is clearly not a topic of discussion for the parent education setting. For example, during a first session a parent may begin disclosing very personal and painful stories of childhood sexual abuse. Reading the nonverbal behaviors of the group may provide clues to the facilitator that they are uncomfortable and looking for the parent educator to provide leadership. When parents share on such a deep level, it is important that a facilitator does not minimize their experience by cutting them off, by asking if others have had similar experiences, or by moving too quickly back to the agenda. Whether appropriate or not, it was most likely very difficult to self-disclose at this level. A strategy that can be helpful is to focus less on the content of the self-disclosure and more on the difficulty of bringing it up in the group. Stating, "That is a hard way to grow up. I know it must be difficult for you to bring this up in group, and I hope you know that we all support you" takes the focus from solely on the content to acknowledging and supporting the parent on the difficulty of sharing this information. A sincere acknowledgment of understanding and an offer to connect privately after the group, when a referral for more intense services may be offered, will allow the parent to remain in a position of respect in the group.

Parents may feel embarrassed after leaving a group when they have over–self-disclosed. They may worry about how they will be perceived with the recognition that they went beyond the expected norm for this setting. It is, therefore, important for the parent educator to practice the art of caring that has been identified as part of developing and maintaining a trusting relationship. If the parent does not return to the next session, a follow-up phone call or note to offer reassurance that he or she is welcome to return may be helpful.

Parents may also begin to self-disclose personal information and suddenly sense that they are going too far. They may look to the leader for guidance and an opportunity to move in another direction. The group leader can offer the parent permission to stop: "You can decide how much you want to share." This allows the parent to make a shift in self-disclosure and may subtly refocus him or her on group norms.

By protecting a parent from too much self-disclosure, group leaders are not showing disrespect. They are not setting strict limits that keep the group at a preventive or purely educational level. A parent educator who takes responsibility for keeping all members in a position of respect for themselves and each other provides a setting where issues can be raised, emotions and feelings shared, and problems solved within the boundaries of the parent education setting.

Expectations for self-disclosure will also vary with the developmental stage at which the group is functioning. Self-disclosure that is seen as very personal in the early stages of group development may make others feel uncomfortable and perhaps apprehensive about what is in store for them. This same disclosure shared at a later stage of group development may be acceptable. Groups that meet only a few times may have limited self-disclosure because a mutual trust level has not developed. Ongoing groups that meet for longer periods of time typically become settings where members get to know each other and feel comfortable sharing information and feelings about themselves and their children at a deeper level.

Depth of self-disclosure will also vary depending on the level of the group. A parent educator in a Level 4 setting for parents with multiple stressors and needs can expect a deeper level of disclosure from members. Parents in these settings have more complex issues that affect their family life, and including them in discussion is appropriate and helpful in making positive changes. For example, the topic of discipline in a Level 2 setting may elicit self-disclosure about trying different methods and determining what works best. Level 3 settings may include self-disclosure that focuses on the parent's frustration at not being able to guide his or her child's behavior and feelings of being a failure. Level 4 settings dealing with the topic of discipline may include the previous examples and also self-disclosures about painful memories of childhood abuse as a means of discipline. It is the role of the group leader to allow what is appropriate for the group, keep the focus on how issues affect parenting, and protect parents from exposing too much in this setting.

CONFIDENTIALITY

Confidentiality is an important ground rule for most groups. Parents need to trust that what is said in the group is not shared outside the group. Though this is often a stated ground rule, it is not possible for the parent educator to ensure that it will be followed. Parents may indicate a willingness to adhere to confidentiality and yet leave the group and share information with others in the community. In smaller community settings where there are more connections between members, this may be more of a challenge than in other more anonymous settings. The parent educator has a responsibility to make sure the group is in verbal agreement about confidentiality and to model appropriate confidentiality in conversations. It may be necessary to remind the group of this expectation, especially after a session where personal issues and challenges were shared. A statement such as the following restates the ground rule in a respectful and clear way: "We've heard a lot of difficult and personal things today about our challenges with parenting and families. This makes our group stronger and we all learn more from each other. I do want to remind you of our rule of confidentiality. What we talked about here today needs to stay within the group. Are we all in agreement?"

Parents also need to know early on in a group that confidentiality does not apply to mandated reporting laws. Professionals who work with children and families are required to report suspected child abuse to authorities. This information needs to be shared with each group member through either a handbook or written program guidelines and referenced verbally so that parents are aware of this exception.

Confidentiality considerations also affect the parent educator when he or she is sharing information about families with other professionals. In parent-child settings, typically the parent educator teams up with a children's teacher. Keeping a clear distinction between what others *need* to know and what they *want* to know is helpful. If a parent educator plans to share information from a session that would be helpful for the children's teacher to understand and better serve the child, parents need to be aware of this. For example, if a parent shares information in the group about a marital separation and the stresses of adjustment for the children, it would be beneficial for the children's teacher to understand how this might be affecting the child's behavior. When ground rules are developed, getting the parent's permission to share only information that would be helpful in working with the child can be requested. Typically, parents are supportive of this arrangement.

When staff members work together with families, clear and distinct roles emerge. One of the challenges of collaborating in our work with families is that certain information may not be appropriate to share with all staff who interact with the family. For example, support staff who play an integral role in programs may not need to know certain details about a family's situation of which other staff are aware. A particular family may be involved in a custody determination, a domestic abuse investigation, or some type of law enforcement intervention. Professional staff will often be aware of details about the circumstances and must determine how much others actually need to know. Respect for the family is always a critical factor in making this determination.

Staff who are given some of the information may feel left out or disrespected in this process. However, supervision that supports their role and encourages them to understand the boundaries of confidentiality is critical. Not everyone involved with a family needs to have all the details about a family's circumstances.

"Need to know" and "want to know" issues can be compared to being invited to an informal dinner party. If some guests are invited for appetizers while others stay for the entire meal, the first group may feel slighted. However, in this analogy, those who stay on for dinner also have a higher level of responsibility. They may be expected to help clean up after the meal. It is similar in our work with families. Along with knowledge or information about families comes a responsibility to be more involved. The most informed staff may need to collaborate more with other professionals, follow up on progress, or be involved in other systems that affect the family. This perspective may help staff sort out what they really need to know about the families with whom they work.

Parent educators who work with helping professionals from other agencies regarding a common family will need to have a signed permission for release of information from a parent before any discussion occurs to assist in coordination of services. This keeps the degree of sharing at a respectful level while maintaining the privacy rights of parents. By strictly adhering to these guidelines, parent educators model behavior that promotes a healthy and trusting relationship between professional and parent.

Parent educators who receive consultation services regarding group challenges can share general information and group dynamics issues for feedback and suggestions without divulging names and personal information. Other helping professionals often work within systems that provide regular ongoing consultation and support. Many educational settings are also realizing the value of this model and incorporating it into their structure, especially in family support and education programs. Staff time is allowed for peer consultation where parent educators are able to bring challenging group situations to a supportive setting for help with problem solving. Supervisors may also offer this type of consultation to keep parent educators grounded in their work. Additionally, success is seen in ongoing consultation with helping professionals who serve in technical support positions, offering guidance and suggestions to parent educators.

HEALTHY BOUNDARIES

Boundaries are limits that both connect us to other people and separate us. They are limits that we hold in place that ensure a connection without enmeshment. A boundary is different from a barrier, which keeps the relationship professional but offers no connection to a parent. Parent educators are often challenged with finding this balance in their interactions with parents. To be involved professionally to make an impact with parents and yet not become overinvolved is the challenge.

Typical boundary concerns for parent educators include

- Doing things for parents they could do themselves
- Self-disclosing too much or too little
- Making decisions for a parent
- Becoming overinvolved with a parent's issues
- Excessively worrying about a parent's choices
- Developing a dual relationship with one or more parents
- Doing favors for parents that are outside the realm of the role
- Discussing information about a parent with others
- Accepting gifts
- Providing services to a parent that are more appropriate from another professional
- Relentlessly asking questions of a parent
- Physically touching parents too soon or too much
- Giving unwanted advice
- Not accepting supervision
- Believing they are the only one who really understands the parent's needs

Working with special populations of parents with multiple risk factors tends to generate more complex boundary challenges for parent educators than experiences with more typical groups (Peterson, 1992). If parents themselves have poor boundaries, they often bring special considerations to groups that make it necessary for parent educators to respond with care.

To understand boundary challenges and violations, it is helpful to consider where we learn about boundaries. Although peers, media, and other sources influence our attitudes about boundaries, the most important influence comes from our families of origin. As children, we observe and practice behaviors that our families model about how connected or disconnected we are with the outside world and with each other. Every family has different boundaries about how connected they are with others, how much nonfamily members are included or invited into their lives, and how much they trust and share with others. Additionally, families set standards for their children as to how connected individual family members are with each other. Unwritten rules govern what topics can be discussed, how much privacy individuals have, whether personal opinions are allowed, whether secrets are kept, or if outside help is accepted. All of these experiences influence our connections with other people. Adults who grow up with healthy boundaries are typically able to develop relationships in groups that respect differences and yet maintain a connection. Those who grow up with an experience at either extreme, with either very rigid controlling boundaries or a lack of appropriate boundaries, may bring many challenges to the parent educator–parent relationship.

Just as each parent brings his or her own unique experiences and family training with regard to boundaries, so do parent educators. It is important, therefore, for parent educators to understand the dynamics of their own families and the impact they may have on their leadership role with groups. Suggestions for parent educators to maintain healthy boundaries with parents include

- Setting professional limits on behavior
- Being a good role model for parents regarding boundaries
- Assertively balancing "I can't" with "I won't"
- Getting one's own needs met in other places than at work
- Utilizing support and supervision to keep boundary issues in check
- Knowing when to refer
- Accepting their limitations and those of the parent educator role

Dual relationships can be particularly devastating to the parent group. If a prior relationship exists between a parent educator and a group member and an alternative placement in another group is not possible, the parent educator has a responsibility to separate the connections related to the parent group from those in his or her personal life. In other words, the prior relationship may stay intact but will exclude conversations about the group experience or other members. Additionally, information about the friendship will not be brought to the discussion of the parent group.

There should be a clear distinction between friendship and friendliness with parents in groups. The leader is friendly to all members of the group but should not develop friendships. Behaviors that are more likely to be found in a friendship need to be kept out of this professional relationship. If a parent educator becomes involved on a personal basis with one or more parents, a different kind of relationship develops with that person. A feeling of being special, of knowing certain things about each other, and of sharing outside experiences will cause an inner circle to form that excludes others. Group leaders have an obligation to make all members feel equally valued. This is not possible if a special relationship develops with a particular parent. Parent educators may feel a stronger bond with a parent who has participated in a previous class with them. Though it is natural for this to occur, it should not interfere with the group experience. This special bond tends to diminish as the facilitator builds helping relationships with new members.

When faced with a boundary issue, group leaders need to carefully consider the impact of their decision. Parent educators can ask themselves the following questions that assist in making decisions that stay within the role of a helping professional and outside the role of a friend:

1. *Whose needs will be met?* Occasionally helping professionals become overinvolved with a parent because they feel needed. It may feel satisfying to know that another person needs them, but this puts the professional's needs above those of the group member.

2. *Are you worried you won't be liked?* Most helping professionals want to be liked. Parent educators may violate a boundary to avoid having a parent reject them or become angry. For example, because a parent educator is concerned about not being liked, he or she may agree to watch a parent's child during nonwork time.

3. *How might this affect the parent educator–parent relationship?* Actions outside the realm of a professional relationship may establish a special quality. Frequently, expectations continue to increase, escalating the relationship to resemble a friendship.

4. *How might this action affect others in the group or other members of the professional team?* Other group members may feel left out or feel that they are less significant to the leader. Other team members who uphold professional boundaries may feel undermined in their efforts to maintain appropriate boundaries.

5. *Can you identify the emotions that you are feeling?* Parent educators should recognize warning signs such as frustration, guilt, confusion, or feelings of importance that they associate with this boundary challenge.

6. *Is there someone you can consult with regarding this issue?* Team members, other professionals, consultants, and supervisors may all provide an objective perspective to assist parent educators in their boundary challenges.

Though it is probably more typical for parent educators to struggle with boundary issues that relate to overinvolvement with parents, it is also possible for professionals to err by having a lack of connection. Unwillingness to go beyond teaching content, absence of any self-disclosure, lack of interest in the parents, and a relationship void of any caring or genuine concern are examples of boundary violations at the other end of the continuum. Each boundary challenge occurs within a unique context and must be considered carefully. Parent educators who attempt to maintain strict professional boundaries

Box 5.1   What Has Influenced Your Boundaries?

Think about your family of origin and what kind of connections and limits were set with others. Boundaries were modeled to you regarding behaviors with the outside world and those within your family. These questions will help you identify what kinds of messages you received about appropriate boundaries.

Boundaries to the "outside world":

- Were you allowed to share information with friends, neighbors, or others about problems your family was having?
- When someone came to your home, were they welcomed in or discouraged from entering?
- Were you able to keep confidential conversations with friends, or did other family members need to know?
- Did you feel obligated to have the same opinions as your parents?

Boundaries within your family:

- Was someone in your family chemically dependent or mentally ill?
- Did you feel that your behavior "made" your parents' lives good or bad?
- Did your parents ever talk to you about their personal problems?
- Were you allowed to express anger?
- Did family members talk directly with each other, or did you sometimes say things to one member, knowing they would pass your message along?
- Did you feel like you were in charge of when and how you were touched?
- Were you allowed adequate privacy when dressing or using the bathroom?
- Were you encouraged to think for yourself?
- Were your individual interests supported by your family?
- Did you feel like someone else often spoke for you?
- Did you feel like you had choices?

After reflecting on these questions, what have you learned about your own issues with boundaries?

SOURCE: Questions adapted from McGuire (1994).

Box 5.2   Boundary Challenges: What Would You Do?

Consider the following six questions to determine how you would respond to each boundary challenge.

1. Whose needs will be met?
2. Are you worried you won't be liked?
3. How might this affect the parent educator–parent relationship?
4. How might this affect others in the group or other members of the professional team?
5. Can you identify the emotions that you are feeling?
6. Is there someone you can consult with regarding this issue?

A. Mary is one of the parents in your weekly parent education group. She is very friendly and spends a few minutes chatting before and after class with you each week. You soon realize that you have much in common. Her children are close in age to yours, she enjoys the same hobbies, and your backgrounds are similar. As you get to know her more, you feel a connection and enjoy the interaction. Mary calls you at home one day and invites you to her home for the afternoon. She suggests you bring your children so they can play with hers and also get to know each other. You know that you'd like her as a friend and think your children would get along well also.

B. Greg is a new parent in one of your groups who was referred by another agency. He struggles with parenting his three young boys while his wife works long hours. Greg is sincere and open in the group about how overwhelming parenting is for him and yet how he wants to be the best parent possible. As part of your job, you have also been home visiting him and the boys to work on specific issues of parenting. One night after class, Greg stays a few minutes and seems almost frantic about a situation the next day that requires him to be gone for a few hours to attend to important business while he has no one to watch the children. You have a home visit scheduled for tomorrow, and he asks if you could please use the time instead to stay with the boys so he can conduct his business.

C. Julie struggles with her role as a parent. She is 18 and the single mother of two children. She attends a parenting program for young parents with a variety of risk factors. Julie feels cheated out of her youth and often takes her resentment out on her children by yelling at them. Although the children are physically well cared for, they seem to lack the nurturing and emotional support they need. You have worked with Julie in the parent group as well as individually on her parenting issues. You find yourself

(Continued)

Box 5.2   Continued

worrying about her for long periods of time. You call her home frequently to see if everything is okay and have even found yourself driving past her home after work. You have made numerous phone calls and contacts for Julie to enroll in a college program and continue her education, but she is not following through. You've called her extended family members to talk about how she is doing and whether they feel the children are all right. You are losing sleep over this family and find yourself thinking that if only Julie would follow your suggestions, everything would be fine.

---

without using common sense, may, in fact, develop rigid barriers between themselves and parents.

Parent educators have a responsibility to understand and be aware of professional expectations regarding boundaries. Codes of ethics for education and other helping professions typically address boundaries in general ways. Agencies and programs must be willing to discuss policies and expectations regarding boundaries with parent educators. Careful examination of the potential results of boundary decisions, along with consultation and supervision, should assist parent educators in maintaining healthy boundaries with parents.

Summary

Developing and maintaining healthy relationships with and between group members is an important priority for a parent educator. Through insight and the use of strategies that support and affirm group members, a sense of cohesion and trust will soon develop. The process in which the relationship develops unfolds as the stages of group development occur. The parent educator gives time and attention to relationship building in incremental steps as the connections with parents become more involved. The open and caring environment that emerges allows parents to trust and participate fully in this unique adult learning experience.

6

Designing Educational Content for Group Parent Education

The issue of balance between education and support in parent education elicits a variety of responses that reflect different perspectives. The question of whether parent educators' primary role is that of facilitator or educator continues to generate debate. Program administrators in Early Childhood Family Education programs in Minnesota have commented that parent educators with teaching degrees tend to be more didactic, structured, and directive in their approach to parent education. They have specific goals and information they want to deliver, and parents are expected to adapt to their style. This describes one end of the educator-to-facilitator continuum. On the other end is the parent group leader who begins a session by asking parents to share joys and concerns and facilitates a discussion around the issues that parents bring up for the next hour without a clear focus on a specific content area. This style honors parents' immediate concerns but may never provide parents with new information or focused content. It is easy to critique the extremes of the educator-versus-facilitator debate and point out the limitations of each approach. Parent educators must develop their own style and sense of balance between being an educator and being a facilitator. The parent educator has to provide a blend of support and education, while following the lead of parents as they share their interests and concerns.

The purpose of this chapter is to shed some light on the educational function of parent education and to examine how this focus can complement the support function. The dynamic and creative balance between education and support in parent education has been an area of tension between the "educators" and the "facilitators." The background and preparation of parent educators often influence which role a particular parent educator prefers and knows how to implement. *Education* and *educators* are value-laden words that carry many images and connotations when applied to parent education (Canning & Fantuzzo, 2000). When it comes to parenting knowledge and skills, everyone wants to claim some expertise. The negative stereotypes of parent education come from those who see parent educators as "narrow-minded experts" who try to tell parents how to raise their children with little understanding of or respect for diverse family and cultural values. This chapter will clarify the role of education and the importance of blending education and support in contemporary parent education.

The chapter will begin by examining different strategies for understanding parent needs, values, and interests. The focus will then shift to designing effective lesson plans, beginning with the articulation of clear learner outcomes for parents. The parent educator is presented as a guide who listens carefully to parent interests and assists them in exploring their values and goals before leading a group to generate and consider concrete ideas for child rearing. Parent education is filled with issues that stimulate strong emotional responses based on diverse beliefs about children, parents, and child-rearing strategies. A careful selection of methods helps a parent educator navigate these emotional issues effectively. This chapter also examines how to match learner outcomes with different methods and stages of group development. The chapter concludes with a practical framework for integrating outcomes and methods into effective lesson plans. Lesson plans are created to guide the process of parent learning and exploration in a parent education session. Some examples of lesson plans will be presented to illustrate different planning principles.

The Design Process

The design process for parent education sessions consists of four stages that follow a clear sequence, from the initial stage of understanding parent needs and interests to the final stage of putting it all together in a lesson plan. The lesson plan is presented here as a guide that is created by the parent educator to coordinate with parent needs and interests. Lesson plans are often seen as general recipes that should work under most conditions with a skilled teacher. The lesson plan process described here is a creative and dynamic endeavor. It is designed to be more group centered, organic, and interactive than the typical generic lesson plans presented in parent education curriculums. The four stages are

1. Understanding parent needs and interests

2. Defining relevant and appropriate learner outcomes for parents

3. Matching methods to learner outcomes and group factors

4. Putting it all together in a lesson plan

STAGE 1: UNDERSTANDING PARENT NEEDS AND INTERESTS

Understanding parent needs and interests is an ongoing process in parent education. Parent needs are not always self-evident or easy for parents to artic-ulate. Parenting itself is a developmental process where parents grow and change through interactions with their children. The growth through experi-ence is not always smooth or positive. Parent education should guide parents through typical transitions and support understanding and skill development to enhance parent growth and change. The parent educator must work with parents to discover and understand their goals and values as well as their uncertainties about parenting. This is a lively, interactive process where a skill-ful parent educator listens to parents in many different ways. Not all commu-nication about parents' needs and goals comes in the form of their spoken words about values, goals, or needs. The processes for discovering and clarify-ing evolving needs and interests can be seen as a complex dance. The skillful parent educator engages parents in defining and reflecting upon their own goals for parenting in light of different perspectives and knowledge about child development and parenting.

Who should make decisions about what parents need, parents as con-sumers or parent educators as experts (Powell, 1986)? There are many possible gradations between these two ends of the continuum, as depicted in Figure 6.1.

Figure 6.1 illustrates some of the possible ways of thinking about parent needs along the continuum from parent directed to educator directed. This way of thinking about parent needs suggests that a balance between parent and educator influence is optimal. Clearly, one end of the continuum represents the expertise that parents bring to parent education and the other end represents the educator's expertise. Parents bring their immediate concerns (e.g., sleep issues, child fears, tantrums). Parents' everyday experiences with their children are the source of this knowledge base. At the other end, parent educators bring ideas for a structured parenting curriculum. The curriculum is developed from generic parenting concerns based on theory, research, and experiences with previous groups of parents. The parent educator who designs a curriculum tries to address concrete parent issues that are reflected in immediate concerns. The sequence of topics is carefully organized to reflect a knowledge base and a logical sequence for learning new information and skills. A skillful parent edu-cator can make some connections between the two ends of the continuum, but his or her influence on defining needs is limited, and the curriculum can dominate the parent and parent educator interaction. On the continuum, the process of defining parent needs becomes more interactive as the parents and

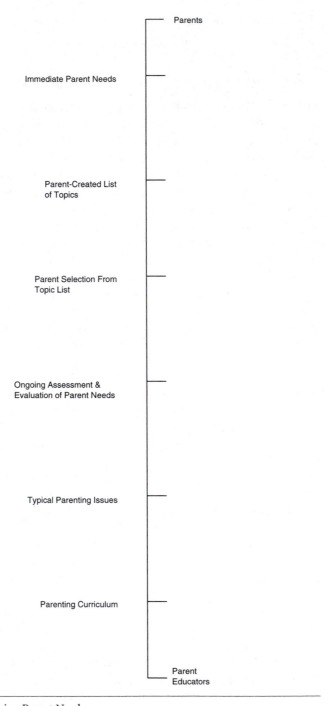

Parents

Immediate Parent Needs

Parent-Created List
of Topics

Parent Selection From
Topic List

Ongoing Assessment &
Evaluation of Parent Needs

Typical Parenting Issues

Parenting Curriculum

Parent
Educators

Figure 6.1   Defining Parent Needs

parent educator meet in the middle in a more equal exchange of areas of expertise. The parent educator has the primary responsibility for maintaining a balance of power between parent expertise and parent educator expertise. This balance ideally leads to a synergistic blend of parent and parent educator knowledge and parent education programs that are both relevant and effective.

The actual process of creating this balance is much more complex than the model suggests. It makes sense to think about what parents bring to this process and what we might expect a professional parent educator to bring. Parents bring their values and images of good parenting. These reflect their current family situation, community, and cultural contexts. The parent educator brings a general understanding of child development, parent-child relations, family dynamics, and the ways culture and social class influence family life. He or she also brings skills to design educational programs and lead parent groups in clarifying values, needs, and interests. The parent educator has the responsibility to create a balance along this continuum and to work at discovering and understanding parent values and needs.

The list that follows describes some ways to discover parent needs that can be used to guide the design of a parent education class. The ability of parent educators to implement these strategies will help them maintain a healthy balance between parent and educator direction in program design.

STRATEGIES FOR IDENTIFYING PARENT NEEDS AND INTERESTS

1. *Interest Checklist.* This is usually done at a first session. It can be generated by parents, with the educator then adding some items, or it can be prepared by the parent educator, who then allows parents to add to the list. It can help parents to see a list of topics to stimulate their thinking about possible interests. The checklist gives a parent educator some clear indicators of parent needs and interests at the beginning of a new group. The results can be used to set a schedule of topics that can be revisited as the group evolves. See Table 6.1 and Table 6.2 for examples of interest checklists. Table 6.1 is a checklist for parents of infants that includes some of the typical topics of interest for this group. Table 6.2 is an example of some of the issues that incarcerated fathers of young children ages 3 through 5 might find interesting.

2. *Icebreakers.* These can help parent educators learn about the parents in their group. They are short and nonthreatening ways to begin a session: for example, "Share a funny incident that recently happened with your child" or "What advice about discipline would you give to your sister who is having her first child?" Responses to these types of questions can help the educator understand parent values and beliefs. They can energize the group and invite participation at the beginning of a session. Icebreakers should be connected to

Table 6.1   Parent Discussion Topic Survey—Infants (Birth to 1 Year)

Check the topics you would like included during parent discussion.

_____ Physical development

_____ Language development

_____ Social/emotional development

_____ Intellectual development

_____ Temperament

_____ Crying

_____ Sleep schedules

_____ Play and learning

_____ Mealtime

_____ Nutrition/feeding concerns

_____ Nurse or pediatric nurse practitioner (available to answer questions)

_____ Baby-sitters/child care

_____ Siblings

_____ Parents' self-esteem

_____ Children's self-esteem

_____ Changes a baby creates in our family "system"

_____ Child-proofing your home/safety

_____ Spoiling

_____ Talking to babies

_____ How babies "talk"

_____ Adjusting to parenthood

_____ "The good parent"

_____ Expectations from ourselves and others

_____ Typical parent feelings during the first year of parenting

_____ Trust and separation

_____ Comfort items (bottle, pacifier, blankets)

_____ Weaning

_____ Family rituals

_____ Discipline (limit setting)

_____ Parenting style, differences between mother and father

_____ Grandparents and in-laws

_____ Infant health concerns

_____ Balancing work and family

_____ Infant massage

Table 6.2   Topics Checklist for Incarcerated Fathers Class

_____ 1. Creating positive images of fatherhood

_____ 2. Understanding children and typical development

_____ 3. What we want for our children—visions and values

_____ 4. Effective communication with young children

_____ 5. Developing respectful relations with child's mother

_____ 6. Nurturing our children from a distance

_____ 7. Understanding family and cultural values

_____ 8. Lessons from our dads

_____ 9. Fathers as protectors—keeping children safe

_____ 10. Supporting a child's self-esteem

_____ 11. Understanding feelings in children

_____ 12. Male issues around control and anger

_____ 13. Developing support systems for good fathering

_____ 14. Discipline and the toolbox of techniques

_____ 15. Adjusting to the outside—reconnecting to children

_____ 16. Rethinking discipline—fathers as teachers

_____ 17. Legal issues—child support, paternity, custody, and visitation

the topic or issue that is the class focus for the day. This provides a smoother transition to the topic than an icebreaker that does not relate to the topic. An effective icebreaker activity engages and energizes parents to get them ready to examine and discuss a topic.

3. *Joys and Concerns.* This technique provides a chance to check in at the beginning of a class to find out about recent events, successes, and challenges that parents may want to share with the group. Joys and concerns help to update changing parent and family circumstances and give parents the opportunity to share immediate concerns that may need to be addressed before planned topics. This type of activity demonstrates the parent educator's flexibility and willingness to listen to new issues as a parent group continues. It also opens up the possibility that parents may spend most of the group time bringing up immediate concerns and never get to planned topics and general information on parenting that some groups members want and need. Parent educators have to recognize the importance of parents expressing immediate concerns and sharing family crises as part of developing group trust and providing support. They also have a responsibility to address the topics that the group has selected for the class. Some ways that facilitators create this balance

Photo 6.1   Parents learn about typical child development as an important topic in parenting classes.

is to set a time limit for joys and concerns or to address immediate concerns during the last 10 minutes of a class. Joys and concerns help parent educators to better understand parent needs and stresses and to consider these as they plan future sessions.

4. *Class Exercises.* There are many exercises in parent education where parents may share their experiences from growing up or current beliefs about parenting that help them describe and examine current attitudes and behaviors. Early recollections, sharing of experiences from childhood, and checklists of values are some common exercises that reveal parents' expectations for their children and beliefs about child development. For example, in a parent group for fathers of young children, participants were asked to reflect back on their childhood and remember a time that their own fathers or grandfathers had read or told a story to them. Their recollections, or lack of recollections, provided insights into male models of early literacy activities and a springboard for the discussion of fathers and their responsibility for early literacy experiences for young children. This information helped the parent educator understand parent beliefs and attitudes about fathers and literacy. A simple checklist on desirable child characteristics (e.g., Crary, 1993) is another activity that can provide some concrete information on parents' values and expectations. The

use of class exercises is a critical part of effective lesson plans in raising parent awareness and assisting parents in shaping their own parenting beliefs and behaviors. Parent responses help the parent educator to better understand parent needs and interests in order to address them in future sessions.

5. *Class Discussions.* Parent sharing of beliefs and attitudes about child development and parenting practices often occurs in the context of class discussions. The more comfortable and safe parents feel, the more they reveal about their own needs, concerns, and dreams for their children. A variety of methods can provide different opportunities for both involvement and sharing of beliefs and values. Clear, focused questions assist parents in expressing ideas and feelings during discussion time. The parent educator can use discussion as a time to listen carefully to parents and gently probe parents' beliefs and attitudes. A basic discussion question such as "What discipline techniques did your parents use with you?" with a follow-up question of "What did you learn from these experiences?" reveals a great deal about parent attitudes about discipline techniques. This provides the parent educator with practical information for planning later lessons about discipline strategies.

6. *Observations of Parent-Child Interaction Time.* Strengths of both parents and children can be gleaned from observations of their interactions. These interactions may also reveal some of the tensions that parents may be experiencing. If a parenting program includes this option, it provides a window through which the parent-child and family dynamics can be viewed. Not all parents are comfortable in the program environment, and most will be on their best behavior. It is the responsibility of the educators to create a comfortable and supportive environment. Nonobtrusive observation can lead to insights about needs that may never be verbally expressed by parents. The parent educator role is not to judge and diagnose parent weaknesses but to understand the child's individual characteristics and to observe parent strengths and better understand parent struggles. For example, observing a father-child dyad experience difficulty with separation helps the parent educator to empathize and better understand the problems that this father has with feeling comfortable with a baby-sitter. There will be further discussion of parent-child interaction time in Chapter 9. This is another opportunity to informally learn about parent needs, interests, and challenges.

This list of informal strategies identifies important sources of information about parent needs, values, and interests. It is an ongoing process of listening and observing with the goal of better understanding parent needs. In some groups where more intense parent services are provided, there may be additional paths for learning about parent needs. In a family literacy program, initial or intake interviews allow the parent educator to meet with parents as individuals and learn more about their current family situation and their reasons for wanting to participate in the program. Sometimes information about parent needs may come from a referral source with a release of information. Home visits are also used in some programs and provide a time and space to learn about individual parents and families. Learning about parent needs occurs in the context of developing relationships between parents and parent educators in the evolving group context. Though understanding parent needs is presented as a first step in designing educational sessions, it is clearly an ongoing task that should continue to shape the content and design of parent group sessions. The process for discovering parent needs will vary depending upon the length of the group, the intensity of the program, and the personality characteristics and the investment of parents.

STAGE 2: DEFINING LEARNER OUTCOMES

Defining learner outcomes is a critical step in any educational process. The educator has the major responsibility for defining clear, pragmatic, and relevant goals for parent education sessions. Working with adults in parent education involves sharing this responsibility with parents. The possible outcomes for parent education encompass a number of different content areas. Defining parent education goals is not a simple task due to a number of factors. Parenting is a complex enterprise that includes multiple roles and tasks. Table 6.3 outlines six general areas that have been identified in the National Extension model of parenting practices (Smith et al., 1994). These are presented as the basic skill and knowledge areas that parents in our culture must learn in order to be effective parents. The examples listed are adapted from the National Extension model and outline the complex nature of parent roles and the functions that parents are expected to perform. These provide a springboard for identifying specific goals for parents in parent education.

Table 6.3 can be used as a starting place for identifying goals or outcomes for parent education. It provides a comprehensive view of the knowledge and skill base for contemporary parenting. The actual session outcomes will be more specific and will describe what the parent educator hopes parents may take away from a specific session. For example, in a session on discipline the outcomes might be:

Parents will examine their attitudes about physical punishment.

Parents will understand long- and short-term consequences of using physical punishment on both children and the parent-child relationship.

Parents will be introduced to a wide range of guidance and intervention tools.

Table 6.3   Important Domains of Parenting Practices

1. Understanding
   - Understand how children grow, learn, and develop.
   - Understand how children interact with and influence their environment.
   - Know and acknowledge child's individuality and unique strengths.

2. Nurture
   - Provide warmth and affection to children.
   - Display sensitivity and responsiveness to a child's feelings and ideas.
   - Provide for basic needs.
   - Teach self-respect.
   - Provide a connection to family and cultural roots.

3. Advocacy
   - Understand and access community resources for children.
   - Help create healthy communities for children.
   - Build healthy relationships within family and community.

4. Guidance
   - Model desirable values and behaviors.
   - Set clear limits for children.
   - Teach and foster responsibility and problem solving.
   - Monitor activities and relationships with peers and other adults.

5. Motivation
   - Encourage curiosity and imagination in child.
   - Teach child about self and others.
   - Select or create supportive learning conditions.

6. Care for Self
   - Manage personal and family stress.
   - Cooperate with child-rearing partner.
   - Set child-rearing and family goals in a thoughtful manner.
   - Know own strengths as a parent.
   - Give and ask for support when needed.

SOURCE: Adapted from Smith et al. (1994).

The main benefit of the model in Table 6.3 is that it provides a more holistic view of parenting and the varied and interrelated functions that form the basis for creating specific parent education outcomes.

Areas of Change

Three areas of potential change for parents are changing knowledge, changing skills, and changing attitudes. In addition to understanding domains

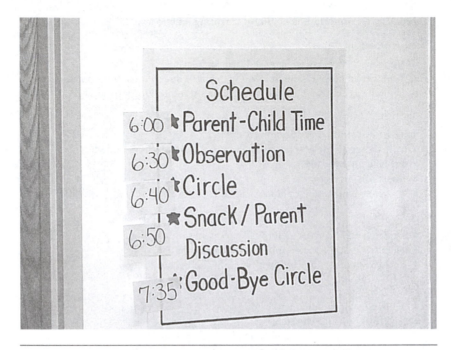

Schedule
6:00 ▸ Parent-Child Time
6:30 ▸ Observation
6:40 ▸ Circle
    ★ Snack/Parent
6:50 Discussion
7:35 ˙ Good-Bye Circle

Photo 6.2   Parent education programs provide parents with many different ways
               to learn, including parent-child interaction and observations.

of parenting practices, parent educators must consider these different types of
change as they design learner outcomes. These three distinct but interrelated
areas of change are discussed below.

1. *Knowledge.* In parent education, *knowledge* refers to our understanding
of specific content areas such as typical child development. For example,
understanding children's typical developmental patterns for expressing anger
from ages 2 to 5 is important and practical information for parents of
preschool children. This type of knowledge can lead to understanding
children's behavior and tempers a parent's response to what otherwise might
be considered "strong-willed" misbehavior. Child development knowledge
helps parents to develop appropriate and realistic expectations for child behavior.
Though child development information may be clearly presented to parents,
they must still incorporate this knowledge into their schema of development.
Helping parents to process new information and understand the application to
child-rearing practices can be a challenge.

2. *Skills.* Skill development in parent education includes a wide range of
parenting behaviors that cluster around discipline and communication. Skills
involve learning specific strategies for effective parenting. Setting clear limits

on a 2-year-old's safe exploration of a home environment by carefully arranging the environment is a skill. Observing and distinguishing different infant cues for hunger or tiredness is a skill. Clearly communicating empathy for a child who is losing a best friend because the friend's family is moving to a new state is a parenting skill. Monitoring an adolescent's peer relationships in a supportive manner is a parenting skill. Parenting skill development is the major focus of many parent education programs. Skills involve the appropriate application of strategies to guide and manage child behavior. Skills are the next step after knowledge and understanding; they are knowledge in action. What makes skill development challenging is that parents may have grown up with poor role models and may have developed habits or behaviors that are not very effective or can compromise parent-child relationships. Old habits must be discarded to make room for new skills. Learning a new skill also takes time for practice, coaching, and encouragement. Parents must be convinced that the new skill is worthwhile and matches their beliefs about children and parenting. Skills must also fit the family and community context to be practical. The presentation and modeling of new skills may be easy for the educator, but parent incorporation, integration, and practice of new skills is not always a smooth or simple learning process.

3. *Attitudes.* In parent education, *attitudes* refers to beliefs of parents that often involve a strong emotional component. For example, parents may believe that young children are intrinsically strong-willed and manipulative and need to be punished so that they will learn to respect adults. The diversity of attitudes and beliefs about parenting makes it difficult to clearly define which attitudes or beliefs to target for change. The parent educator's role is to help parents carefully examine their attitudes and, when appropriate, consider alternative beliefs and practices. This is the most difficult area to change, but it is critical to address in parenting programs. It may be futile to teach new discipline skills or strategies if a parent strongly believes that children can learn respect for parents and other adults only through physical discipline and intimidation.

These three areas of change must all be addressed in a careful and systematic manner. Sensitivity to group process is one important consideration for how to approach each area of change. Sometimes it can be safer in a group to address and discuss knowledge of development before moving into attitudes that evoke strong feelings—although most child-rearing issues can stimulate strong feelings in parents. The learner outcomes must be carefully defined with regard to content, change areas, and stages of group development. Lesson plans can address all three areas of change in one session or provide some time to focus on attitudes before moving into specific strategies and skills. For example, with topics like spanking or sexuality, it helps to elicit parent attitudes and have parents consider their goals for children before the group moves into specific strategies and skill development. All three areas of change fit together and need to be examined in designing effective sessions to promote parent growth and development. This conceptual model for educational change is both simple in defining three specific areas of change and complex in how these areas interact with each other.

STAGE 3: MATCHING METHODS TO LEARNER OUTCOMES AND OTHER FACTORS

The use of a variety of methods has been a hallmark of best practices in parent education (Braun et al., 1984; Kurz-Riemer, 2001). It is assumed that a variety of methods is the best strategy to meet different learning styles and thus engage everyone in the group. Variety also keeps the attention of participants who might become bored with a limited number of basic teaching methods. Methods like an occasional game or more interactive exercise help to bring a different level of energy to a group as well as a different level of engagement. Though variety of methods in and of itself has some merit, matching of methods to areas of change and to group development is a critical step in designing effective parent education sessions (Table 6.4).

Table 6.4 is presented as a practical guide for thinking about different areas of change and which specific methods may be most effective in promoting change in these areas. It also illustrates the wide variety of methods that can be used in parent education. Videos have become a popular tool and can be used in many ways, depending upon the intended outcome. For instance, if the goal is to give parents information about different levels of social play, an instructional video with clear examples of child behavior will be an appropriate choice. Alternately, a video clip from a popular movie or TV show can be used to trigger discussion on male and female communication styles. Curricula such as Early Childhood STEP (Dinkmeyer, McKay, & Dinkmeyer, 1989) use video clips of specific parent-child situations for practice in identifying child feelings or problem-solving typical behavior problems with new techniques. Table 6.4 can be used as a general guide to help parent educators think about their intended outcomes by asking, "What educational changes am I targeting?" and "What methods are best suited for facilitating these outcomes?" In effective planning, it is essential to ask what the desired outcomes for this session are and what types of change the parent educator wants to address. Table 6.4 reminds parent educators that a variety of methods can be used and that methods should be carefully selected to promote different intended outcomes.

Another important factor to consider in selecting appropriate educational methods is the stage of group development. In Chapter 3, the stages of group development were outlined as a way to understand how groups typically cycle through different stages. Table 6.5 outlines the stages of group development and

Table 6.4   Parent Education Methods of Promoting Adult Change
in Knowledge, Attitudes, and Skills

Knowledge, Information	Attitudes, Predispositions	Skills, Applications
Lecture/Minilecture	Case Study/Critical Incident	Suggestion Circle
Reading Materials Parenting books Articles from magazines/ newspapers Pamphlets	Stories	Games
	Structured Exercises Checklists Family sculpture	Demonstration/Modeling
		Video Clips Situations to apply new knowledge

Audiovisual/Media
Audiotapes
Videotapes
Visual aids
   – Posters
   – Overheads
   – Cartoons
   – Chalkboard or
     other erasable
     board
Computer programs
	Guided Imagery	

	Panel Presentation	Homework Practice Learning kits
	Trigger Video	
	Early Recollections	Video Feedback
	Role Play Emphasis on child's feelings	Role Playing as Practice
	Journals	Guided Observation

Table 6.5   Parent Education Methods for Each Stage of Group Development

Forming	Norming	Storming	Performing	Adjourning
Icebreakers to share information	Informational videos	Stories	Games	Informal evaluation
Checklist of topics	Minilecture	Panel presentation of different perspectives	Early recollections	Minilecture summary
	Structured exercise on values and goals	Trigger videos	Role plays	Formal evaluations
	Observations	Critical incidents	Suggestion circle	Linkage to other learning opportunities
	Readings articles on development	Brainstorming	Home assignments	Affirmations
			Guided imagery	

some of the educational methods that may be most effective at different stages. The first stage of forming and last stage of adjourning are more focused on initial relationship building and bringing closure to a group and are less focused on new content and on processing ideas, attitudes, and feelings. The middle three stages of group development provide space for parent learning. At each phase of group development, different methods are listed to identify which might be most effective at that specific stage. While the group is "norming," it is important to use methods that help group members to share basic values and goals and develop common ground. Information can be provided about less controversial topics through videotapes on development or short interactive minilectures on topics such as typical sequences of language development.

As a group moves into the storming stage, recognition of group differences is likely to emerge, and a different set of methods can be used. The set of methods listed under this stage can provide opportunities to explore different perspectives and attitudes respectfully. The panel presentation can be used to present different perspectives to parents of 4-year-olds who are concerned about their child's readiness for kindergarten. Stories or trigger videos can be used to bring up more emotionally laden issues while providing some distance and safety in discussing someone else's situation. A method like brainstorming encourages parents to express different ideas through a structured and safe process.

The stage of performing includes another set of methods that assumes that parents have developed a sense of trust and are able to share information and feelings at a deeper level, including some early recollections or even guided imagery. Parents are also ready to engage in more focused problem solving such as suggestion circles. The methods that are listed in Table 6.5 are presented both as suggestions that fit different group stages and as a reminder that educational methods are powerful tools that can complement and support group dynamics.

Several other important factors should be considered in selecting educational methods for group parent education in addition to parent outcomes and group development. One factor that is mentioned most frequently is different learning styles (e.g., visual, auditory, and kinesthetic). Awareness of these different styles reminds parent educators that each parent may be processing information differently. Visual learners process information by seeing, so visual aids such as videotapes, chalkboards, and cartoons are effective ways to convey information and ideas. Auditory learners learn through listening, indicating the use of minilectures and discussion as appropriate techniques. Kinesthetic learners learn best by doing and need to be more actively involved through activities such as parent-child interaction, role playing, or games. In most parent groups there will be a range of learning styles, and the parent educator should carefully observe which methods are most effective at engaging different members. Learning style surveys can also be used to identify parents' preferences. This activity can be integrated into the topic of understanding children's learning styles, as well as giving the parent educator valuable information about the group members. Using a variety of methods and remembering which methods address different learning styles is a key to keeping parents engaged. It is easy to slip into one's own comfort zone of methods and avoid those that you don't like or are not comfortable using or don't feel are very effective. The parent educator's sensitivity to different learning styles makes learning more comfortable for parents with different learning styles.

Other factors that must be considered are cultural backgrounds, literacy levels, learning disabilities, and gender. Each of these areas can pose significant challenges for selecting and using different educational methods. Different cultural norms may exist for sharing feelings and discussing problems even after a group has built a sense of trust and a genuine sharing of differences has begun. It can be helpful to acknowledge both differences and similarities in a group early in the group process. Sensitivity to cultural differences is essential for parent educators. Selecting methods that build a common understanding and establish an ethic of respect for differences can help diverse parent groups to function effectively and synergistically.

Literacy is also an issue that has received more attention in parent education during the past decade (Brizius & Foster, 1993). The issues around parent or family literacy come from two different directions. First, the family literacy programs established during the past decade have sensitized parent educators to the fact that many parents have limited literacy skills. The initial response to this awareness was to simplify language and limit the use of written material or rewrite materials at a lower reading level. Family literacy programs have provided an alternative to this approach by focusing on improving parent literacy skills as a direct way to help both parents and children. Sensitivity to literacy levels is still important in groups, and written materials should match the reading levels of the group. A common myth about illiteracy is that parents who

Photo 6.3   Children learn with their parents as they participate in circle time
activities.

struggle with reading have limited cognitive abilities. Many parents with
literacy issues have a deep understanding of the complexity of parenting issues.
A group of families that raise a different set of questions about parent literacy
are English as a Second Language (ESL) families. The use of English is a major
barrier to parent education. This also affects our use of methods in ways that
are very similar to working with parents with limited literacy skills. Parenting
issues are both complex and emotional, and limited language skills pose a
major barrier in sharing of ideas, discussion, and processing of new information. It is important not to oversimplify parenting feelings and knowledge in
these types of parenting groups. It may be better to use a translator with ESL
parent groups than to oversimplify concepts. This is one way to respect parent
understanding and to facilitate a deeper level of discussion. The development
of programs like Even Start Family Literacy has helped advance our understanding of parent education in these two populations. Parents in these programs also have diverse learning styles and will benefit from a careful selection
of methods to match group goals and group development.

The final factor that should be considered is the gender of the parent groups
or the gender mix of the group. Parent groups have tended to serve mothers
(Palm & Palkovitz, 1988), and most parent educators are women. The development of groups for fathers (Johnson & Palm, 1992; Klinman & Kohl, 1984;

McBride, 1989) has generated some insights into the educational methods for parent education. Men, in general, may not be as direct in expressing feelings and may be more reluctant to share problems. Some activities (methods) that may be very comfortable and effective for most mothers may not be comfortable for most fathers. In a recent parent session observed by one of the authors, the topic for the day was "Taking Care of Ourselves" and addressed managing stress. One of the closing activities was to pass around hand lotion to use as an example of taking care of yourself. Because the parent group consisted of mothers, this was an effective method. However, if a father had come to the class that morning, this activity would most likely have been uncomfortable. Gender mix should be considered when deciding which activities and methods to introduce to a group.

This section on selecting methods has outlined a number of specific factors to consider in designing effective parent education sessions. The goals of the session and the stage of group development are major areas to address, but other factors may also influence the selection and use of methods. It is evident that the selection of methods and design of effective parent education sessions is a complex but important process.

STAGE 4: PUTTING IT ALL TOGETHER: CREATING A LESSON PLAN

The lesson plan is the actual blueprint for organizing a class. It is the integration of steps outlined in the previous sections of this chapter. There are a number of reasons for investing time in creating lesson plans. A well-designed lesson plan ensures that the session will have a clear focus by articulating specific learning outcomes. It also helps the parent educator to think carefully about matching methods and outcomes and to think about how to present new information in interesting ways while meeting the needs of different learning styles. Careful lesson planning also can help to avoid or prevent common group process problems such as a quiet or tired group or a few individuals who tend to dominate parent discussion time.

Lesson Plan Format

There are many ways to organize or structure lesson plans. The following format is simple and has four basic components that should be included in planning parent education sessions.

1. *Learner Outcomes.* A clear description of two to four different educational outcomes provides the major focus for the session.

2. *Introductory Activity.* The introductory activity engages the group in the topic and encourages active participation at the beginning of a session.

Box 6.1   Lesson Planning Tips

1. Give parents information/ideas that are new for them.
2. Clarify issues that parents have around a topic before creating a plan.
3. Stay focused on two or three important points for parents to take away.
4. Adapt topics for different ages of children.
5. Provide information that will reassure parents.
6. Present something that interests you.
7. Don't try to discuss/cover everything you know.
8. Clear up misconceptions that parents bring to the group.
9. Adapt materials to different learning styles.

---

3. *Session Activities With Discussion Questions.* This section includes a clear outline of the sequence of activities to be used in a class session. Related discussion questions can be included to help initiate and guide the processing of major ideas and related feelings.

4. *Closure.* There are many different ways to end a session, from summarizing discussion points to encouraging parents to try out new strategies from the session. This component ensures that closure will be considered as an essential part of the class, and some specific strategies for closure should be included in a lesson plan.

These four components allow parent educators to outline a clear plan starting with the description of learner outcomes. The format also includes the opening activity and closure because both are essential to an effective session. The session activities should be carefully outlined using the planning principles that have been outlined earlier in the chapter. This format is not as detailed as the typical lesson plan in a published curriculum, which may include a more detailed script, resources for background information, and a list of materials. It is presented here as a basic guide to assist parent educators in outlining and designing their own sessions.

Table 6.6 is a list of practical tips to use in planning effective and engaging parent education sessions. The tips stress the major points from the chapter in simple terms and strive to balance education and support. They also are reminders of ways to use parent input to ensure that the information presented is relevant and interesting. Three different lesson plan outlines are presented as examples of how to use the lesson plan format. Table 6.6 outlines a lesson plan for an initial session with a group of parents of young children. This session emphasizes the initial goals of getting parents to know each other, understand

Table 6.6   Lesson Plan for Parents of Young Children: Program Orientation

I. **Learner Outcomes**
    A. The parents will get to know each other and their children.
    B. The parents will know program philosophy and goals.
    C. The parents will help develop guidelines for discussion.

II. **Opening Activity**
    Have many items on the table. Ask parents to share their name, their children's names and ages, and whether they have been in a group before. Also ask them to choose one item on the table that in some way represents their child—and explain why.

III. **Session Activities**
    A. Have schedule on board. Describe different components of the schedule, pointing out "who's in charge" during different components of the program.
    B. Group discussion guidelines
        1. Introduce bright-colored card activity with statements that will help us feel comfortable sharing. Ask parents to choose the statement that "speaks to them" and share why.
        2. Mention important group guidelines if not mentioned (right to pass).
    C. Program philosophy and goals.
        1. Review program goals and basic beliefs of the program about importance of parent education and support.
        2. Time for any questions about the program.

IV. **Closure**
    A. Ask parents to comment on their child's reactions or feelings about coming to the program.
    B. Remind them that next time the group will be choosing topics.

SOURCE: Developed by Jane Ellison, Sauk Rapids ECFE

the program, and set up group ground rules for discussion. This beginning session is for a 45- to 60-minute time period in a program where parents and children come together for a 2-hour session and spend the first hour together in parent-child interaction time. In longer initial sessions of 1½ to 2 hours with only parents, some educational content would also be included.

Two other sessions are outlined in Tables 6.7 and 6.8. Table 6.7 outlines a plan that introduces some basic information on early literacy to a group of Early Head Start parents. The parent educator uses observation of the early childhood teacher as a way to introduce parents to specific literacy strategies. The session includes a book-making activity to engage parents in an active way to create a book to bring home and extend the learning about early literacy.

The final lesson plan in Table 6.8 is for a parent group for couples that is meeting for the third of four sessions. The plan focuses on helping couples to understand some of the typical tensions they may experience based on some general gender differences. The plan incorporates a minilecture and

Table 6.7   Parent Group for Early Head Start Families: Lesson Plan
               for Introducing Books to Infants and Toddlers

A. **Learner Outcomes**
   1. The parent will know the importance of reading to young children.
   2. The parent will know how to introduce books to infants and toddlers.
   3. The parent will understand differences in interest, development level, and personality and how these affect reading.

B. **Opening Activity**
   Discuss how reading was approached in their homes while growing up.
   1. Were there books and other reading materials around?
   2. Did your parent(s) enjoy reading?
   3. Did your parents read to you? What kind of books?
   4. How do you feel about reading now, as an adult?

C. **Session Activities**
   1. Minilecture on reading and young children
      a) Share what statistics and reading specialists say about the benefits of reading:
         2–10 minutes a day = 4,000 vocabulary words at start of school
         50 minutes a day = 10,000 vocabulary words
         70 minutes a day = 12,000–16,000 vocabulary words
      b) Learning words must be in context: Activity: Parents read aloud together:
         "John says, 'Does are in the park, aren't they?'"
         "Though smelly and ugly to look at, the sewer makes beautiful clothes."
   2. Observe Early Childhood teacher reading to some of the children. When reading to infants and toddlers:
      a) Watch for how he or she approaches using books.
      b) Watch child response to being read to.
      c) Some reminders:
         • Just introducing the book to touch is enough.
         • Let toddler turn pages.
         • Don't try to read a story: Just point to picture, say words.
   3. Debrief the observation
      a) How did the children respond?
      b) What did the teacher do to involve the children?
   4. Make animal books for our kids: Parents make books by cutting out animal pictures and using contact paper and 5 to 10 tagboard pages to create a picture book. Pages are held together with rings.

D. **Closure**
   1. Any new ideas for reading to children from today's class?
   2. Reminder to try new books and report back next week on child's response.

SOURCE: Jane Ellison, Sauk Rapids-Rice ECFE.

brainstorming as a way to introduce the content. It also ends with some practical strategies for addressing tensions and creating more balance. This plan uses parent input as a primary source of information about strategies and then complements this with a written handout to remind parents of important

Table 6.8   Lesson Plan for Parent Group for Couples of Young Children:
                 Gender Tensions and Paths to Balance

I. **Learner Outcomes**
    A. Parents will understand tensions around sharing household responsibilities
        and the feelings that these create for men and women.
    B. Parents will gain some practical ideas about small changes they can make
        toward more balance in household responsibilities.

II. **Activities**
    A. Gender Tensions Around Household Responsibilities
        1. Introduction to Issues: Minilecture—Main Points
            a) Different expectations—Mother knows best
            b) Women's endless list—never enough time or help
            c) Men don't listen/don't show feelings
            d) Disagreements about who is on duty
            e) Fathers' feeling left out—don't take time for kids/family
        2. Brainstorming: What are the feelings that come up? Ask for the feelings
            that are generated. Examples:

Men	*Women*
Left out	Angry, unfair
Defensive	Unsupported
Guilty	Overwhelmed
Inadequate	Inadequate, unorganized

        3. Discussion Questions
            a) How do these feelings get in the way of working together as parents?
            b) How do you deal with these feelings in a constructive manner?
        4. Summary of Important Points
            a) Families often stressed with too much to do
            b) High expectations and economic realities
            c) Lack of role models for current family pressures
    B. Roads to More Balance
        1. Brainstorm ideas: What kinds of strategies have been helpful in gaining
            some sense of balance in your families?
            a) Give an example: Deciding on Saturday morning to make a list of
                what we want to accomplish for the day, clarifying agendas and
                setting priorities
            b) Make a list of ideas generated by the group on the board
        2. Review handout on roads to more balance and notion of small changes

III. **Closure**
Role of love and caring for the other person as a motivator. It can be hard to get
through early years and to work out roles.
    1. Handout on nourishing each other
    2. Sharing a new appreciation or understanding about partner/spouse

SOURCE: Lesson plan developed by Jane Ellison and Glen Palm, Sauk Rapids ECFE, for a
couples class. This was the third of four sessions.

ideas from the session. These lesson plans were chosen to provide examples from different groups at different points in group development to demonstrate how some of the principles outlined in the chapter are practiced. All of the sessions were planned for parents of young children where parents and children come together for a parent education program that has an early childhood component as well as parent-child interaction time. Lesson planning demands an investment of time using the matching process that has been discussed. It is assumed that parent educators can creatively blend their knowledge of group process with content and use a variety of methods to help parents grow and develop their skills and confidence.

Summary

Designing effective parent education sessions to guide parents in groups toward learning new ideas and skills and clarifying their beliefs and goals around child rearing is a complex process. This chapter was included in this book, which focuses primarily on group process and facilitation, to emphasize the importance of integrating educational goals into parent group sessions. The process for understanding parent needs and interests and translating them into concrete educational goals for parent groups has been described. The chapter has also introduced the reader to a variety of methods to consider in planning stimulating and effective parent education sessions. The lesson plan format and examples are presented as models of careful planning and design of group parent education sessions that incorporate parent needs and interests as well as group process dynamics.

Discussion Questions

1. Why is there tension between the parent educators who stress education and those who stress support?

2. Where would you place yourself on the continuum from educator to facilitator?
   Why?

3. Which strategies for identifying parent needs and interests are most useful for planning content for parent education sessions? Why?

4. Why are lesson plans important for group parent education?

5. Why is it useful to identify areas of parent change when designing parent sessions?

7

Facilitation Skills

Though parent educators need general facilitation skills for working with any group, each level in the levels of involvement model (see Chapter 4) requires a different set of competencies. As group facilitators move from education to support to intervention, the necessary skills become more complex. Level 2 groups require solid teaching and presenting skills that share information with parents in a clear and understandable manner. Level 3 experiences require more involved relational skills that elicit and respond to feelings and emotions in a supportive atmosphere. Finally, Level 4 groups require interventive skills that assist parents with addressing challenging issues and formulating a plan for change. This chapter will deal specifically with the skills required in Level 3 settings that aid leaders in providing a meaningful experience for participants.

Group Leadership Skills

In addition to the many personal and professional qualities and characteristics that parent educators must have, a variety of specific leadership skills are needed. These skills can be classified into two categories. One set can be described as external and active; these skills are obvious to the group and are related to content and goals. They fit well with the task functions in functional theory. The other set of skills are more subtle and are internal and reflective. These maintenance skills require insight, evaluation, and internal direction, of which group members are not always aware. The challenge to parent educators is that they need to function within the two categories simultaneously.

Photo 7.1   Parent educators adapt leadership skills in different physical settings.

The *external/active leadership skills* include

- Leading the discussion
- Keeping the group focused and engaged
- Posing questions that generate dialogue
- Moving toward a goal
- Sharing information drawn from a solid knowledge base
- Teaching and engaging with a variety of methods to meet the needs of varying adult learning styles
- Problem solving

The *internal/reflective leadership skills* include

- Assessing progress
- Observing, interpreting, and reacting to nonverbal signals
- Choosing appropriate communication strategies
- Encouraging member-to-member interaction
- Leading indirectly by allowing self-exploration and discovery
- Assessing parents' responses and level of understanding
- Planning the direction of the remaining session

EXTERNAL/ACTIVE SKILLS

Foundational to the external/active skills is a solid knowledge base in order to develop sessions based on current information and research. Beginning parent educators often feel as if they must know everything about parenting, children, and families to lead groups. In reality, group leaders can give themselves permission to say, "I'm not sure about that, but I can check on it and get back to you." As parent educators grow into their professional role, they become more confident and continue to be exposed to new information on a variety of topics that increases their knowledge level, as well as their self-confidence. There are, however, particular content areas in which it is necessary to be well versed. Parent educators need to know about child and adult development, family life cycles, family systems dynamics and diverse family structures, parenting strategies, cultural diversity, social issues affecting families, and community resources. Information and trends change rapidly; new parenting approaches are recommended, and research influences current thinking. Therefore, it is critical for parent educators to keep themselves informed on new research and emerging issues.

Parent educators are group leaders and facilitators, but they are also teachers. Leading parent groups involves sharing some content. Presenting information in a clear and concise way is necessary so that parents understand the content. Additionally, group process skills are required that encourage dialogue and discussion to guide the group toward growth and learning. Group leaders, therefore, need organizational and presenting skills. The skill of cognitive organization helps parent educators to design sessions that are productive and have purpose (Clarke, 1984). Clarke's steps in cognitive organization for parent educators are

- Having clear objectives
- Dividing learning into orderly steps
- Having knowledge categorized to be able to respond to questions
- Being clear and willing to admit what one knows and doesn't know

INTERNAL/REFLECTIVE SKILLS

The other set of leadership skills, internal/reflective skills, are those that often go unnoticed by group members. They are related to the maintenance function skills and include observation, interpersonal communication, and group process skills that guide the group toward growth and learning. These skills allow the facilitator to influence the direction of the group to encourage optimal functioning.

Parent educators typically teach parents to observe their children's behavior as a means of understanding and responding to them better. A parallel can be made to the group setting. Observational skills that allow a facilitator to note behaviors, both verbal and nonverbal, help group leaders form appropriate responses to individual members and to the group as a whole. Observational skills, combined with the ability to interpret behavior on the basis of knowledge of human development, assist the facilitator in guiding group process.

It is this set of internal skills that allows parent educators to assess what is currently happening as the group progresses and to redirect, if needed. The skills involved in reflection and insight blend to assist the facilitator in taking action. On one hand, the group leader is guiding the discussion in a leadership role. At the same time, he or she is evaluating the progress of the group and making decisions about what happens next.

The skill of indirectness is also one of the internal skills of a group leader. With this skill, a confident group leader allows members to discover things for themselves (Clarke, 1984). Adult learners prefer to explore options, consider resources, and make their own decisions rather than being told what to do or given "the answers." A parent educator demonstrates professionalism by including indirectness in his or her work with parents. Although it may be easier to teach content to interested learners, it is more meaningful to provide a guided experience of growth and learning.

Strategies that utilize indirectness include giving a variety of parenting methods and facilitating a discussion that allows parents to choose those that fit best with their values, family, individual child, and parenting style. Statements such as "Consider which methods you feel most comfortable using" or "Think about what strategy would work best with your child" encourage parents to make their own decisions about how they will parent. Questioning techniques that gently probe to get more information and guide a parent to formulate a desired model of parenting also allow the facilitator to function indirectly and assist parents to make changes. Questions that invite self-exploration, such as "What kind of parent would you like to be?" or "What is most important to you in your relationship with this child?" encourage parents to examine their behavior and values in order to determine what parenting approaches are most compatible.

ACTIVE LISTENING SKILLS

Level 3 groups require active listening skills from the facilitator. Parent educators must learn to listen empathetically, attend with their whole body, and respond with statements that support and encourage group members to openly explore their parenting issues. Level 3 skills also require a parent educator to universalize normal experiences, engage parents in problem-solving discussions, and refer the parent to another source beyond the scope of parent education when appropriate.

Listening skills require more than hearing what someone is saying. By actively listening, parent educators listen to the words, observe nonverbals, attend and focus, and respond in a reflective and supportive manner. Group members have a greater tendency to discuss their issues when the facilitator practices active listening skills. In the field of counseling, listening skills are

Box 7.1   Just Like a Duck

Watching a skilled parent educator is much like watching a duck swimming effortlessly down the river. Barely a ripple appears as the duck serenely floats along. He moves his head from side to side occasionally but has a clear vision of where he is going. The part of the duck that we see hardly shows any effort at all. In fact, as we watch, we assume that this effortless act uses little or no energy or thought.

What we don't see is that under the water, the duck's webbed feet are moving furiously through the water to propel him to where he wants to go. These bright orange feet are hidden under the surface, but their quick movements not only keep the duck afloat but steer him in the right direction. The duck is aware of everything around him and ready to change directions in a moment.

An experienced and skilled parent educator is much like the duck. She makes her work look easy as she leads the discussion, keeps the group focused, responds to difficult situations, and meets the individual needs of everyone in the group. This parent educator appears calm, relaxed, and very self-assured. What we don't see is that she is "paddling furiously." She is assessing the group's progress, gauging individual needs and reactions, determining what direction to go, choosing strategies to address challenging behaviors, and deciding how much to deviate from the careful plan she has prepared for the session.

Parents and observers may believe leading a parent group is an easy task. Until they take on the role of a parent educator and understand the complex skills involved, they may believe it is as easy as a duck swimming quietly downstream.

seen as prerequisite in the client-professional relationship (Cormier & Cormier, 1998). If enough active listening is not done with the client and the professional moves too quickly to finding solutions, it is likely that resistance will occur. Individuals need to feel heard before they can truly move forward in self- exploration. The same concept applies to parent education. When leading groups, it is necessary for the parent educator to listen first and then assist the parent in finding solutions for change.

Attending Behaviors

For group leaders to truly listen, they must use attending skills that convey a message of full attention and care to individuals. Group leaders attend to parents by maintaining eye contact, leaning in toward the speaker, and using facial and other gestures that communicate understanding and generate trust. These attending behaviors tell group members, "I am being heard. This person is giving me his or her full attention." Without the connection that attending behaviors make, it is unlikely that parents will fully participate in the parent education and support experience.

Eye contact is an important attending behavior. When a listener looks away from a speaker, the connection is broken. When the leader avoids eye contact or is distracted by notes or other things in the room, the speaker begins to wonder if he or she is being heard or being dismissed as unimportant. Because cultures vary in their practice of nonverbal behaviors such as eye contact, it is an important factor to consider for group leaders. Typically, however, group members feel a connection to a leader who maintains eye contact when they are speaking.

The use of the body can be very influential in using attending skills. We listen, not just with our ears, but with our whole body. The acronym SOLER refers to physical attending skills that remind facilitators to communicate an empathetic connection as they listen to others. Face individuals SQUARELY. Adopt an OPEN posture. LEAN toward the speaker. Maintain good EYE contact without staring. Remain RELAXED as you interact (Egan, 1994). Although it is not helpful for facilitators to focus too intently on orchestrating the use of their body and therefore appear unnatural, attention to the power of attending behaviors assists in relationship building and facilitating discussion.

Just as using helpful nonverbal attending skills can make a connection with parents, the wrong ones can easily show judgment and interrupt the parent's involvement in learning. Group leaders whose nonverbal and verbal messages are not in agreement with each other may confuse parents or make them ambivalent. Delivering supportive or affirming comments when facial gestures or body language show negative judgment typically stops the parent from communicating openly. Keeping verbal and nonverbal messages congruent is essential in healthy communication.

Active Listening Responses

After group leaders listen to parents, they need to respond verbally in ways that confirm that they have understood the message and are supportive. Several communication strategies are used by facilitators as active listening responses. They are reflecting, clarifying, paraphrasing, and summarizing (Cormier & Cormier, 1998), and they precede problem solving. A common error that group facilitators make is to move too quickly to problem solving. Parents need time to express their concerns and feel they are understood and supported before they are ready to look for solutions. In addition to these active listening responses, parent educators also use universalizing as a supportive skill in Level 3 interactions.

Group leaders listen for feelings and reflect them back to the parent. A parent may not name the feeling he or she has, but it is often clear to the listener. A reflecting statement rephrases the affective part of the message. "You sound frustrated about how your child responds to discipline." This statement tells parents that you have heard what they have said and you understand how they feel. Reflection of feelings should not be stated definitively, as in the statement "You feel frustrated . . . ," but rather more tentatively. No one knows exactly how another person feels, but careful listening allows facilitators to identify and name the feeling they believe is present.

Clarifying statements are phrased in the form of questions and are often used following an ambiguous message. "Do you mean . . . ?" or "Is what you're saying . . . ?" or "Could you tell me what you mean by . . . ?" are all ways to begin a clarification. These statements encourage elaboration, check for accuracy, and may clear up confusing messages. Using clarification also tells the parent that the facilitator is listening carefully and values the information enough to ask for a clearer picture. Group leaders often use clarification to make things clear not only for themselves but for the other group members and for the individual parent as well.

Group leaders paraphrase as they rephrase the content part of the message. This may help the parent focus on the content of the message and allow him or her to hear the message in someone else's words. By paraphrasing, parent educators show that they are being attentive and genuine while listening. "So, single parenting leaves you little time for yourself and you need a break." This statement paraphrases what the parent has been saying and focuses on content, not feelings.

Summarizing statements are also helpful to group leaders as they tie together multiple ideas expressed by a parent. A group member may ramble about a particularly challenging parenting issue. The parent educator listens for a common theme or pattern and forms a statement or two that pulls the message together in a condensed way. Summarizing can refocus the parent, who may feel overwhelmed after speaking in detail about a concern. It can assist the parent in seeing the issue more clearly and prepare him or her to move to action. Summarizing statements are typically two or more paraphrases or reflections and are used toward the end of a parent's disclosure. Additionally, the facilitator may engage the group in summarizing the material at the end of a session or ask an individual to summarize what he or she has just said. A statement such as "If you could put that into one or two sentences, what would you say?" invites the parent to condense his or her thoughts into a short focused statement or two.

A final strategy that is used in Level 3 and conveys support to the parent is universalizing. This technique helps parents to see that some of their problems are common to all parents. Many times parents have unrealistic expectations of their children and of themselves as parents. They may describe behaviors of their children that are fairly typical of a particular developmental stage. For example, they may share feelings about being overwhelmed by the role of being a parent and feeling incompetent in their skills as they describe a struggle with bedtime issues. A parent educator can build relationships and also encourage and affirm a group member by pointing out the universal qualities of this issue with other parents. This needs to be done without minimizing the parent's concern, so it is often combined with a reflection-of-feelings statement. "You sound very frustrated with how things are going at bedtime. It may help you to know that what you are experiencing is fairly common in households with 2-year-olds." This acknowledges the group leader's attention and caring regarding the issue and also affirms the parent in recognizing that he or she is not alone. Frequently, in a supportive group setting, other members will assist a parent by making statements that universalize the experience. "I know what you mean. We went through the same thing at our house." This not only builds rapport between members but promotes an environment where members trust that they will be supported.

Problem Solving

Parents in group settings present issues of concern. Though support, empathy, understanding, and universalization are helpful strategies, parents also are looking for solutions. Problem-solving skills assist parent educators in working with the individual and the group to generate possible solutions.

FOUR-STEP PROBLEM-SOLVING PROCESS

The parent educator can use a fairly structured four-step problem-solving process described by Dr. William Doherty of the University of Minnesota (Minnesota Department of Education, 1995):

1. Clarify the problem or situation.

2. Elicit and acknowledge the parent's feelings.

3. Discuss the child's feelings.

4. Generate solutions.

Note that generating solutions is the last step in the process. Frequently, as mentioned, group leaders move too quickly to this step, while parents are not ready. The first three steps involve active listening and responses that are supportive and encouraging to the parent.

Example of Four-Step Problem Solving: A group of parents of 4-year-olds has been meeting for the past several months. This week's topic is kindergarten readiness, which was identified by the parents as an important issue. The group has received information on developmental characteristics of children ready to enter school and helpful skills and ideas for activities to assist with the transition. As the discussion evolves, Jane begins to voice ambivalence about sending her son, whose fifth birthday is this coming summer. "He has no interest in anything related to school, he is small for his age, and all he wants to do is run and play with his toys." Other parents join in the discussion and describe concerns they also have, but Jane seems "stuck" and keeps coming back to her dilemma of sending her child or waiting another year. She acknowledges that it would be easier for her and her family if this child started school because child care costs would be eliminated and it would allow her to return to work full time. She is, however, concerned about her child succeeding in school.

Begin by clarifying the problem and asking for more information. "Tell me more about what you are seeing." "What happens when he does try some of the table activities?" "How do others in your family feel about this issue?" These clarifying questions provides a more detailed description of the concern for the leader, as well as the other group members and the parent herself.

Next, elicit and acknowledge the parent's feelings. "It sounds like you are very unsure of which choice to make." "I can understand why you would feel concerned about this. You want your child to succeed and yet you are unsure if he is really ready." There is a tendency for both parent and group leader to become stuck in this stage. It feels good for the parent to be affirmed and understood, so she may keep the focus here. The facilitator may also believe that support is enough, when in this situation there is a clear challenge for the parent to address and a need for a solution.

The facilitator then encourages the parent to consider the child's feelings. "How do you think your child might be feeling?" "What does your child say about this?" Empathy building for parents allows them to see things from their child's perspective and may assist them in making difficult decisions that are in the best interest of the child.

Finally, the parent is ready for solutions. "Would you like some ideas?" It is advisable for the parent educator not to move into solutions until he or she believes the parent is ready. Asking permission not only is respectful but also subtly signals the parent that you are moving into the action phase of the process. "What have others done with your older children? " "Some people suggest . . . " "There are some alternative experiences for children before kindergarten that might be helpful. They are . . . " Now the parent feels she has been heard and is ready to consider alternatives and make a decision.

SUGGESTION CIRCLE

Another common facilitation technique that guides a process of problem solving is the suggestion circle. This fairly structured method, described by

Jean Illsley Clarke (1984), is useful when a group member repeatedly returns to a particular issue, does not respond to ideas or support from the leader or other group members, and appears to be stuck. Verbal or nonverbal behaviors of the group members may indicate to the leader that they are ready to move on. The parent with a concern typically appears frustrated, and the direction of the group becomes stagnant. In this situation, the parent educator becomes fairly directive, refocuses the group, leads a process of problem solving, and then moves the group along with its agenda.

Steps in leading a suggestion circle are:

1. Acknowledge the feeling of being stuck.

2. Clarify the situation.

3. Ask for permission.

4. Set ground rules for the process.

5. Facilitate, keeping things moving and adhering to ground rules.

6. Give closure.

7. Offer to check in next time on progress.

Example of a Suggestion Circle: The topic of the parent education group is sleep issues. The facilitator presents some information and then asks what group members are experiencing at their homes regarding sleep issues. Mary, one of the parents, describes her struggles with her toddler regarding bedtime. She is clearly frustrated with how things are going. Other members join the discussion with supportive comments and several ideas on things they have tried. Mary repeatedly returns to her concerns and responds to any new ideas with resistance.

The parent educator soon recognizes that the frustration level is rising in the group, both from Mary and from other parents. She says, "Mary, it's clear to me that you are very frustrated with how things are going. I can understand how you might feel, since it seems like many parents of toddlers go through this." She then quickly clarifies the situation. "What I'm hearing is that your child's bedtime is becoming very stressful for everyone in your house, and I think there may be some useful ideas from the group that could be helpful." The facilitator waits for acknowledgment from Mary and then asks for permission. "Would you like to try something that often works in groups that's called a suggestion circle? It's another way of generating solutions, and there may be a few ideas that could work well for you." After Mary agrees, the parent educator gives the group the ground rules for the process. "We are going to go around our circle and each of you can give your best idea to Mary. You can say it in one sentence, and Mary will say, 'Thank you,' after each idea. We will not discuss the ideas or decide if they would or wouldn't work, and we will make sure everyone has a chance to give their best idea." The parent educator reminds the group members that they always have the option to pass and also asks for a volunteer to record the ideas on paper that will be given to Mary at the end of the process.

The suggestion circle begins in a structured format that gives each parent an opportunity to give a suggestion. If someone passes, he or she will have another opportunity at the end. Typically, the parent with a concern, in this case Mary, will attempt to pull the group back into a discussion about her concerns and try to evaluate each idea by sharing why this would not work. The facilitator's role during a suggestion circle is to demonstrate more control and direction, keeping the process moving. Helpful statements are "Remember, just one sentence, describing your best idea," or "Mary, I need to remind you that you can only thank each person for their idea. We won't take the time now to discuss them." These statements keep the suggestion circle from breaking down and the group from returning to the feeling of being stuck.

At the end of the process, the facilitator thanks everyone for his or her helpful suggestions, encourages Mary to take the written list and decide which ones would be most helpful, and invites her to try those that fit for her. An offer to check in next time on how it went lets the parent know that both the facilitator and the other members are genuinely concerned. The parent educator, however, must be very cautious that the same issue does not dominate the next session. A check-in must be quick, and it must be made clear that the group will move on with the designated topic.

Suggestion circles are helpful when a parent appears to be stuck on an issue and resistant to ideas that are offered. Group members immediately notice the change in tone when the facilitator firmly takes control of the group's direction. This strategy is respectful to all members. The parent with a concern gets the suggestions he or she needs, other group members appreciate that one individual's needs do not impede the progress of the session, and the group facilitator demonstrates leadership in a challenging situation.

Referrals

Most parent educators find making referrals challenging. Deciding if the issue is of great enough concern, anticipating the parent's response, and finding the right words require many skills. In this section, we will examine the issues involved in referrals, look at possible reactions from parents, and provide a process for parent-, family-, and child-related referrals.

Parent education cannot meet every need of every family. There will be times when a parent educator must accept the limitations of his or her role and recognize that a parent and/or child require services beyond what can be

Photo 7.2   Referrals are conducted on an individual basis to discuss needs that may not always be met in a group setting.

offered in this setting. Mental health counseling for a child or parent, special education or speech services, domestic abuse protection, and family or marriage counseling are examples of possible referrals.

When deciding whether to refer, parent educators must rely on the information they gather from parents in the group setting or from observations of children in programs that combine services for both children and adults. The levels of involvement model (Chapter 4) states that skills in a Level 3 setting require the ability to identify family dysfunction and psychological dysfunction. Typically, universalizing the concerns of parents is a supportive and affirming method of interaction. When the issue is beyond the realm of normal functioning or development, however, it can be inappropriate to universalize and even detrimental to the parent. When parent educators use their solid knowledge of normal family functioning and typical child development to identify a concern, it is their responsibility to approach the parent to offer information about further services. Referrals are not done within the group setting, but rather, privately with the parent.

The following questions can help a parent educator make decisions about referrals:

- Is this issue of enough concern and likely to be a problem?
- Do I have enough information? What else do I need to know?

- Do I know what services are available in my community?
- What is my relationship with this parent? Is there a level of trust present?
- Am I the best person to approach him or her regarding this issue?
- What might the parent's reaction be?
- Am I aware of my own feelings about this issue and able to keep them separate?
- How can I approach this parent privately, and what words will I use?
- How would I want to be treated if this were me?

Different types of referrals present the need for varying skills and considerations. Initially, some referrals may seem easier for a parent educator to make than others. For example, approaching a parent about concerns of domestic abuse and possible community interventions probably appears much more difficult than suggesting speech services for a child who has articulation problems. However, any referral can be difficult. Though a speech concern may seem uncomplicated, it can be traumatic for the parent to address. Being approached regarding any type of developmental concern or delay that shatters the parent's dream of his or her child can be challenging (Bowman, 1994).

For example, like all parents, Carol, an elementary teacher, enjoyed watching her toddler grow and develop into a happy, healthy preschooler. Carol had a vision of what this child would be like as an older child and adult, the success he would have in school, and the social and developmental milestones he would achieve. As her son reached the age of 3½ years, she noticed that other people often commented that his speech was difficult to understand. Carol, however, had no problem understanding him.

At his first preschool experience, both the early childhood teacher and the parent educator had concerns about his speech development. When the parent educator approached her and asked if she had any concerns about her son's speech, Carol immediately began crying. Intellectually, Carol knew that a delay in language development could most likely be helped by speech therapy. Emotionally, she felt devastated as the perfect image of her child was shattered. Bowman (1994) referred to this as "loss of dreams." Parents who are approached about a referral for what may seem like a nontraumatic issue may experience great anxiety and distress.

In this situation, it is helpful for a parent educator to be supportive in acknowledging the parent's feelings. At the same time, it is helpful to be positive and realistic about the likely outcome of the suggested services.

Depending on the issue of concern and the type of referral, there are a number of possible reactions from the parent. When parent educators approach a parent about a referral for his or her child, the parent may be relieved that someone has finally acknowledged the problem and opened the door for help. Or the parent may not be ready to consider the referral and become defensive or evasive. When referrals are made for parents to access counseling or address domestic violence issues, they may suddenly appear uncomfortable with the facilitator. It may feel as if the relationship with the parent educator has now changed and the parent has been exposed and identified as someone with a complex problem. The parent may feel embarrassed and withdraw from the group. He or she may respond in a defensive way and become resistant. Or, hopefully, he or she will listen and accept the suggestion of the parent educator.

If a parent becomes defensive or resistant to the concerns of the professional, the parent educator needs to stop the referral. Continuing makes a power struggle likely to occur, which typically guarantees that the parent will not cooperate. It is difficult when a professional firmly believes there is a problem and a referral to another service is in the best interest of the child or parent, yet the parent is the only one who can make the decision. Parent educators may need to pull back from the process. Statements like "It sounds like you don't feel there is a problem. I'm still concerned, but let's give it a little more time and I'll check back with you" give the parent time to take in the information, reconsider, and perhaps be more receptive at a later time. When parents do not see a need for change or services, attempts by the parent educator to "assist" will not be productive and can, ultimately, damage the relationship between parent and professional (Dunst, Trivette, & Deal, 1988).

Before approaching a parent, several strategies should be considered. First, the concern should be stated from the perspective of the parent educator. "I'm noticing that it is hard for me and the other children to understand Marie's speech. Have you had any concerns about this?" This approach is less threatening than language that states, "There is a problem with your child's speech." It also clearly conveys concern and asks for the parent's reaction. It is important for the parent educator to use positive attending skills and also read the nonverbal language of the parent at this time. Does he or she take a step back from you? Sigh in relief? Look confused? By assessing where he or she is at that moment, the parent educator can decide how to proceed.

It is also critical for parent educators to keep their own values and experiences out of the referral process. A professional who has a child with attentional difficulties and has had a positive experience with medications and medical interventions needs to keep that bias out of the referral. Each parent and child situation is unique, and parents need to make their own decisions. Though it is appropriate to use self-disclosure to assure the parent that you may have gone through a similar experience, it is not acceptable to try to influence others' decisions on the basis of your own situation. The values, beliefs, and experiences of the professional should not be used to sway parents in their decision making.

Example of Referral for a Child's Concern: Larry's son is 4 years old and is having difficulties in the preschool program. The parents of the children meet weekly and discuss parenting challenges and strategies with the parent educator. The early childhood teacher has noticed delays in development, both physical and cognitive, and is beginning to be concerned about his child. The parent educator has a good relationship with Larry, and there is a high level of trust between them. She approaches him after group one day and states, "Larry, we are really enjoying having Matthew in our program. We're noticing a few areas where things seem to be somewhat difficult for him. When he runs, he often trips and falls. He also has trouble with many of the table activities, like putting the puzzles together and matching games. Have you noticed any of these things?"

Larry responds by saying that he, too, had noticed his son seems slower than the other children and was beginning to wonder if there were problems. The parent educator says, "Would you be interested in having someone meet with you to see if there are any areas of concern? Many times there are things early intervention teachers can do for young children to help before they start school. We have teachers who can work with your son if you think that would help."

Larry seems relieved that help is available and readily agrees to having someone contact him with more information. The parent educator affirms his decision to check things out and stays in touch by checking in from time to time on Matthew's progress.

Example of Referral for a Parent Concern: Shelly is a young mother of two little girls. She has been attending parent education classes, and the facilitator has noticed bruises on her arms and face several times. Shelly has confided to the group that her relationship with the children's father is violent and that they often fight. She arrives at class one night with fresh bruises on her face. She keeps covering her face with her hand during the class and afterwards stays late to help the parent educator clean up the room.

The parent educator, approaches her and says, "Shelly, I'm concerned about you. I know that things have been difficult for you at home lately. Would you like to talk about what is happening?"

At first Shelly seems embarrassed and makes excuses for the bruises. But as they begin to talk, she opens up and admits she is being abused. She indicates that the children are present during these outbursts but are never physically abused by their father.

The parent educator focuses on Shelly's well-being but also asks, "Are you worried about your children watching this happen? It can be pretty devastating for children to be present and watch one of their parents being hurt by the other."

Shelly and the parent educator continue the conversation, and Shelly admits she doesn't want to live this way any longer and is concerned about her daughters growing up in this environment.

"There are people in the community who can help you. Would you like some information about where you might go?"

Shelly agrees and makes the phone call to a women's shelter from the classroom. The parent educator assists her, as needed, and supports her in her decision.

These referrals demonstrate situations where services are needed beyond what traditional parent education has to offer. The relationship between educator and parent is strong, and the parents trust the educator and are responsive to suggestions.

Approaching a parent for a referral for either the child or the parent can be very challenging. Consideration must be given to whether a referral is warranted, what the most appropriate services are, how the parent may respond, and what is the best way to bring up the concern. Parent educators rely on their observation and listening skills as they assess developmental issues of the child, family dysfunction, or personal or marital issues that affect family life or parenting. Referrals are made when the parent educator believes that additional services beyond the scope of parent education are warranted, are available, and would benefit the parent and/or child.

Summary

In summary, a variety of leadership and facilitation skills are necessary for the parent educator to be successful. Skills that focus on presenting content and leading discussion are important competencies that help make group sessions productive. Additionally, parent educators utilize skills that are more reflective, deal with the affective aspects of group process, and focus on the interconnectedness of parents as they share in the group learning experience. It is by blending these two skill areas that parent educators are able to provide quality opportunities for parents to grow in their role through participating in group parent education.

Discussion Questions

1. Choose a challenging parenting situation. Role-play the four-step process to assist the parent.

2. Choose a reason for a referral that you think might be easiest to conduct with a parent. What issues might make it more complicated than might seem obvious?

8

Managing Difficult Moments in Parent Groups

P arents exhibit a variety of behaviors in groups that create challenges for group facilitators. Disruptive behaviors can impair group process, cause conflict between members, and make other parents feel resentful and dissatisfied with the group experience. The parent educator has an obligation to monitor the disruptive behaviors and respond to them, depending on the impact on the group. Group members quickly lose respect for parent educators who ignore their duty to address disruptive behaviors (Curran, 1989). As groups develop beyond the beginning stages of development, it is common for some challenging behaviors to occur. Groups that function beyond Level 2, as described in the levels of involvement model (Chapter 4), also tend to experience more of these challenges, as parents feel comfortable discussing and sharing their views and experiences. In these settings, group topics cover more personal and intense issues that allow members to share feelings and emotions related to the parenting experience.

This chapter will identify common challenging behaviors in groups, propose possible explanations of why they occur, and suggest helpful responses from the group leader. It is beneficial for facilitators to understand likely dynamics that often cause these behaviors. However, it is also important to note that each parent is unique and that the reasons behind behaviors are speculations based on analysis of typical human behavior. Although disruptive behaviors of group members may be directly related to lack of skills in the leader or deficits in the relationship between leader and parent, frequently these behaviors are ingrained in a parent's style of interactions in multiple settings.

Parent educators who observe disruptive behaviors in their groups must decide if and when to intervene. Responding to every behavior that is not deemed acceptable will cause other parents in a group to feel uncomfortable, unwilling to share, and fearful that they too will be "corrected." Waiting too long or not responding at all sends the message that this behavior is tolerable. The group leader has a responsibility to maintain group process that is productive, functional, and positive for all members. Deciding when and how to intervene is a very challenging group leadership task.

These questions may assist a parent educator in determining a response to a disruptive behavior:

- At what developmental stage is this group?
- What are the norms for this particular group?
- Does the behavior seem to be affecting other group members? What nonverbal or verbal responses do I see?
- What is my relationship with this particular parent?
- Is this something I need to respond to immediately?
- Can I intervene in the group or should I approach the parent individually?

Monopolizing

WHAT IS IT?

A parent dominates the group with his or her issues, comments on everything being said, shares personal experiences at length, and talks significantly more than others in the group. This parent moves from one issue to the next and gives little opportunity for others to step into the conversation. He or she will often respond to what someone else has said, then quickly turn the focus to personal experiences or ideas.

WHY DOES IT OCCUR?

A monopolizing group member may actually be very insecure and need to feel in control of the group situation. By monopolizing, this parent feels a sense of security in that he or she knows what is happening in the group. Allowing the facilitator to lead or other parents to participate makes the parent uncertain of what may happen next. A monopolizing parent may also have an unfulfilled need for attention and validation (Rothenberg, 1992) or may lack opportunities in his or her life for interactions with other adults. It is also possible that an overly talkative group member has a personality type that is more verbal and outgoing than that of others in the group.

SUGGESTIONS FOR LEADERS

- Avoid or limit eye contact with a monopolizer.
- Increase your awareness of your own body language to be less open to that parent.
- Add more structure to the group session.
- Avoid open-ended questions for this person.
- Post an agenda, and refer to the progress of the session.
- Read nonverbal behaviors of others to invite their ideas.
- Use a structured suggestion circle if this parent gets stuck on a particular issue. Each member quickly contributes an idea, and then the group moves on without further discussion (see Chapter 7).
- Consider whether this parent may benefit from one-to-one support rather than, or in addition to, the group experience.

HELPFUL COMMENTS

"Excuse me. I wonder if anyone else would like to comment on that."

"Could you finish that thought and then we'll move on?"

"What you are saying fits well with something we heard earlier." (Ask another member to comment.)

"If you could put all those thoughts into just one sentence, what would you say?"

Interrupting

WHAT IS IT?

Interrupting is similar to monopolizing behavior, except that the parent repeatedly cuts off the leader or another parent during discussion.

WHY DOES IT OCCUR?

An interrupter may be self-centered or have poor social skills. He or she may also be an eager parent who is excited about participating and enjoys being an active group member. Someone who repeatedly interrupts may have problems following a discussion or challenges with staying attentive.

SUGGESTIONS FOR LEADERS

Gently but firmly interrupt the parent and give the other parent permission to continue.

HELPFUL COMMENTS

"Could you hold on to that for just a minute? I'm not sure Tom was finished."

"I'm feeling like Mary still wants to hear more from the group. Let's back up a minute."

"I'd like to get back to Elizabeth's comment. Elizabeth, did you have anything else to add?"

Engaging in Side Conversations

WHAT IS IT?

Typically, side conversations involve two group members sitting near each other who engage in a quiet exchange of conversation while the leader or others in the group are talking. Their discussion may or may not be related to the topic. Side conversations are distracting to the leader and other members and undermine the cooperative spirit of a group.

WHY DOES IT OCCUR?

Parents who engage in side conversations may not realize that their behavior is disrespectful to the rest of the group. Like other parents who exhibit disruptive behaviors, they may lack social skills. They may be bored or feel they are above the others in the group. By engaging in this type of interaction, parents separate themselves from the rest of the group, a course of action that often stems from a feeling of not belonging. Side conversations may also be a learned behavior from earlier years of being a student in a traditional school setting. Parents who are reluctant or uncomfortable sharing in the larger group may feel it is safer to share their experience quietly with someone near them. Groups where some members know each other well or have developed close relationships within the group are particularly prone to side conversations.

SUGGESTIONS FOR LEADERS

- Address side conversations during the early stages of group development when ground rules are set.
- Consider activities at the beginning of a group that divide members into other seating arrangements.
- Use silence to get everyone's attention.
- Gently confront with an "I message"—that is, a statement from your own frame of reference.

HELPFUL COMMENTS

"Excuse me, I'm having trouble hearing Michael."

"I'm feeling distracted. Can everyone hear what is being said?"

"It sounds like you have a good example. Would you be willing to share with all of us?"

"Let's try to stay focused on one person at a time."

"Let's wait until everyone is ready."

Silence of Members

WHAT IS IT?

Silent members are either unable to participate verbally in a group, unwilling to participate, or uncomfortable about participating. A distinction is made between active quietness and passive quietness (Bowman, 1987). Actively quiet members follow the conversation and are nonverbally responsive. They attend with eye contact, facial expressions, and gestures that indicate that they are actively listening. Passively quiet members, on the other hand, show few clues as to their level of connection and appear preoccupied and disengaged.

WHY DOES IT OCCUR?

Parents who are silent may have a temperament that makes them shy or naturally quiet. They may be participating by listening intently and learning in their own way. They may lack the social skills that enable adults to speak comfortably in group settings. Or they may have low self-esteem and be fearful of saying something wrong or being judged. Silent group members may also have limited cognitive abilities and find it difficult to understand the discussion. By reading nonverbal behavior and getting to know parents well, facilitators may also surmise that parents are silent because they are not comfortable in the group, are reluctant participants, or are being mandated to attend. Court-ordered parents may initially begin a group with a negative attitude and unwillingness to participate. Crossing arms, physically sitting back from the rest of the group, and using facial expressions that imply annoyance are strong cues that this parent does not want to participate and does not feel a sense of belonging. "Spouse-ordered" parents may also feel resentful for being made to attend parent education groups and can sabotage the group process (Curran, 1989). Other parents need more time to process information and formulate their thoughts in words. They may feel left behind in fast-paced groups where others share quickly. ESL (English as a Second Language) parents with limited English skills may be silent as they struggle to comprehend what is being said. Other quiet members may have an idea to share but may wait to be asked. Finally, some group members may be distracted and consumed by other issues in their lives and unable to participate beyond being present. This may be a chronic condition or simply a stressful time when one withdraws from group participation.

SUGGESTIONS FOR LEADERS

- Consider whether full participation is a realistic goal for all groups (Bowman, 1987).
- Ask parents to write down their thoughts, or give them a short time to consider their ideas before asking for responses.
- Watch for nonverbal behaviors of members who are quiet to determine why.
- Allow for small-group or dyad work where a quiet member may feel more relaxed.
- Connect with silent members before and after the parent session to strengthen the relationship.
- Accept quiet learning as a style.
- Help group members get acquainted through activities that strengthen the bonds of the group.
- Model that differences of opinions are valued.
- Ask a quiet member to help you with simple tasks such as refreshments, listing items on a board, or setting up a display.

HELPFUL COMMENTS

"There are a few of you we haven't heard from yet tonight. What would you like to add?"

"I know this is something Ben has dealt with successfully with his children. Would you be willing to tell us how you've handled this issue?"

"It looks like you have something to add about this. Would you care to comment?"

Silence of the Group

WHAT IS IT?

Another issue related to silence involves a group that is generally quiet and relies heavily on the parent educator. When a question is asked, no one responds. This type of group is especially challenging for a group leader who relies on active participation, especially in Level 3 and 4 groups.

WHY DOES IT OCCUR?

Quiet groups may be tired groups. Parent groups that meet in the evenings, especially later in the week, may be made up of parents who have low energy. They may expect to sit back and absorb information, whereas the parent educator has planned an interactive session. Quiet groups may be unclear about the norms and expectations of this particular experience. Often a pattern has been established where the parent educator does the majority of the talking in early sessions. Quiet groups may consist of people who have not had enough time to get to know each other and feel rushed with a premature expectation of self-disclosure or sharing of ideas. It is also possible that a particular group is made up of quiet personalities.

SUGGESTIONS FOR LEADERS

- Plan for active participation early on in the group to set an expectation of meaningful involvement by the parents.
- Ask parents to jot down their reactions; then ask, "What did you write?"
- Use open-ended questions to encourage verbal responses such as "Tell us how you deal with this."
- Include dyad or small-group work.
- Allow for some open, free conversation before beginning the topic.
- Consider leaving the group alone for a few minutes before beginning, while you tend to other tasks. This often encourages members to connect with each other.
- Avoid "yes/no" questions.
- Model respect and nonjudgmental attitudes when members share their ideas.
- Avoid talking every time a group member finishes speaking. This encourages member-to-member discussion.
- Allow for some silence; do not fill in the silence with your own voice.
- Use humor.
- Use energizing activities or icebreakers that get members talking and laughing early in the session.
- Offer refreshments at each session.

HELPFUL COMMENTS

"There is a lot of thinking going on in here right now. Let's hear your thoughts."

"I'd like to hear what you think about this."

"Who has experienced this? Tell us about it."

"Who will share?" rather than "Does someone have a comment?"

Resistance

WHAT IS IT?

Resistance is a defensive reaction a parent may exhibit to the group that indicates an unwillingness to fully participate. It may be reflected in nonverbal behavior that resists listening to or considering the leader's or other members' ideas. Resistance may also occur when parents refuse to accept assistance or try new strategies, even when asking for help. Although resistance may exist within a person as a learned means of coping, it is often something that occurs between people. Therefore, it is important for the parent educator to examine his or her relationship with the parent to determine if a power struggle exists and if nurturing the relationship might diffuse any tension.

WHY DOES IT OCCUR?

Parents who are resistant may see themselves as holding onto a self-image that says, "There is nothing wrong with me!" By accepting an idea or buying into the concept of parent education and support, the parent may feel an admission of personal limitations and vulnerabilities. This view of the parent education experience originates from a deficit model. It is important, therefore, for the group leader to reframe the meaning and purpose of parent education as a positive and supportive experience. Group members are often resistant in order to avoid change. As systems theory states, individuals have a need to keep their lives in balance, and possible changes coming from the group experience threaten that equilibrium (Cormier & Cormier, 1998). Resistant parents may also be feeling resentful toward a spouse, friend, or relative who is pressuring them to attend parent education classes. Or they may have personality traits or learned behaviors that make them respond quickly to anything new in a negative way.

SUGGESTIONS FOR LEADERS

- Nurture your relationship with this parent.
- Reframe ideas to which you feel they are resistant.
- Use storytelling and metaphors in your teaching.
- Use humor to build rapport and energize the relationship.

- Give more control and choices to this person.
- Acknowledge resistance to defuse it.
- Challenge "always/never" statements.
- Suggest small changes that offer less to resist.
- Use kinesthetic activities that divert attention from the resistance.
- Avoid personalizing the resistance; this only encourages a power struggle.
- Spend time talking about the purpose and meaning of the group to eliminate a deficit model impression.
- Allow adequate time to listen before moving to problem solving. Parents need to feel heard before they can abandon resistance and take the next steps.

HELPFUL COMMENTS

"Let's look at this in another way."

"I can tell you just aren't buying this."

"We've talked about several different ideas tonight. Which one could you try?"

"If you tried this, what is the worst that could happen?"

Conflict

WHAT IS IT?

Conflict typically occurs in the storming stage of group development. It is a common component of most active, productive groups and is frequently seen as differences of opinions emerge among members and/or between members and the parent educator. Family-of-origin issues seem to influence how adults handle conflict, a characteristic that is important for parent educators to consider. Each of us has a different threshold for conflict; some group leaders are comfortable with its presence, and others avoid it at all costs. Conflict in itself is not necessarily negative. In fact, it can energize a discussion and bring it to a deeper level of understanding. However, when it is accompanied by anger, judgmental comments, sarcasm, and other negative behaviors, it can be damaging to group process.

WHY DOES IT OCCUR?

Certain behaviors or comments of members tend to elicit negative feelings from others that may result in conflict (Corey, 2000). They include remaining aloof, observing the group experience rather than participating, talking too much, constantly questioning, giving abundant advice, dominating the group, using sarcasm, or demanding attention. When parents have differing opinions, they may feel attacked by others who disagree in a judgmental way.

SUGGESTIONS FOR LEADERS

- Adhere to ground rules regarding respect.
- Agree to disagree.
- Promote an atmosphere where differences of opinions are accepted.
- Use group activities that allow members to know each other and build on similarities.
- Acknowledge differences in backgrounds, beliefs, values, and perspectives.
- Don't always align yourself with the values of the majority group.
- Keep conflict focused on issues, not people.
- Recognize your own issues with conflict.
- Emphasize the insights and important points from differing perspectives and invite parents to make their choices about what fits for their situation and values.

HELPFUL COMMENTS

"Differences of opinions make our group interesting, and yet I want everyone to feel respected."

"That's one way to look at it. Others may not agree."

"It's my job to make sure all members are respected, so I need to remind everyone about our ground rules."

Bringing Couple Relationship Difficulties Into the Group

WHAT IS IT?

One or both parents may attend a parent education group. Occasionally, when both parents attend the group together, they bring their own relationship issues to the group in a more intimate way. Though the focus is on parenting, a couple that is in need of therapeutic intervention may use the group as an opportunity to vent or explore issues that are beyond the scope of parent education.

WHY DOES IT OCCUR?

Couples who may need therapy to address difficulties in their relationship may be avoiding their perceived stigma of seeking the help of a therapist.

Though couple relationships are definitely affected by the parenting experience, a parenting group may seem like a safer place to start. The couple's intention may be to address challenging parenting issues with the hope that this will help their relationship with each other.

Couples who share personal challenges of their relationship within the context of a parent education can make other participants uncomfortable and change the dynamics and process of the group. Though they may be unaware of the inappropriateness of their disclosures, others may choose not to continue attending because the experience is not providing what they need.

SUGGESTIONS FOR LEADERS

- Keep the focus on issues of parenting and family life.
- Gently challenge the parents to consider how their relationship issues are affecting their parenting.
- Clarify the purpose of this particular group—what it is and what it is not.
- Privately, refer the couple to counseling or to another more intensive intervention.

HELPFUL COMMENTS

"How does your relationship as partners affect your parenting?"

"While the relationship between the adults in a family is crucial to the children, we want to make sure our focus in the group stays on parenting issues."

"Some of the issues you are raising, while they are very important, are beyond what we can address in this group. If you are interested, I can give you some suggestions for other programs that might be of help to your family."

Making Politically Charged Statements

WHAT IS IT?

Parents make strong statements in a group that the leader and others would judge to be inappropriate. They may be sexist, racist, or political and may cause offense to others. For example, a mother in the group may make a derogatory comment about men and their inherent inability to care for children. Another parent may use an offensive slang term to refer to an ethnic or racial group. A negative comment may be made about a particular group of immigrant families in the community.

Additionally, statements may be made that touch areas of personal sensitivity of the leader. For example, a parent may make a negative and judgmental comment about gays and lesbians, and the facilitator may have a close relative who is gay. Though the leader has a responsibility to respond, he or she must also deal with personal, and often intense, feelings of anger, hurt, or being judged by the person speaking.

A judgmental statement about particular group members is a common source of conflict. A person who makes negative statements that disrespect the views or behaviors of others can cause great conflict in groups. Others in the group may challenge those judgmental comments, or they may internalize them, which creates an uncomfortable tension in the group atmosphere. The presence of these types of statements should send a signal to the parent educator that the atmosphere in the group has suddenly changed and that group members are carefully watching and waiting for a response.

WHY DOES IT OCCUR?

Group members who make strong politically charged statements do so either intentionally or unintentionally. They may enjoy making outrageous statements to spark a response from others. Their social interaction style may be that they "say what they think" and relish the attention it brings. Their statements may also be made without the intention of offense. These parents may have been raised in a racist or homophobic environment, and making offensive comments may reflect their value system. They may assume that everyone in this setting agrees with them, just as others in their social system appear to.

SUGGESTIONS FOR LEADERS

- Separate yourself emotionally from the comments being made.
- Pay attention to others in the group.
- Use a moment of silence to bring stability to the group and give members a chance to respond.
- Remind the group of ground rules that support respect for everyone.
- Gently challenge the group members to consider what they want their children to learn about accepting others and how this thinking affects that goal.
- Make a statement that does not place judgment on the speaker but expresses the opposing personal values you have.
- Give a sense of immediacy to what is happening in the group right now.
- Provide a statement of research or fact that challenges this view.
- Depending on the relationship with the group and stage of development, use a comment of self-disclosure that expresses your own experience and challenges the other.

HELPFUL COMMENTS:

"How are others of you feeling right now?"

"I'm sensing that not everyone agrees."

"We've enjoyed an atmosphere in our group where we can agree to disagree. I have to say that my views are very different on this issue."

"Does anyone have other ideas or thoughts about this?"

"We've talked before about helping our children be accepting of others. I'm wondering how these statements would fit with that goal."

"My family is biracial, and what you are describing hasn't been my experience at all."

Expressing Intense Emotions

WHAT IS IT?

In any parent education group, intense emotions may surface. Parents may cry, become extremely angry, express great sorrow or regret, or display other feelings that change the typical emotional level of the group.

WHY DOES IT OCCUR?

A parent may begin to cry when the content triggers an emotional connection. For example, the topic of explaining and helping children cope with the death of a loved one is often a session when parent educators can expect someone to cry. This topic can easily elicit feelings from parents who are dealing with or have dealt with the death of someone close to them. Childhood memories also can result in emotional intensity for parents. An unsuspecting parent educator might ask parents to recall holiday traditions when they were growing up. For some parents these memories are painful, and it is not uncommon for someone in a group to respond strongly in recalling memories of his or her childhood.

SUGGESTIONS FOR LEADERS

- Be prepared for the possibility of strong emotions, particularly with certain topics.
- Acknowledge the pain or sorrow being expressed.
- Focus on giving the parent your support.
- Read the body language of other group members to determine their level of comfort.

- Focus on the difficulty of remembering and sharing these feelings.
- Refocus the parent on the present and how these experiences affect how he or she parents.
- Universalize the emotion without minimizing the experience.

HELPFUL COMMENTS

"It must be very difficult for you to share some of these experiences."

"This must have been a significant part of your growing up. How do you think it affects how you parent your own children?"

"These are difficult feelings that many parents struggle with."

Some parents who attend parent education groups may, because of their mental health issues, current life challenges, or styles of interaction, be contraindicated for continued participation. If a parent is suffering from a major mental illness that manifests itself in disruptive behavior in the group, it is in the best interest of that parent, the other participants, and the leader to find an alternative experience. A parent who is belligerent or confrontational to the leader and others in the group does not belong in this setting. In these cases, it is the responsibility of the parent educator to guide that parent toward getting his or her needs met in another way. A referral to a mental health center and a targeted parent group for those with mental health issues is an appropriate option. A parent who destroys the parent education group experience for others with aggressive and negative behaviors may need to be asked to leave the group. These are exceptional circumstances and occur infrequently, but if typical strategies to address difficult behaviors in parent education groups fail, the leader must take responsibility for the well-being of the entire group of participants.

Summary

As parent education becomes more commonplace in our society, it attracts participants from a variety of backgrounds. Parents bring not only their values, beliefs, and parenting experiences to the group but also their insecurities, past relationships with authority figures, and varying levels of social skills, and their own personal and mental health issues. Though parent educators must always examine the role they play in the expression of disruptive behaviors and their relationship with a parent, they may also assume that frequently these behaviors stem from the parent's issues outside the group. Parent educators must be willing to evaluate their role but also to acknowledge that they cannot be responsible for each individual's behavior choices. Though it is difficult not to take some behaviors personally, they often are not intended that way.

Disruptive behaviors in parent education groups can have devastating effects on the morale and success of the group. Application of family systems theory to parent groups suggests that the behaviors of one member can drastically affect everyone else in the group as well. Members who are invested in the experience may bring conflict to the group as they confront the offending member, or they may decide to exit the group in search of another, more rewarding learning opportunity. By setting a positive tone in the beginning and developing ground rules that support functional roles for all members, one can prevent many disruptive behaviors (Braun et al., 1984). However, when these behaviors do occur and threaten the cohesiveness of the group, the role of the facilitator is to monitor and intervene in order to maintain an atmosphere of respect for individual members and the group as a whole. When a parent educator is able to successfully guide the group through a difficult moment, the group may develop a stronger sense of trust and greater cohesion. This may enable the group and the facilitator to address other emotional issues with more confidence.

Discussion Questions

For each situation below, consider the following two questions:

1. What questions do you need to ask yourself before responding?
2. How might you address this behavior?
   A. Tonya and Marietta have attended parent groups together for several years. They register together and enjoy attending as friends. During the group, they typically sit together and have recently begun chatting quietly with each other during the discussion.
   B. Carlos faithfully attends parent group each week. He is pleasant and seems interested in the topics that are covered. During the group he appears to be listening intently, but he never volunteers his opinion or verbally joins into the discussion. You have noticed that if the group is divided into dyads, Carlos participates and shares his experiences freely.
   C. Elaina is a court-ordered parent in one of your groups. Currently, her children are placed in foster care, and she is required to attend parent education classes each week. Elaina attends, but her nonverbal behavior indicates that she is bored and annoyed with having to be in the group.

She often argues and disagrees with the information that is being presented. Her favorite response is "That wouldn't work for me."

D. Marie is an enthusiastic and outgoing member of your parent group. She often comments on how important this group is to her and how much she enjoys coming each week. Marie likes to talk and is the first to volunteer her opinion or bring up a challenging parenting issue. You have noticed that each week she seems to dominate the class, leaving little time for other parents to discuss their issues.

9

Parent-Child Interaction Time

Laboratory for Learning

Parent-child interaction time has become an essential part of many parent education programs over the past two decades. Kristensen (1984) referred to parent-child interaction time as the heart of Early Childhood Family Education programs in Minnesota's program for parents with young children. Family literacy programs in Kentucky have designed Parent and Child Time (PACT) as a key component of their family literacy model (Darling & Hayes, 1989). During parent-child interaction time, parents and children come together in schools and other settings to participate in group and individual early childhood activities. There are also some parenting skills classes (e.g., Brock, 1989) where parents bring children to class to practice some of the skills that they learn in parenting sessions. Parents Are Teachers (District 742 Parent-Child Program, 1993) uses parent-child time as a time for parents to observe their young child and follow the child's lead in exploring the early childhood environment. There are also some prison programs (e.g., Moore & Clement, 1998) that incorporate parent-child visitation time as part of a parent education program. Parent-child interaction time is both a laboratory for parent learning and a quality time experience for parents and children (Palm, 1992). The focus on parent-child interaction time in this chapter will be on how to design and integrate these experiences into group parent education classes.

This chapter will explore the different goals of parent-child interaction time, with an emphasis on young children birth through 5 years old, although programs could extend activities through age 8, as some Even Start Family Literacy programs do (St. Pierre, Layzer, & Barnes, 1995). Parent-child time has many potential benefits for both parents and children. Parent roles vary according to program philosophy, beliefs about children, and specific program goals. Designing parent-child interaction time often is a team effort between a parent educator and an early childhood educator. In this chapter, some basic design principles will be outlined, along with favorite parent-child activities for various age groups. The integration of parent-child interaction time with parent education will also be discussed, giving examples of parent-child interaction as an opportunity for parent observation and for linking parent-child interaction time to parent discussion. Finally, this chapter will examine some typical difficult moments in parent-child interaction time and possible responses that can turn potential problems into opportunities for parent learning.

Examples of Parent-Child Formats

PARENT-INFANT SESSION FOR 6- TO 12-MONTH-OLDS

Seven mothers and one father of infants 4 to 8 months old sit around the edge of a large rectangular area with gym mats covered with sheets and sprinkled with infant toys, rattles, bright-colored balls, and teethers. At the beginning of the session, most parents put their babies down on the mat in front of them. Some of the infants are sitting up, and others are on their stomachs exploring the toys. The parent educator greets each parent and baby as he or she enters the room and asks how he or she is doing today. After everyone arrives and has had a few minutes to settle in, the parent educator begins a circle time routine of short songs and finger plays. The group has been together for 5 weeks, and when the songs begin, the babies become quiet and attentive, watching as the parent educator and parents sing "Twinkle, Twinkle, Little Star" with hand movements. When the songs are over, the parent educator goes around the group to check in with each parent about any new changes in their babies or any new issues that they are dealing with since the last time they met. The babies continue to explore the toys that are on the mat. Some infants stick close to their parents, while the two oldest venture out into the middle of the circle and explore other toys and babies. Parents occasionally redirect an infant who may be too rambunctious and invade another baby's space or take away a toy. The parent educator talks about emerging social skills with a few posters on the wall that outline these skills and how parents can support these emerging skills. The interaction of the infants provides a rich set of examples to weave into the discussion on social skills.

Photo 9.1   Parents and children have fun and learn together during parent-child time.

SUPER SATURDAYS: FATHER AND CHILD PROGRAM

Another example of a parent-child interaction time comes from a Saturday morning program for dads and their young children aged 2 through 5. This group meets twice a month, and many fathers come to this program to spend quality time with their young child. The parent-child interaction time takes up an hour and 15 minutes of the 2-hour-long session and is the main attraction of the program for many fathers and their children.

"My daughter looks forward to this time that she has together with me without the distractions we have at home."

Some of the members of this group have been coming to the Super Saturday class for 2 to 3 years. The children walk in with a smile and work on making a name tag while their dads sign up on the registration sheet. The parent educator greets the dads and kids and tells them about the activities for the day, giving them a sheet that describes the special activities for the day. Today the activity is cooking with kids, and seven different food projects are spread out in the two early childhood classrooms and the hallway. Some of the children run ahead of their dads and go down to the gym to play floor hockey or ride a tricycle down the long hallway at the other end of the building. After about 15 minutes, the children and dads gather in one of the classrooms for circle time. There are 13 dads and 18 children today. The dads introduce themselves and their children. One 4-year-old boy decides to change his name to Sam during introductions today, and everyone chuckles. The early childhood teacher plays his guitar and sings a song about Herm the worm and what he will be eating. Children volunteer an odd assortment of worm food as they join in the silly song. After a couple of songs, the parent educator and the early childhood teacher take turns describing the seven different food projects. Today the menu includes a banana yogurt milkshake in a blender and trail mix with dried fruit, peanuts, cereal, M&M's, and raisins. Out in the hall, children are rolling out tortillas from round balls of dough into flat, thin pancakes. They will fry them in an electric frying pan and then cover them with cheese to make quesadillas. At another station, dads and kids chop up apples and place them in a blender to make applesauce. Finally, a small group of dads and their children are making chocolate pudding by shaking milk and pudding mix in a small jar. The dads with younger children do most of the work but find ways to engage their children, such as putting the apples into the blender and pushing the button. The children and dads sit at small tables in one of the classrooms and sample their creations before moving to the next activity or taking a break by going to play in the gym. Most dads are attentive to their children's interests and follow their lead in selecting the next activity. As the activity level winds down, the dads take their children to the first classroom, where the early childhood teacher and two assistants have set up activities for the children, while the dads join the parent educator in a room down the hall for parent discussion time.

Goals for Parent-Child Interaction Time

The various goals of parent-child interaction time reflect the program philosophy, the target group of parents, and the age of the child. The focus in this chapter is on the parent and what the parent can learn from parent-child interaction time. There are three general goals for parents with a number of important direct and indirect benefits for both parents and children.

The first goal is *to create "quality time" for both parent and child.* Parent-child interaction time provides a special time for parents and children to be together in a supportive environment created for children, with limited distractions. Parents, especially those who work outside the home, appreciate this time together where they can enjoy being with their children in a child-oriented environment without some of the stresses and distractions that creep into time at home.

A second goal is *to provide time and a comfortable environment to practice parenting skills.* For example, parents learn to be better observers of children and become more sensitive to child cues. Parents observe which activities are most attractive to their children. They also may observe how their child slowly moves into new activities and may learn new information about their child's temperament. Parents may get a chance to guide their children through an art activity of making hand prints and have to set limits about using the paper, not the table or the wall, for their project. There are many opportunities for practicing a variety of parenting skills during parent-child interaction time. The parent educator can model ways of talking to children about their artwork or redirecting a child to a more constructive activity.

The third goal of parent-child time is *to provide parents with ideas for developmentally appropriate learning activities that can be extended into the home.* This is done by creating a child-centered environment with a variety of fun, stimulating activities where children learn by doing. For example, this can be accomplished by setting up a post office dramatic play area where children can "write" letters or postcards and sort mail into different categories. Simple art projects can be prepared for children to experiment with cutting and pasting different materials. Cooking with kids provides parents with new ideas for healthy snacks to make at home.

Benefits to Parents and Educators

Parent-child interaction time provides direct opportunities for parent learning as well as some indirect benefits to parents. Parents are able to observe their children in a social context with other children. In the process, they learn about the range of typical behaviors as well as different learning styles. Parents also learn more about a child's perspective by being in a child-oriented environment and observing how the educators organize this environment. The variety of parenting styles and strategies, as well as the modeling of program staff, exposes parents to new parenting ideas and approaches in a natural environment. This experience provides a range of choices for parenting behavior and the message that there are a variety of choices for parents. Parents are encouraged to select the strategies that reflect their family values and goals for their child. They also observe that a child's temperament is an important factor in selecting effective parenting strategies. These indirect messages can be explored during parent discussion time to take advantage of the rich group dynamics between parents, children, and educators during parent-child time.

The parent educator also benefits from participating in and observing parent-child interaction time. This is an opportune time to observe parents in a variety of interactions with their children. They may observe the parent encouraging the child in the gym in a game of catch. They watch parents structure a task that is too difficult by breaking it into simple steps, thus making it easier for the child to succeed. Two parents work with their children as they build a set of train tracks in a corner of the room. These observations can lead to a greater understanding of parent strengths. Watching a mother who is really patient with her son who is moving nonstop from one activity to another raises the educator's awareness and appreciation of the parent's strengths. Parent educators may observe parent-child tensions as a mom attempts to persuade her 2-year-old daughter to share the painting easel. The parent educator also has the opportunity to observe children and their style of interacting with other children and adults and how they approach new activities. Parent-child time provides numerous teachable moments where parent educators can model respectful but firm limit setting with children. Sometimes a parent needs a subtle suggestion to make a project work better, like adding food coloring to the water before mixing up the play-dough recipe. Other times parents need an empathic or reflective response: "Jeremy looks like he is having a hard time connecting with the other children after being gone for 2 weeks." Parent-child time can be an appropriate opportunity for parent educators to videotape parents and children in interaction (Erickson & Kurz-Riemer, 1999). These videotapes can be used to point out parent strengths and unique child characteristics. Parent educators who can directly observe and interact with parents and children together have a deeper understanding of the unique strengths and tensions around parent-child relationships.

Designing Effective Parent-Child Interaction Time

SELECTING AND ADAPTING PARENT-CHILD ACTIVITIES

There are a number of important considerations for creating parent-child activities that work for both children and parents. The environment should be sensitive to child development, with appropriate and engaging activities for different age groups. The boxes that follow (Boxes 9.1 through 9.3) list some examples of favorite activities for different age groups.

It is helpful to balance projects that are sensitive to both parent and child interests. Although the child's abilities and interests have to be the primary focus, it is also important to observe parents and select activities that will be appealing and engaging for both the parent and the child. It sometimes works to give parents specific instructions about their role in doing an activity with their child. More challenging activities that are just beyond a child's ability in a specific age group can be completed only with a parent's assistance. This creates a role for parents to guide and work with their child in completing an

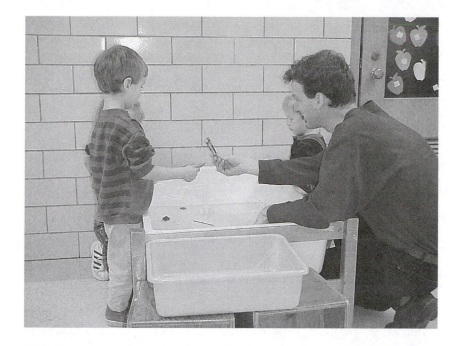

Photo 9.2   Parent strengths can be observed during parent-child interaction time.

activity. Parents are thus challenged to practice modifying an activity to match a child's ability.

Offering a variety of activities is usually a good idea to meet the needs and interests of different parents and children. This may include balancing active with quiet activities and open-ended or process-oriented with product-oriented activities.

It is most important to design activities that will be fun and enjoyable for both children and parents. Activities that are simple, provide some challenge, and promote feelings of competence help both children and parents to enjoy themselves. Parents like the feeling of doing something with their child in which the child has fun and feels successful.

PREPARE THE ENVIRONMENT

Parent educators who team up with early childhood educators can work together to select activities to engage both parent and child. Once activities have been chosen, the next step is to prepare the environment. Activities must be arranged to indicate space boundaries while also considering activity and noise levels. Parent-child activities should also be presented in an appealing or attractive manner. This can be done by arranging materials in new ways,

---

Box 9.1   Favorite Activities With Parents and Infants (Birth
to 12 Months)

1. Mats with boxes of different sizes for babies to crawl into and
   through.
2. Mirror Play: Set up different sizes of mirrors around the room for
   babies to explore.
3. Crawling on different textures that are taped to the ground for
   babies to explore with their hands as they crawl.
4. Peek-a-Boo game with colorful silky scarves.
5. What Makes Baby Laugh: trying out different activities written on
   cards for infants 4 to 12 months to see which ones make them laugh.
6. Sensory table with small soft toys inside for babies who are
   beginning to stand and walk.

---

adding a new twist to a favorite activity, and carefully organizing materials into classroom spaces. For example, making name tags for parents and children is typically part of a "registration routine." The program has used masking tape and markers but recently decided to use colored shapes of animals, apples, and badges instead of tape. The children are more excited about making name tags from specific shapes and colors. The aesthetics and detail of preparing an attractive environment for parents and children convey messages of "We care," "Welcome," and "Have fun."

INTRODUCE AND MODEL ACTIVITIES

The parent educator can be involved in explaining the specific parent-child activities so that parents have an understanding of how to do an activity and the purpose of the activity for child learning. This can be done verbally before beginning parent-child time. It also can be written on small cards or signs for parents to read when they go to an activity area, or parent and early childhood educators can circulate and assist parents as necessary, explaining the purpose of each activity.

SET A POSITIVE TONE

The parent educator can set a positive and fun tone for this time by his or her own attitude about parent-child time and by helping parents understand

---

Box 9.2   Favorite Activities for Parents and Toddlers (12 to 30 Months)

1. Sensory table filled with rice and containers, cups, and funnels for pouring.
2. Art collage with pieces of tissue paper and sticky contact paper; toddlers can rip paper and stick onto the contact paper.
3. Shaving Cream: Parents can squirt shaving cream on clean surface for child to explore. Can add food coloring to make different colors.
4. Dramatic Play: Washing babies at the water table. Set up the water table with some soapy water, and use washable dolls with towels for the children to bathe and dry off.
5. Trains: Children like to set up train tracks with small wooden trains to move around the track. Parents can offer guidance and support in setting up the tracks.
6. Pounding: can set up pounding area with golf tees and small wooden hammer to pound into styrofoam.

---

the expected roles and appropriate behavior. Because parents are in the program or educators' environment, they need clear descriptions and explanations about the purpose of parent-child time and expectations for parent and child behavior. Parent educators can model respectful interactions with children and also describe how parents can help their children with an activity. For example, what are the expectations during circle time? Should all children come to the circle and participate, or can they just watch? Do children need to try all of the activities, or can they spend the whole time with one activity? When parents know the rules and expectations, they can relax and have fun and not worry about being judged.

CLARIFY PARENT ROLES

Programs may have varying philosophies about parent roles during parent-child interaction time. Some programs want parents to be relatively passive observers. Parent-child time is a time to observe children interacting with the social and physical environment. This role allows parents to observe their child's behavior in a different social context with peers and provides parents with opportunities for new insights into their children. In other programs, parents are expected to be cooperative playmates who follow their

---

Box 9.3   Favorite Activities for Parents and Preschoolers
(3 to 5 Years)

1. Cooking—Painted Toast: Child can paint a piece of bread with a small paintbrush and a mixture of food coloring and milk. Toast and eat.

2. Art Mural: Put a large piece of paper on a wall, and use a variety of media (chalk, markers, crayons) to make a mural.

3. Wood Project—Magic Wands: Begin with a small dowel rod about 18 inches long. Make a notch in the top of the dowel rod about 1/3 inch deep. Cut small colorful ribbons of three or four different colors about 12 inches long, and place in the top slot with glue. Can also trace a small star on card stock and cover with glitter to place in the same slot with the ribbons.

4. Dramatic Play—Camping: Set up a camping area with two or three tents and a pretend campfire with props (sleeping bags, cooking pots and pans, flashlights, etc.). Turn down the lights and play a nature tape as background noise.

5. Cooking—Purple Cow: Mix 1/2 cup of grape juice, 1/2 cup of milk, and three to four ice cubes in a blender to make a purple cow. Blend until smooth.

6. Science Parachutes: The parachutes can be made from plastic garbage bags cut into large squares (12–18 inches). Tie a piece of string to each corner of the plastic square. Then attach all four strings to a wooden clothespin. The clothespin can be decorated with markers to make a person. Fold up and throw into the air.

---

children's lead. Parents in this role may be encouraged to practice reflective listening, encouragement, and expansion of a child's dramatic play.

Another role that parents may play is the teacher/guide who demonstrates to a child how to complete a task and encourages his or her efforts. Parents in this role are expected to teach through modeling or scaffolding tasks such as putting together a puzzle or working on a collage of different fabric pieces.

Parent educators sometimes express impatience about parents not exhibiting appropriate role behavior during parent-child interaction time. A parent may spend more time talking to other adults than following his or her child with attention and encouraging statements. It helps when the program is clear and explicit about the roles that parent educators want parents to play during parent-child time. This can be conveyed in a number of ways. One way is

Photo 9.3   Circle activities build a connection between parents, children, and staff.

through an initial orientation to the program and the purpose of parent-child interaction. The role expectations can also be addressed in a handbook. The parent educator must also model the roles that they would like parents to play during the parent-child time. This information and demonstration of appropriate role behavior will help the parents feel more comfortable and be aware of the program goals and role expectations for parents.

CIRCLE TIME: CREATING A GROUP FEELING

Circle time can be an important component of parent-child activity time. It provides a time for the group to come together and connect around a shared activity. It can provide a routine for both younger and older children. It should be engaging and fun for both parent and child. The length of circle time should vary with the age of the child. The pace and variety of activities, from songs to finger plays to stories, will change with the age of the child.

Circle time often begins with recognizing each child by name through a song or chant. Some children like to hear their name and are pleased to be recognized and acknowledged in the group. Other children hide their faces when their turn comes. Not all children like to be the center of attention, and

---

Box 9.4   Circle Time Favorites for Young Children
and Parents

1. Name Songs to greet and welcome children and parents:
   - Chant: "_____ is here today, _____ is here today . . ."
   - Song: "Oh I see _____ over there sitting . . ."

2. Action Songs to engage parents and children in actions and interactions:
   - Raffi's "Bumping Up and Down" (child sits on parent's lap and gets a ride)
   - Ella Jenkins's "Stop and Go": Different actions can be incorporated—clapping, jumping, dancing
   - "Row, Row, Row Your Boat": Parent and child row facing each other and holding hands
   - "Skip to My Lou": A circle song with holding hands and various actions

3. Animal Sound Songs, asking children for animal ideas and the different sounds that each animal makes:
   - "Old MacDonald's Farm"
   - "When Cows Get Up in the Morning, They Always Say Good Day"
   - Raffi's "Down on Grandpa's Farm"

4. Finger Plays:
   - Criss-Cross Applesauce
   - Itsy Bitsy Spider, Great Big Spider

5. Parachute Games with small parachute:
   - Popcorn with balls
   - Dome house

---

educators should be sensitive to inviting children to participate but still give them a choice not to be part of a name song. The parent educator has the task of engaging both children and parents in the circle time activities through creating both a feeling of safety and sense of fun. Circle time itself should become a comfortable routine for both parents and children. Box 9.4 presents some favorite ideas for circle times for parents and young children together.

SELECTIVE INTERVENTION DURING PARENT-CHILD TIME

Parent educators can intervene in a number of different ways during parent-child time. It is important not to disrupt parents and children who are engaged in an activity. Parent educators can watch to see if parents need help with a project or need materials to complete the project. It is easy to disrupt the parent-child connection during this time. Though it is important to connect with parents and children, it helps to keep a respectful distance from parents and children who are working together on an activity. Sometimes educators feel awkward or left out to be only observing parent-child activities. Other times they may be concerned about being too intrusive. This time can be an opportunity to note parent strengths to acknowledge at a later time, or child behaviors that can be discussed with parents during parent discussion time.

Sometimes parents and children may be struggling with their own interaction, and parent educators can intervene by making a simple comment to a parent to support their efforts or redirect both the parent and child. The final section of this chapter will address a number of common difficult moments between parents and children that occur during parent-child interaction time. These interventions can be seen as opportunities for learning and can be resolved with a variety of effective strategies.

Guided Observation of Child Behavior

Group parent education offered in settings that include children provides a unique opportunity for parents to learn from observing their children in an environment with other children and adults. Just as teachers of young children learn observation skills, parents can learn to observe in ways that provide insight into their children's behavior, development, temperament, and skills. In these programs, typically offered for families with younger children, parent educators not only facilitate group discussion but also structure and guide a process of observation for parents (Independent School District 742 Parent-Child Program, 1993). This section will address methods of designing, guiding, and debriefing observations to enhance the experience of parent education.

SETTINGS FOR GUIDED OBSERVATION

Guided observation is designed for parent education settings that include children. Programs where parents and children attend together include parent-child activities as well as a separate time for parent education that provides a rich opportunity to learn through a combination of observation and discussion.

Children's environments that include a separate viewing area with one-way windows and sound systems are most effective for guided observation. However, many parent-child programs include guided observation without these facilities. Parents can separate within the same room as the children, by gathering in a corner to watch with the parent educator. Classes with very young infants and toddlers may struggle with separation issues and find that even with separate viewing areas, parents and children are most comfortable and secure within the same room. Either way, a structured time for parents to pull back from their children and observe with guidance from the parent educator can provide another way of learning about their own and other children.

Settings such as these typically include a children's teacher who can work with the parent educator to facilitate a positive observation experience for parents. The children's teacher will need to know what the parents are observing in order to facilitate an environment that supports the observation focus. For example, if the focus is on language development, the children's teacher may demonstrate particular communication strategies that encourage young children's speech. Collaboration between the parent educator and the children's teacher is critical for a successful observation experience.

VALUE OF OBSERVATION AS PART OF PARENT EDUCATION

Including guided observation as part of the parent education experience allows an immediate and individualized opportunity for parents to learn about their children by watching them. It provides a practical reinforcement of concepts and ideas covered in the discussion group as parents learn about development through observation of their children. There are a number of benefits of guided observation for parents. They include

- Learning about child development through demonstration
- Seeing their children within a social context with peers
- Gaining insight about learning styles, conflict resolution skills, and temperament
- Gaining observation skills that can be applied in other settings
- Experiencing a more objective perspective and understanding of their children
- Gaining new insights into their child's behavior from the parent educator who interprets behavior
- Understanding their child's perspective or view of the world

PARENTS' AND CHILDREN'S REACTIONS TO OBSERVATION

The concept of observation may be very foreign to parents in educational settings. Parent educators may hear comments such as "I spend all day with him. Why would I want to observe?" Observing may seem like a waste of time or like something that may put parents in an uncomfortable or embarrassing situation if their child misbehaves. These reactions are not uncommon, and the parent educator can acknowledge and support parents when introducing the observation time.

Without careful guidance during observation time, parents may lose interest and begin interacting with each other or become distracted. Some parents may begin visiting about unrelated events and disrupt this quiet time for others. It is the responsibility of the parent educator to keep parents focused and involved in the observation process. Commenting on what is happening, moving between parents, and encouraging parents to put themselves in their children's shoes will help to keep parents' attention on their children.

Children may also have reactions to observation time that can cause challenges. Issues of separation may be disruptive as children move from the classroom environment to their parents during this time. They may realize they are being observed, especially during the early stages of this activity, and "act out" for attention. Children may embarrass their parents by misbehaving, being aggressive or emotional during observation. Teamwork between the children's teacher and the parent educator is important during these times. The children's teacher can demonstrate appropriate responses to the children, and the parent educator can identify these strategies while affirming and universalizing the situation for the parent. For example, a child may hit or bite another child while parents are observing. The children's teacher can use this as a "teachable moment" by modeling appropriate limit setting, guiding, and comforting responses to both children. At the same time, the parent educator may point out what is happening, provide insight into developmental behaviors, and reassure parents. Overall, these issues may present challenges for the parent educator, but they also provide an opportunity for learning for the parents.

STRUCTURING AND GUIDING OBSERVATION

Structuring a guided observation includes thought and care from the parent educator. Selecting the right focus, designing and maintaining "ground rules" for observation, and guiding the actual observation are necessary skills. With careful consideration, observation can become an important part of the learning process for parents.

Steps for effective observation include:

1. *Select a focus for observation that matches the topic of group discussion.* For example, if the session's topic is social development, the focus may be to observe signs of social skills with other children and adults. An observation for the topic of self-esteem could be for parents to watch the ways their children demonstrate confidence and how the children's teacher fosters self-esteem.

Photo 9.4   Parent educators guide observations to help parents gain insight into their children's development.

2. *Post the focus where parents can read it.* The language used in the focus should be simple, easy to read, and without jargon or questions. Questions may intimidate parents who feel they are being tested or instructed to find the right answer. Statements such as "Notice how your child gets his/her needs met" and "Watch for new skills your child has acquired" are good examples of observation focuses that encourage parents to look for specific behaviors or skills. Occasionally, the parent educator may have a particular focus in mind that just doesn't happen. Parents are watching for social skills while children are playing alone. A confident guide of observation will focus on what is happening at the time and use it as a spontaneous learning opportunity.

3. *Keep parents focused during the observation.* Parent educators need to give guiding comments regarding what is happening with the children, as well as statements that challenge parents to put themselves in their child's place. Parents can be given the option of taking notes during the observation that can be used later during a debriefing time. The parent educator might provide clipboards to facilitate note taking. Attention and sensitivity should be given, however, to parents with low literacy levels as well as to varying learning styles. A creative alternative method of note taking might be to provide a general floor

plan of the room. Ask parents to move the pencil across the paper to "track" where their child moves during the observation time. This activity could be linked to the discussion of motor development or activity levels in children.

4. *Design and maintain ground rules of observation.* They may include:

- Observation is quiet time.
- Put yourself in your child's place to understand him or her.
- Watch the children and listen to their words.
- Avoid judgment about your child, as well as others.
- Note your own feelings as you observe.
- Respect all of the children as you observe.

5. *Focus primarily on "what" is happening, not "why."* Although this is often difficult for parents, it keeps the observation objective and helps to avoid judgment. During the debriefing time, the parent educator's tentative interpretation may be helpful for the group.

DEBRIEFING THE OBSERVATION

Generally, after the observation, parents will gather to begin their discussion group. A good strategy for bridging the observation with the topic is to begin with a short debriefing of observation. During the watching time, parents are encouraged to watch, not talk. Debriefing offers an opportunity to discuss what they saw, how they felt, and what they learned about their children.

During the debriefing time, the parent educator should try to include everyone by checking in with each parent and commenting on something he or she observed about each child. These comments can be as simple as noting what a particular child played with or a particular interaction between two children.

Debriefing time can also offer an opportunity to address a difficult situation that may have occurred during observation. An affirming or universalizing comment regarding a child's behavior can assure a parent that everyone understands and that this behavior is not uncommon.

During the guided observation, the focus typically remains on what is happening. By including a debriefing time within a discussion with parents, the facilitator can offer tentative interpretations of particular behaviors that occurred. Parents may wonder, for example, why their child responded in a particular manner. The parent educator can draw on both experience and knowledge of development and behavior to offer possible explanations. This insight offers parents an opportunity to learn about their child from another perspective.

The end of the debriefing time should flow directly into the topic of the session. By carefully designing an observation focus that matches the session's topic, the parent educator can move the group directly from observation to discussion. Reversing the order of discussion and observation is also an option. The parent educator may lead a discussion on a particular topic and end by offering parents an opportunity to observe their children as a way to demonstrate a particular concept or idea.

Including observation in groups where parents and children attend together has many benefits for parent learning experiences. Observation can strengthen the group discussion as parents and educator share a perspective of each individual child. Designing, guiding, and debriefing observation requires different skills from those involved in group process. A competent parent educator will combine both observation and discussion to enhance the parent learning experience.

Linking Parent-Child Time to Parent Discussion

Another advantage of parent-child activities in parent education programs is the potential impact on parent group discussion time. Parent-child time can be used by the parent educator as an opportunity to build relationships with parents and children. It can provide a means to initiate deeper involvement with parents with greater needs through referrals or more intensive services. Parent educators can link parent-child time to discussion by debriefing the experience and connecting it to the discussion topic. This section will explore the role of the parent educator during parent-child activity time and address the positive outcomes that are possible by linking this experience with group parent education.

The Role of the Parent Educator During Parent-Child Activity Time

RELATIONSHIP BUILDING

Though parent-child time is typically planned and facilitated by the children's teacher, the parent educator also plays an important role. Parents and children spend time together actively engaged in a variety of learning opportunities. It is a special time for parent and child to enjoy each other's company, as well as to complete developmentally appropriate activities or stations. Though it is important for the parent educator not to intrude into this special interaction time, an opportunity exists to connect with each family and strengthen the educator-parent relationship.

The parent educator moves through the classroom setting, checking in, cautiously joining in the play, affirming, and commenting on the interaction that is occurring. A few minutes with each family strengthens the relationship, which will enhance participation in the parent group. A parent who has not connected with the educator before separation time may be less likely to openly share and participate in the group experience. This brief but important connection between the parent educator and each parent builds trust and rapport that follows the parent into the parent group setting. Comments that support the parent and encourage the child help to build a positive relationship. This preliminary connection affects the quality of interaction during parent discussion. Parents who feel close to the parent educator, who feel affirmed, supported, and comfortable, are more likely to engage in open discussion later in the session.

Example: Mary is a parent educator in a group of parents and preschoolers. The parents and children have arrived to find a variety of activities set out for them to enjoy during the first part of the class. The room is comfortable and inviting, with soft background music playing as parents and children move from station to station. Mary greets each family as they arrive. When everyone is settled in with activities, she slowly moves through the room, sitting near each dyad, yet being careful not to intrude. She joins Amy and her daughter Aisha as they play together in the sand table. Mary makes affirming comments about what they are making, how soft and smooth the sand feels, and how much they are enjoying playing together. She is careful not to intrude in the play between parent and child but may linger nearby, observing the interaction. The focus of Mary's involvement is primarily on the play that is taking place. Amy begins to draw Mary into a conversation about a parenting issue. Mary assesses the situation and decides that Aisha is content pouring sand from one container to the other and that Amy seems to need this time for one-on-one parent education. Mary keeps in mind that she wants to avoid talking about Aisha in front of her, and because Amy's concerns are general, she responds to her questions. After a few minutes, Aisha clearly wants her mother's attention for another activity, and Mary says, "Mom, it looks like Aisha is needing you right now. We'll talk more later." She moves on to another parent-child dyad to connect before parent discussion time begins. These few minutes together have connected the parent and educator and will help them begin the group experience on a closer level.

MODELING BEHAVIORS

The parent educator can also use parent-child interaction time as an opportunity for modeling positive relationship-building skills. Though it is important not to interfere in the play between parent and child, it may be appropriate to provide a model for a parent who is uninvolved with his or her child or for one who is clearly struggling with a behavior issue.

Example 1: Max is a parent educator with a group of young fathers. Some of the dads bring their children to the group each week and are actively involved in their lives. Others attend sporadically and have limited involvement. Brad attends today with his daughter Brittany. She is an active 3-year-old who loves art activities. As Brittany approaches the art table covered with a variety of materials, Brad settles back in his chair. Brittany wants to paint but needs an apron. She begins to pull some of the art supplies toward her but clearly needs assistance. Brad seems distracted and unaware that she needs his help. Max moves closer to the table. He senses that Brad doesn't realize what is happening. "Brittany," he says, "You can ask Dad for help rolling up your sleeves and putting on the apron." Brad looks up and moves closer, taking the verbal cue from Max. Max mentions Brittany's interest in painting and use of bright colors, which helps Brad become engaged in the painting activity.

Example 2: Judy is a parent educator in a group of parents and children who are between 2 and 5 years old. Kia and her 2-year-old son Matt are attending the group for the first time. Matt is a very active 2-year-old who occasionally is aggressive with other children. Today Matt is playing next to Timmy, who is also 2 years old. Timmy is playing with a little truck that Matt wants. Matt eyes the truck, hits Timmy, and grabs it from him. Timmy begins to cry. Kia looks embarrassed by her son's behavior but doesn't respond. Judy is nearby and moves in a little closer. She gently pats the backs of both boys and says, "Timmy is upset. We can't hit people. That hurts." She continues to talk gently to both of them, comforting Timmy, who begins to calm down. Matt moves in closer with the truck. He holds onto the truck but keeps watching Timmy's reaction. Judy says, "Let's look for another truck for Timmy. Matt, can you help us?" Kia watches in amazement, and Judy comments that they can talk about this later during parent group.

In this example, the parent educator sensed the parent's uncertainty of how to respond to a difficult situation. She was clearly embarrassed and unsure of what to do, especially in a group setting with other parents watching. The parent educator provided a positive model for intervention. She comforted both children and helped them work out a solution in finding another similar toy. She modeled respect and elicited a gentle response from the child. The mother had the opportunity to see a different way of responding. Parent education can sometimes occur through modeling, sometimes in one-to-one interactions, and sometimes in groups. During the parent group, the educator can later use this example in a universal way to talk about realistic expectations of children, common 2-year-old aggression, and the importance of intervening calmly and gently.

UNDERSTANDING PARENTS' NEEDS

Parent-child time also provides an opportunity for the parent educator to observe the relationship between parents and children and the strategies employed by parents to nurture, guide behavior, and gain cooperation. Knowing what challenges exist for individual parents will help the parent educator plan topics. For example, observing attachment behaviors between parent and child offers valuable insight into their relationship and also assists the parent educator to assess the needs of group members. It is important for the parent educator to observe informally and unobtrusively during parent-child interaction. This will lessen parent feelings of being observed and judged. This type of observation can also offer the parent educator opportunities to share affirming comments with individual parents.

Example: Lydia is a parent educator in a group of parents and infants. She notices that one of the parents, Maria, does not seem emotionally connected to her infant son, Juan. Maria does not always respond to his cues, often holds him at a distance, and seldom strokes or cuddles him in nurturing ways. Lydia observes informally during interaction time and throughout the session. She had planned several topics on infant attachment and nurturing behavior, but because of Maria's behaviors, she adjusts her plans to include more basic information. She also brings in a videotape for the parents about the importance of touch. During play time, Lydia holds Juan for short periods of time. She models good eye contact and positive connections and then comments on how well he engages and enjoys this type of interaction. Maria seems more interested in what is happening, and Lydia notices that she is soon trying some of the behaviors Lydia has modeled. When a strong trust level has been established, Lydia approaches Maria after class one day and tells her about a series of home visits that are available to parents and their infants. Maria explains that these visits include some play time, as well as an opportunity for the parent and teacher to talk one on one about parenting issues. She will also bring a video camera along each time to tape Juan and Maria together. At the end of the series, Maria can keep the video as a keepsake. Maria is interested and agrees to the visits. Lydia feels encouraged that she will be able to work closely with this parent and child and hopeful that she will continue to see changes in attachment and nurturing behaviors.

DEBRIEFING PARENT-CHILD INTERACTION

Occasionally, parents have difficulty seeing the value of parent-child interaction time. "We play at home all the time." "I thought we would do more here than just play together." Parent-child interaction can be validated when the parents gather for discussion by debriefing what occurred. Each session might begin with a short check-in as an opportunity for parents to share their impressions and gain insight into this part of the session. If debriefing is to be meaningful, therefore, the parent educator needs to have played an active role and be aware of what happened. The following are sample questions for debriefing parent-child interaction time:

- "What was it like for you playing with your child today?"
- "What did you notice about your child's choices?"
- "How have things changed from earlier in the year during this time?"
- "How is it different playing here with your child than it is at home?"
- "What surprised you as you played together?"

Finally, linking parent-child interaction time with discussion allows the parent educator to use professional judgment in tailoring topics and sessions to meet the needs of a particular group. If there appear to be power struggles during interaction time, the discussion group can focus on appropriate strategies. If the educator observes parents whose expectations are unrealistic about what their children should be able to do in the classroom, a time of focusing on child development is appropriate. In the absence of strong trust and rapport, it is difficult for the parent educator to focus individually on challenges of a particular parent. Bringing the information into the parent discussion group in a more universal way allows everyone to learn without targeting or overemphasizing the needs of a particular person.

The time spent by the parent educator during parent-child interaction is a solid investment in the quality of the parent discussion group. Building a relationship before the group, learning as much as possible about each parent and child, and sharing insight about this experience all have a positive impact on the parent group. Parent-child interaction provides an opportunity for the parent educator to know the parents in a way that would not be possible within a typical discussion group. Seeing the parent-child relationship in action provides a more accurate understanding than relying on information gathered through parent reports. Parent-child interaction is not only an enjoyable component of many parent education programs but also a valuable opportunity for the parent educator to connect with and understand parents and their children.

Difficult Moments as Teachable Moments

Parent-child interaction time is not always fun or easy for parents and children. Like any parenting of young children in public, it involves trying and embarrassing moments for parents. The educator can see these times as opportunities to intervene with support and empathy. Other times, modeling ways to guide or redirect a child or set limits can be appropriate. Difficult moments between parent and child during these young ages are typical and to be expected. Though some preventative measures can be taken to limit the number of difficult moments, they are inevitable, and the parent educator's skill in intervening is crucial. These tend to be times where parents are emotionally invested and real learning can occur or, conversely, parents can leave a class feeling incompetent and embarrassed and not wanting to come back. A number of typical problem scenarios will be described. There are a number of possible strategies for successful intervention that can be used in different combinations. It helps to consider options that may fit different parent personalities and different parent educator–parent relationship levels.

SITUATION 1: SEPARATION BLUES

Parents in a 3-year-olds' group are getting ready to go to the parent discussion in another room. Jamal protests when his mother starts to leave and grabs her leg and begins to cry. Tenisha looks embarrassed and uncertain about what to do. She enjoys parent discussion time and could use a break, but she feels guilty leaving Jamal.

This is a typical situation for young children and is likely to occur when a new class is beginning. A number of suggestions for addressing this situation follow.

1. *Reassure the parent that Jamal will be okay* and that if he doesn't calm down in a couple of minutes, the staff will come to the parent discussion room to get her.

2. *Give mom the option to stay if she feels this is best for Jamal.* Leave the decision to the mother, and let her know that Jamal's behavior is a typical reaction for some children at his age. Children will get more comfortable as they come to understand the program routine and develop a trusting relationship with the early childhood teacher. Sometimes it helps for a parent to stay for a while until the child calms down. It can be easier to say good-bye when the child is engaged in an activity. Child teachers can help by working with the parent to help the child find something to do and by being with the child when the parent is ready to leave.

3. *Spend some time with Tenisha after the session to share information from the parent discussion.* The parent educator could also spend time with Tenisha planning a strategy for her to help Jamal to feel comfortable so that she can begin to join the other parents. Possible alternatives might include showing Jamal where mom will be, leaving her jacket or other personal item in the room so that he remembers she has not left, or encouraging her to stay in the room as an observer without playing with him to encourage him to explore other play opportunities.

SITUATION 2: CIRCLE TIME WANDERER

Parents and children ages 2 to 3 are singing songs and doing finger plays during circle time. Judy tries to get 2-year-old Josh to join in. Josh says no and runs off to a corner of the room to play with the train set. Mom yells at him to come back to the circle and sing with the rest of the children. He ignores her, and Judy is both angry and embarrassed. The positive energy in the circle begins to fade.

1. *Assure mom that it is okay for Josh to be on his own* if he is safe. He will come to join the group when he is ready.

2. *Change the activity level in the circle time to a more active song* that might be inviting for Josh and that keeps the other children and parents focused on circle time.

3. *Talk to Judy privately about circle time.* Discuss the purpose of circle time and expectations for children who are Josh's age. Josh's behavior can be described as typical for some 2-year-olds. This helps to normalize the behavior and helps Judy feel assured that Josh is not a bad child and that she is not a bad parent because her child is not participating in circle time. The parent educator can address the issue of circle time in the group setting and discuss the purpose, expectations for children this age, and ways to help children with the transition to circle time and what to do if a child doesn't want to participate.

SITUATION 3: INATTENTIVE PARENTS

Five-year-old Amanda is working on making play-dough cookies. She keeps trying to show them to her dad. Dad is talking to another parent, whose daughter Felicia is clinging to her leg and whining to go play at the water table. Both parents seem oblivious to their children's demand for attention and continue talking about the upcoming school bond issue.

1. *Model a positive response to the child.* The parent educator can come over to Amanda and tell her, "Your cookies look delicious." This may get the parent to also pay attention.

2. *Redirect the parent's attention to the child's activity with a comment.* The parent educator can ask the parent to "check out" the cookies Amanda has made. Gently guide the parents to refocus on their children without making them feel they are being corrected.

3. *Affirm the importance of the parents' concerns.* The parent educator may join the two parents and ask them if they would like to talk more about the bond

issue during the parent group time. The parent educator can affirm that it is an important issue and also note that the children both look ready to play right now.

The goal in this situation is to help the parent and child reconnect and interact around an activity. This means that parent educators have to redirect a parent's attention and still give time for the adults to connect in other ways. Sometimes parents don't have the skills to interact with their children in a child-oriented environment, and educators need to model interactions. Other times parents are bored with child activities and find it more interesting to talk to other adults. They may feel that they spend enough time paying attention to their child at home. If this is the situation, the parent educator must help the parent to understand the purpose of parent-child interaction time and what children gain from getting this focused attention from their parents. Programs may also try to create a space during parent time for informal sharing that promotes connection between parents.

SITUATION 4: THE BORED CHILD

Seven-year-old Ramón is looking bored while his mother Maria finishes a book-making project. He refuses to help her and wants to go play outside with his friends.

1. *Redirect Ramón to help his mother finish the book* so that he can go join his friends outside. Make a suggestion about a specific task that Ramón could do to help his mother finish the book.

2. *Engage Ramón in a conversation.* Find out what activities Ramón likes to do and look for opportunities to create parent-child activities that would be more engaging for Ramón in the future.

Designing parent-child activities for older children can be more challenging. If activities are too much like "school projects," they may not be appealing to some children. A child may also not feel successful at certain activities and avoid them. It can help to provide a range of activities so that children can have some choices that are more appealing and more likely to match with children's interests. The goal in parent-child interaction is to support parents and children in having a good time doing activities together. It helps to have projects that are both novel and challenging for children and parents. Parents may also need some modeling about how to engage children in an activity and work with the child to finish the activity.

SITUATION 5: REFUSING TO SHARE

Sharon, the mother of 2-year-old Angela, asks her daughter to stop painting and let another child who has been waiting have a turn. Sharon begins to take the brush out of Angela's hand, and Angela tries to hit her with a messy paintbrush and gets paint on her mom's shirt. Sharon gets mad and smacks Angela on her bottom. Angela begins to cry.

1.   *Assist the parent and child in calming down.* Move closer to the parent and child and talk in a calm voice. You might offer to help mom get the paint off her shirt or to stay with Angela while Sharon goes to clean the paint from her shirt. Some distance between parent and child may help both cool off at this point.

2.   *Help the mother to understand the child's behavior.* Describe how sharing is difficult for most 2-year-olds, and talk about the process of learning to share. Assist Sharon in thinking about how to encourage Angela to share, focusing on supportive strategies and realistic expectations.

3.   *Set clear limits for parents about physical punishment in the program.* Parents need to know program rules about spanking children in "school." Sharon can be reminded about this rule when she calms down. Parents in a situation like this can be angry and frustrated and feel that the program is not allowing them to discipline their own child. Sharon may also be embarrassed if she lost her temper and didn't really want to hit her daughter. It helps to know how the parent is feeling to decide what to do next.

In a situation with an angry parent and child, the most important goal for the parent educator is to remain calm. The parent in this situation may not be able to hear about appropriate child development, alternative strategies for teaching sharing, or program rules about hitting. The parent educator can move in and help to deescalate the conflict by helping the child to calm down as well as listening to the parent's version of what happened. Once the parent has calmed down, you can address other issues, knowing which areas are most important to emphasize with this parent. If a trusting relationship has already been established, the parent educator can help the parent to understand his or her child's behavior and other ways to handle this situation. This should be done in a tone of caring and concern. Parents may be stressed out and need support for their own issues. They may also be defensive about their actions. Remaining calm and respectful will help create a space to talk about this situation and make it easier to talk about program rules and support alternative discipline strategies.

SITUATION 6: THE LITTLE PERFORMER

Pam wants to show the parent educator Joanne how her 5-month-old daughter Alicia has learned to crawl. She puts Alicia down on the floor and takes a rattle away from her. Alicia tries to get the rattle but only manages to go backwards. Pam continues to prod Alicia, who gets frustrated and begins to cry. Pam says one more time, "You know how to crawl."

1. *Redirect the parent to try another activity.* "It's okay, she may not be up to crawling today, but it looks like she really wants her rattle." The parent educator can move the rattle into baby's reach and let her calm herself.

2. *Use reflective language with the baby to model how to get a child to calm down.* "You're feeling frustrated that you can't get your rattle. Let's try a new position." Parent educator can move the baby to a different position.

3. *Help the parent understand the process of how a child learns to crawl.* The parent educator can explain that some children end up going backwards until they are a little older and have the coordination to get all parts of their body moving in the same direction. The parent educator can focus on other new abilities that Alicia has acquired.

In this situation, the parent wants her baby to perform and is not being sensitive to her baby's cues. She may need some help to appreciate what her baby can do and how to read her baby's cues when she is frustrated. Clear information about development of motor skills can also help Pam understand the sequence and range of developing skills.

Summary

The following tips summarize important ideas from this chapter for creating effective parent-child interaction components for parent education programs:

1. Parent-child interaction time can address a variety of goals in a parent education program. Parent educators should consider both parent and child needs and clearly articulate the program goals for both parents and children.

2. The expectations for parents and children should be explained to parents. Parents will appreciate knowing what roles the program wants them to play and what rules or limits the program has for their children.

3. Parent-child interaction should be designed to bring parent and child together with activities that require active participation for both parent and child.

4. Parent-child interaction time can be threatening to some parents who are concerned about being judged. Sensitivity to parent feelings of embarrassment when children "misbehave" can support parents through difficult moments.

5. The tone and energy in parent-child time should be light and fun. Careful design of activities that incorporate parent and child interests can increase the likelihood that both parents and children will have fun and enjoy their time together.

Discussion Questions

1. What can a parent educator learn about a child during parent-child interaction time?

2. What roles does the parent educator play during observation time?

3. Give examples of observation questions that may be coordinated with specific discussion topics.

4. Discuss difficult moments at the end of the chapter and brainstorm additional responses to each of the situations.

10

Leading Groups
With Complex Issues

Parent education programs frequently reach out to diverse populations by forming collaborative relationships with other family support agencies. Either in these partnerships or in other programs that target special populations, parent educators find themselves working with parents who have more complex issues. Trained to facilitate traditional groups, professionals are often challenged by the intense needs facing families in these settings. Programs for teen parents, parents who have children with special needs, incarcerated parents, or those with low education levels tend to deal with issues beyond typical parenting concerns. Parents who enroll in these programs often have multiple stressors and risk factors that present complex challenges for parent educators both within and outside the group setting. This chapter will describe programs designed for special populations, examine family issues and dynamics common to these settings, and address intervention and problem-solving skills useful in facilitating groups of parents with complex issues. Additionally, benefits and challenges for parent educators in collaborative programs will be examined.

Special Populations

Though many parent education programs offer universal access so that any parent can participate, a growing number are designed specifically for special populations. Universal access is reflective of society in that all families are

Photo 10.1   Parent groups for fathers provide an opportunity to explore the unique challenges of fatherhood.

welcome. The philosophy is that healthy families, as well as those with challenges, can benefit from participation as they learn from each other and the parent educator. This model works well in many cases. However, for some parents, particularly those with specific challenges or concerns, a targeted parent education program can address their issues more directly.

For example, a teenage parent is welcome to enroll in a typical parent education class for parents of infants. However, when she arrives she may feel insecure and out of place in a group with older, more mature parents. In many cases, this young parent either will not enroll or, after attending once or twice, will drop out of the program. A group designed specifically for young parents that focuses on topics relevant to her situation will be much more appealing and appropriate for this young mother. In this setting, the parent educator will need to have a good understanding of adolescent development when structuring a group that is supportive to young parents. Topics such as living in intergenerational families, supporting a relationship with the baby's other parent, decision making, continuing education, and accessing community social service resources will be of particular interest. Parent educators may collaborate with public health nurses, social workers, and high school teachers to serve teen parents.

Parent education groups also exist for those whose children have special needs. Again, although these parents are welcome in any parent education program, they often prefer time with others who share their common challenges (Ellison, 1997). Participating in typical programs that include children can be a wonderful opportunity for these families to enjoy time together. Or it can be a painful reminder of how different their parenting experience really is and may accentuate the developmental delays of their children. Targeted groups for parents of children with special needs provide support from others who truly understand and can empathize. Typical topics in these groups include dealing with questions about your child's differences, guiding behavior of a child with special needs, supporting the sibling relationship, and advocating for your child. Parent educators may work collaboratively with special education teachers and others with expertise in working with children with special needs.

Group parent education is also offered in jails and prisons for incarcerated parents (Palm, 2001). Skilled facilitators of these groups focus on developing and maintaining parent-child and family relationships during this difficult time of separation and family crisis. This may also be an opportunity for parents to gain a better understanding of the impact of their families of origin on their ability to parent. Groups for parents who are incarcerated cover a wide range of ages of children and a variety of family structures and cultural differences. Some typical parenting issues that are important for this group are understanding development and having appropriate expectations, developing effective communication, and understanding positive discipline strategies. These topics must be adapted to the circumstances of the incarcerated parent. Topics of special interest to this group will also include legal issues around paternity establishment, child support orders, and visitation. Parent education must also address emotional development in children, anger management in adults, and developing respectful co-parenting relationships. One dimension of punishment for incarcerated parents is the separation from their children and the discounting of their role as parents. A parenting class becomes an important setting to be affirmed as a parent and encouraged to be a good parent, even behind prison bars. Parent educators in this setting may work in conjunction with Adult Basic Education (ABE) programs, vocational training, and substance abuse programs (Palm, 2001).

Family literacy programs are offered throughout the country, serving parents who have not completed their high school diploma or General Equivalency Diploma (GED). Along with adult basic education, early childhood education, and parent-child interaction, parents participate in group parent education. This targeted program typically serves parents with multiple stressors and risk factors that include low education levels, low income levels, and other social and emotional challenges that have kept them from succeeding in education and employment settings. Topics focus on the development of

literacy skills for both the parent and the child, parents as partners in their child's education, healthy family interactions, and positive parenting strategies. In family literacy, a variety of collaborative relationships may exist. Parent educators may team up with Head Start teachers, therapists, social workers, public health nurses, adult basic education teachers, and welfare-to-work counselors.

English as a Second Language (ESL) families represent a growing number of parents participating in parent education groups. Predominantly foreign-born immigrants, these families originate from a variety of countries. Typically, ESL families participate in programs like family literacy that allow them to enhance their language skills, pursue citizenship, and assimilate into the community. Adult learners tend to be conscientious about their education and committed to succeed. They are also interested in helping their children succeed in school. In addition to the adult education component, programs are designed to include group parent education. A variety of challenges exist for the parent educator of ESL families. Language and cultural barriers present hurdles for even the most seasoned parent educator. The rewards, however, tend to be great.

ESL parent groups in larger communities may consist of families with the same language and culture. For example, a community may have an influx of Hmong families who are interested in participating in classes. If Hmong educators are not available, interpreters can be utilized in group discussion. The parent educator in this group becomes immersed in the Hmong culture, learning from the students while teaching and supporting positive parenting skills.

In smaller communities, ESL parent education groups may include a variety of different cultures and languages. Hispanic, Vietnamese, Somali, Russian, and other parents participate in the same sessions. Clearly, this presents unique challenges for parent educators. A greater focus lies on language acquisition, and topics may include securing medical services, meeting immunization requirements, navigating the school system, preparing children to enter school, attending parent-teacher conferences, and other practical content. Because there are many cultural differences in this type of group, a wide variety of parenting practices and values will exist. The parent educator must respect and learn as much as possible about each cultural perspective, while sharing the information and philosophy of the program. In this setting, parent educators must be willing to learn as much from the participants as they are learning from the group experience. A cross-cultural perspective will assist the leader in remaining nonjudgmental in viewing parenting as a cultural phenomenon (Bennett & Grimley, 2000). Because most of the research on children and parents has been dominated by studies within Western culture, it is important for group leaders to avoid interpreting results as universally applicable to all cultures. One of the primary challenges in working with parents of varying

Photo 10.2   Literacy activities help parents prepare their children for school
success.

cultures is to help them learn new patterns of parenting that do not violate the
principles of their culture (Bavelok, 1997). ESL parents also must learn about
the culture of the school system to support their children, who face the challenges of learning another language and the changing culture of American
schools with its recent emphasis on high standards and accountability.

Additionally, because the focus of ESL groups is often on sharing information, the primary methods used by the parent educator may be related more
to teaching and less to facilitating. Parent educators who work with ESL
parents often include hands-on experiences, sharing of practical content about
parenting, language skills, and school success. These methods, rather than
facilitating discussions about challenges and strategies of parenting, are often
more meaningful and relevant to the ESL parent. Though group discussions
may occur on some level, language differences often limit the depth of sharing
that occurs in groups where most participants and the facilitator share the
same language and culture. Parent educators of ESL groups often struggle in
their attempts to replicate the more typical parent education group for this
population when a different approach would be more appropriate. The parent
educator may find that the initial trade-off for limited depth in discussion is
the provision of practical information on safety, school rules, and practice in

learning English. As ESL parents become more proficient in English and parent educators learn more about the cultural values and parenting practices, the depth of discussion may increase. The use of translators and the hiring of paraprofessionals from specific cultural groups can be effective strategies for improving communication with ESL families.

Parents living in poverty can also present challenges to the parent educator. The culture of poverty is described as having hidden rules that reflect differing social values and behaviors (Payne, 1998). Approaches to family life, relationships, and parenting by those living in poverty may be very different from those of the middle class. Parent educators, especially those who have not experienced poverty, would benefit from learning about the culture of poverty. Working with families living in poverty often links parent educators with other agencies and programs. Social workers, Head Start teachers, family advocates, and others may team with parent educators to provide a continuum of programming to families.

From these descriptions of the wide variety of special populations served in parent education groups, it is clear that as collaborative programs are developed for targeted populations, the role of the parent educator requires a deeper level of involvement with families. The issues of parents in these programs are typically more complex and require more teamwork and intervention on the part of the collaborating partners. The role of the parent educator is expanded from one who facilitates groups to one who works in tandem with a variety of professionals to meet the immediate and long-term goals of the family.

Benefits and Challenges of Collaborations for Parent Educators

Collaborative family support programs are often formed to increase the efficiency of services, to eliminate duplication of those services in a community, and to offer more options to families. Grantors encourage family support programs in search of supplemental funding to join with other agencies and programs. Each agency brings strengths, varying services, and opportunities that, when offered jointly, expand the options for families.

For example, a parent education program offered through the public schools may focus on providing a parent educator to teach parents positive parenting strategies and support them in their efforts. It may not be the program's mission or within its financial abilities to provide transportation, social services, or ongoing home visits. Targeting particular populations, typically lower-income families, may not be successful because of the additional needs of families for these supplemental services. Another community family support agency may be able to offer these options but may not offer formal parent education.

Collaborative partnerships provide opportunities for the families to participate and take advantage of a full range of appropriate services of both agencies.

There are, however, many challenges in collaborations. Because each collaborating partner has particular mandates and regulations that govern funding, eligibility, mission, and scope of services, challenges can occur in collaborative relationships. Direct service staff, as well as administrators, may differ on philosophy and approach for serving families. Local, state, or federal requirements may add stress to the partnering relationship as staff attempt to adhere to standards and expectations. For example, school-sponsored programs may have strict boundaries that keep services focused on education. Parent educators may not be allowed to transport families or provide case management because other agencies take on this role. Head Start teachers often provide rides for families to receive services and adhere to program performance standards that include a social service component. These issues may cause tension in a team relationship when boundaries are set at different places for staff working with the same families. Differences in salaries and status of positions between professionals from partnering agencies can also cause tension among team members. Finally, as in any system, a variety of problems can occur that result from poor communication, lack of time for team members to meet with each other, misconceptions about or differences in philosophies, and ownership issues.

It is clear that collaborations require a commitment from all partners. It is not enough for the decision makers or administrators to be committed to working together. Without a commitment from all staff involved, a collaboration will not succeed. Ongoing support and team meeting opportunities for direct service staff, including parent educators, are crucial. Regular staff meetings that focus on debriefing and updating regarding families' needs and progress and on learning about each agency will assist staff in becoming a real team.

For programs to succeed, supervisors need to choose staff who are open to working collaboratively and who are flexible in their approach. Parent educators and others who can approach a new challenge in a positive manner and are able to put the needs of the families first are good candidates for collaborations. Those who think that their methods are the only ones that work and that their agency is the most important will not be good team members. Careful attention to staff selection for collaborative projects is a key factor in designing a partnership.

Collaboration typically makes emotional energy and time demands on parent educators. However, the benefits of working together for families outweigh the challenges. Approaching parent education with a recognition of the importance of varying the delivery of services to meet the needs of diverse families should result in quality programs and appropriate options for all families.

Within collaborative programs, parent educators may expand the teaming relationship with professionals from other agencies. In some programs, parent education groups may be co-facilitated. This type of group leadership requires a different perspective of group process. The relationship between the co-facilitators is critical to the success of the group. The parent educator may focus primarily on parenting issues, whereas the other facilitator, perhaps a therapist, may take on leadership when personal or more intense issues arise. A public health nurse may co-facilitate groups and bring a medical perspective to parenting topics; a social worker will bring a wealth of information about community resources.

Co-facilitation requires both facilitators to work in tandem with each other and agree upon roles and expectations for leadership. Will one person take on more leadership than the other? Are both willing to share responsibility and ownership? Who will plan the sessions? Are both facilitators accepting of the other moving the discussion along, adding immediacy to a situation, changing the flow of the group, or interjecting another point of discussion not on the agenda? Co-facilitators who work well together will need to openly discuss their expectations and perspectives about group leadership.

Although co-facilitation of parent education groups is not the primary model of most programs, in collaborative programs it may be more practical and likely to occur. There are advantages for groups that are facilitated by two group leaders (Corey, 2000). Participants can benefit from the insights of two perspectives rather than one. Co-facilitators can also complement each other's strengths and expertise, as well as consult, debrief, and plan together. When facilitators respect each other and approach co-facilitation in a positive manner, group members can benefit from this experience.

Understanding Family Issues, Dynamics, and Influences of Family of Origin With Special Populations

Participants in parent education groups, particularly those in settings designed for families with higher needs and multiple stresses, tend to include a variety of familial experiences that can have adverse effects on a group. Challenges arise for the group leader on two levels. First, the parent educator encounters parents' perspectives and behaviors that may have a negative impact on group process. Understanding the origin of these attitudes and behaviors provides insight and enables the facilitator to manage and, if necessary, address them. Second, parent educators need to have a broad understanding of healthy family functioning, with respect to culture and diversity, to identify generational

Box 10.1   How Do Parent Educators Feel
About Collaboration?

In June 2000, the Minnesota Department of Children, Families, and
Learning commissioned a study of service integration in Minnesota's
early childhood programs. Interviews were conducted with staff and
administrators of programs serving young children and parents, as well
as other school and community representatives. All were involved in
programs that collaborate to serve families. Following are excerpts from
their responses to a variety of issues:

Mission Focus: "We've really gone beyond our home organizations in
our thinking. We've taken components of different programs and new
ideas and formed a new entity. . . . We don't have much to do with money,
and that is helpful to us. Administrators deal with resource issues. We share
families and children. What we do for families and children is our priority."

Flexibility: "Everyone has to give. In dealing with conflicting rules
among programs you get around it with flexibility and communication,
keeping focused on working together for families and children."

Relationships: "There are differences in pay and supervision. It's not
always clear whom you go to if there is a problem. You have to work
through these things. . . . Pay scales are different. These things can poi-
son the process if not worked out in a positive way. Administrators play
a key role here."

Connections: "We get to know more about each other's programs.
We are able to streamline access, provide consistency of messages to
parents, and reinforce those messages. We are able to have really solid
knowledge to base referrals. Our work is like an airport terminal, a place
to make connections."

Benefits of Collaboration: "Money, I suppose, was initially a motivat-
ing factor. We have moved beyond money. For us, collaboration just
makes sense, and it is better for families. In the 8 years we've been working together, it made a huge difference."

SOURCE: Mueller (2000).

patterns that may impair family relations. Ethnicity and culture greatly influence
family dynamics, behavior patterns, values, and perspectives (Goldenberg &
Goldenberg, 2000). It is important, therefore, for group facilitators to consider
the possible impact of these factors on family functioning, rather than to
prematurely interpret them as problematic.

By understanding the source and meaning of particular behaviors and attitudes, the parent educator can make decisions regarding respectful confrontation and referral that can assist parents with positive changes. This section will examine recurrent patterns of behavior, attitudes, and values typical of parents with multiple risk factors in order to provide insight and strategies in addressing and understanding them within the group context. The focus, therefore, will remain primarily on how these common issues affect group dynamics.

COMMON CHARACTERISTICS

Not all parents with multiple stressors and risk factors share the same familial experiences. However, many parents who attend parent education groups for targeted audiences tend to share commonalities in their backgrounds and experiences. For example, parents in family literacy programs who are undereducated and working on high school diplomas may have higher rates of teen pregnancies, low income, stresses of single-parent family structures, and struggles with domestic and chemical abuse (St. Pierre, Swartz, et al., 1995). Parents in programs for low-income families share many experiences and characteristics, which can provide a variety of stresses and risk factors that may originate from a generational pattern. A family system that operates dysfunctionally has been described as a multicar pileup on the freeway, causing damage generation after generation. It results from accumulated feelings, rules, interactions, and beliefs that have been passed along for generations (Forward, 1989). The information included in this section is presented as common characteristics but is not intended to describe all families with multiple risk factors.

Families of different cultures may also approach and define stress in different ways. What may be perceived as a mildly stressful situation in one culture may be viewed as more significant in another. However, according to Olson and DeFrain (2000), certain characteristics of stress and family responses are common across cultural groups:

1. Families from all cultural groups experience stress.

2. All stressors either begin or end up in the family.

3. All families must find resources, either internal or external, to help them cope with stress.

4. All families have some internal strengths for managing stress in their family system.

5. Families tend to use internal resources before seeking external resources.

Adult children of dysfunctional families share many characteristics that affect the way they participate in group education experiences and the way they

---

Box 10.2   Parenting Issues That Affect Adult Children
of Dysfunctional Families

1. Being normal
2. Perfectionism
3. Control
4. Hypervigilance and anxious overparenting
5. Underproduction and underparenting
6. Enmeshment, dependency on their children
7. Isolation, not being able to ask for help
8. Chaos versus rigidity
9. Peace at all costs
10. Narcissistic parenting
11. Black-and-white thinking or all-or-nothing behavior
12. Difficulty setting limits
13. Boundary problems
14. Lies, deceit, and denial
15. Unreasonable expectations
16. Blaming and criticism

---

parent their children (Kristensen, 1991). According to Kristensen, there are 16 common issues that affect these parents. Box 10.2 lists the common issues that affect adult children of dysfunctional families.

Some other characteristics that tend to surface regularly also affect group process. Two of them are issues of fairness and being crisis oriented.

EFFECTS OF DYSFUNCTIONAL FAMILY-OF-ORIGIN ISSUES ON PARTICIPATION IN GROUPS

Because parents may act out roles and patterns of behaviors in parent groups that are similar to those of their family of origin, it is helpful for the parent educator to be able to identify and anticipate them. In a group process approach with a systemic perspective, the group is a system, much like a family. It is natural, therefore, for group members to replicate some of the experiences, roles, attitudes, and behaviors from their family of origin. For it is in that context that they were socialized to behave in a system.

Though all of the parenting issues noted by Kristensen for adults from dysfunctional families can affect group process, there are several that are most likely to cause challenges for the facilitator. Issues of control, isolation, having peace at all costs, black-and-white thinking, boundary problems, deceit and denial, and being crisis oriented are of primary concern to the parent educator in the group context.

Control Issues

Parents who struggle with control issues can require careful attention from the parent educator. Often without a conscious awareness, they manipulate group process in order to know exactly what will happen next. These parents often grew up in homes where adults were unreliable; they learned that if they surrendered control, they were not safe. In their adult lives, if they become vulnerable, others will see them as they really are. Control, therefore, offers a buffer of safety in the group setting. A controlling parent may monopolize, insisting on addressing personal issues, even if it is not what other members want. He or she may be resistant to the educator's suggestions or may use passive methods of control like emotionally withdrawing from the group. Ultimately, controlling behaviors come from a lack of self-confidence. They provide a shield of protection against being exposed. Parent educators can help controlling parents learn to let go of having to be in control at all times. Modeling spontaneity as a positive approach to relationship building may help parents take small steps toward eliminating their need for control. Parent educators can also wean controlling members by offering choices that still allow parents some feeling of control, rather than expecting immediate change. For example, a controlling group member may be given a task in the group such as choosing refreshments, deciding on the topic, or acting as a small-group leader. Additionally, it is helpful for the parent educator to let parents know what will happen next by posting agendas and sharing topic lists. If parents with control needs feel safe because they know what to expect, their negative behaviors may be limited.

Isolation

Isolation and not being able to ask for help are other issues that can emerge in the group setting. Children who grow up in dysfunctional families often become adults who have learned that asking for help indicates weakness. They may have been shamed by their families if they admitted feeling vulnerable or needing help from others. They are unlikely to trust others, especially professionals who seem threatening and ready to expose them. These parents may have difficulty opening up in discussion and have learned to keep family secrets. Just as in their personal lives, they struggle with issues of intimacy (Blume, 1989) and may carry that fear into the group setting. Parent educators can focus on issues of trust with these parents. Helping them feel safe, modeling appropriate self-disclosure of shortcomings, helping them connect with other parents, and teaching the notion of interdependence may assist isolated parents.

Peace at All Costs

One of the primary goals of the parent educator who works with adult learners is to challenge them to participate not only cognitively but also emotionally. Adults learn best when they participate on a feelings level. Parents with multiple risk factors may have come from families where no one was allowed to express feelings. As a coping mechanism, they have learned to deny and avoid anything that deals with emotions. These parents strive for peace at all costs. Whereas some have learned to deny the existence of feelings, others have learned that feelings lead to rage, which leads to violence and abuse.

It is not surprising, then, that in the group context these parents feel extremely anxious when any type of conflict or difference of opinion occurs. Yet conflict is part of healthy group development, and parent educators must learn to welcome divergent thinking and, at the same time, manage conflict as part of group process. Teaching the difference between anger and rage offers a new perspective to these parents. Modeling that disagreement is healthy and interesting in the group setting may allow them a new way of learning that includes depth as well as safety. From this experience, parents can learn to survive and grow from an exposure to conflict without loss of self-esteem or fear of damaged relationships.

Black-and-White Thinking

Another common issue of parents from dysfunctional families that affects the group experience is black-and-white thinking. Their experience may have taught them that people are either all good or all bad, that an idea is either good or bad, and that there is only one right way to handle a situation. As a professional, the parent educator may feel accepted by this parent one day and an enemy the next. This can be particularly confusing for group facilitators, who may feel as if they never know what to expect. These parents also have a need to find "the answer" and seem frustrated with choices and alternatives that parent educators may present. In their families of origin, decisions were often made for them, and they had little practice considering options. Facilitators can help parents see that there are more ways than one to handle parenting challenges. They can propose choices and alternatives and draw on the experiences of the group to share successes.

Boundary Problems

Boundary problems typically occur with more frequency for parents with multiple risk factors. These parents often either have few boundaries or many barriers in their interactions with others. They have difficulties separating themselves from others emotionally or may show no empathy or compassion for other parents in the group. The latter type of behavior, when applied to their own children, can be linked to abusive parenting behavior. The parent who is unable to empathize with others, who seems to have no compassion and typically blames the victim, may have a greater than average likelihood of exhibiting abusive parent behaviors.

Parent educators can teach about the needs for clear boundaries, as well as model appropriate boundary behavior within the context of the group. Protecting members from too much self-disclosure and limiting personal sharing within a balanced approach will help parents learn appropriate social boundaries.

Lies, Deceit, and Denial

Parents in families with multiple needs may also use lies, deceit, and denial in all aspects of their lives. Within the group this becomes especially problematic because it erodes the atmosphere of trust that is crucial to a healthy adult learning environment. These parents use pretense to present themselves. They pretend that everything is fine. They say and do the right thing in front of others, but in fact their lives are often unhappy. Shame has been a major emotion in their families of origin, and the family rule has been that lies and deceit are the only way to protect family secrets. Parent educators and other group members may not recognize this behavior immediately. These parents have spent a lifetime presenting themselves in a deceitful manner, and they have mastered the act. However, given time, the facilitator, as well as the other parents, begins to realize that something doesn't add up. Other group members may begin to challenge the inconsistencies, and often as a result there is conflict and finally the parent in question withdraws from the group. It is important for the parent educator to realize the stress under which this parent operates and the enormous need for self-protection. Gentle and private confrontation may be necessary in some circumstances. Modeling honesty and affirming members who share their problems can expose this parent to another way of being.

Crisis Orientation

Finally, being crisis oriented is an issue that can be problematic for the group. A parent who comes from a family where one crisis follows another quickly learns to need the stress and chaos of crises. Attention from others, the separation from other, less exciting aspects of life, and the distraction from what is really important can all provide a way of living that revolves around a continuing list of challenges. Within the group, this parent may quickly emerge as someone in need of attention and assistance. The parent educator may move quickly to involve the group in offering suggestions for this very overwhelmed parent. Initially, other members may show true concern and be willing to forgo their own issues to help. However, very quickly everyone realizes there is no resolution that will really make a difference. This parent moves from one crisis to the next and is in constant need of guidance, which often goes unheeded. In this situation, the parent educator will need to balance the needs of the entire group with the needs of one parent. On a one-to-one basis, it may be advisable to help the parent identify the pattern that has been established. Furthermore, constant crises are indicative of a need for a referral to other services within the community.

It is helpful for parent educators to understand how the past experiences, attitudes, and behaviors of parents can affect the group experience. Though insight into the origin and purpose of each behavior can give greater understanding, it is also important to assess what responsibility the parent educator has in addressing them within the confines of his or her professional role. Many of the behaviors described in this chapter can be better and more comprehensively addressed through therapy. However, parents may choose not to utilize individual or family therapy and yet continue to participate in group parent education. It is not the role of the parent educator to address personality issues of parent participants in a group. Nor is it appropriate to delve deeply into painful family-of-origin issues. This role is reserved for the therapist. However, understanding the probable origin of certain behaviors that affect group process can provide helpful insight for the group leader. At times disruptive behaviors can have very little to do with the parent educator's skills in group facilitation and more to do with the experiences and patterns of behavior that a parent brings from his or her past.

Parents with multiple stressors and risk factors are like all parents in that they struggle with the day-to-day challenges of raising children. They bring many common experiences from their own families of origins that can affect their participation in group learning. Understanding these complex behaviors and their origins can assist parent educators in working with the most challenging parents in groups and offer these parents the support and learning that group parent education can provide.

INTERVENTION SKILLS FOR SPECIAL POPULATIONS

Parent groups that are designed to address the needs of families with multiple risk factors typically require skills associated with Level 4, brief focused intervention (Doherty, 1995). (See Chapter 4.) Within these groups, there is usually a heightened intensity of emotions, issues are more pressing, and there is a need for intervention rather than prevention. Child abuse or neglect, chemical dependency, incarceration of family members, grief and loss, lack of adequate food or housing, and concerns about developmental delays of children are typical issues that arise in these groups. Although at-risk parents

Table 10.1   Parenting Issues That Affect Adult Children of Dysfunctional
                  Families

Issue	Description	Strategy
1. Being Normal	Has no blueprint for "normal" Uses TV families/friends for model Desperately wants to appear normal	Teach normal child development Help find a middle ground Give specific, concrete answers
2. Perfectionism	Was often "parentified" as child Needs to please authority figures Looks for approval, judges self harshly	Reassure, support Help see value of mistakes Self-disclose some mistakes
3. Control	Family life was chaotic—little control as child Feels safe when in control Is addicted to control Parents "by the book"	Help them let go of some control Encourage spontaneity Affirm attempts at letting go
4. Anxious Overparenting	Reacts too soon and too extremely Interferes with child's learning Has lack of trust in others	Create a safe group environment Use case studies and examples Work on relaxation and trust
5. Underparenting/ Underprotection	Doesn't know how to protect self/child Often comes from neglectful home	Help recognize dangerous situations Help understand source of their underparenting
6. Enmeshment/ Dependecy on Their Children	Overdoes closeness with family Fears abandonment Avoids relationships with other adults	Encourage boundaries with children Help establish bonds with other adults
7. Isolation/ Unable to Ask for Help	Feels unsafe when vulnerable Keeps family secrets Has difficulty opening up in group Doesn't trust others	Teach value of interdependence Stress strong people ask for help Address trust issues in group
8. Chaos vs. Rigidity	Has trouble finding middle ground Follows compulsive rules, no joy, rigid schedules or Has complete disorder in life Uses no self-discipline, viewed as freedom, free spirit	Work on "trying another way"

Issue	Description	Strategy
9. Peace at All Costs	Avoids conflict, denies emotional reality Equates conflict with violence from past family experiences	Reflect feelings Manage conflict in group Teach difference between anger and rage
10. Narcissistic Parenting	Lives through their child's achievements Shows poor boundaries	Assist with emotional boundaries Teach healthy family systems
11. Black-or-White Thinking	Sees people as good or bad (friend one day, enemy the next)	Teach about "gray" areas Stress multiple solutions/options Help find a middle ground
12. Difficulty Setting Limits	Cannot follow through on limit Is too patient/nonassertive Wants to be liked, friend of child Shows separation anxiety from child Tries to avoid parenting role	Distinguish between role of parent and child Teach difference of separation and abandonment Teach/model assertive skills
13. Boundary Problems	Has either no boundaries or strong barriers Feels everyone's pain or no empathy for anyone Sees children as constant reminders of their pain Blames their children May be abusive or neglectful	Teach/model boundaries Model respect for individuality of family and group members
14. Lies, Deceit, Denial	Hides problems, keeps secrets, pretense Lies and says the right thing in front of others May look very good, but something seems wrong	Model honesty Self-disclose shortcomings
15. Unreasonable Expectations	Is self-centered, meets own needs, not child's	Teach appropriate guidelines Help build a child-centered family
16. Blaming and Criticism	Doesn't take responsibility for self Blames others, often children Has a negative perspective	Confront destructive effects of criticism Model ownership of feelings and responsibility for failure

(Continued)

Table 10.1 Continued

Issue	Description	Strategy
Others:		
17. Issues of Fairness	Watches to make sure things are fair/equal Inequities trigger memories of the past Competes for attention	Be fair, but realistic Avoid "counting and measuring" Acknowledge feelings about childhood inequities
18. Crisis Oriented	Moves from one crisis to the next Obsessively talks about current crisis Is not happy unless something is wrong Feeds on attention from others	Avoid overinvolvement in crisis Use referral system Help to focus on things that are going well Affirm accomplishments/ success

still deal with universal parenting issues, each challenge can be made more complex by the lack of understanding, and often lack of empathy, demonstrated by the parents for their children. Frequently these parents did not receive the positive parenting they needed as children and may be unable to meet the emotional and physical needs of their own children. It is as if they are "parenting in the dark" (Kristensen, 1990). Although many of these parents have the potential and desire to make positive changes, without the experience of being nurtured, it is very difficult for them to provide what is needed for their own children. Therefore, the job of the parent educator is more complex than in other group settings. Additional challenges arise when unhealthy generational parenting patterns, lack of self-esteem and confidence, unrealistic expectations, and unmet personal needs are brought to the group setting.

The skills necessary to work with higher-need families are more complex and involved. Utilizing opportunities for consultation and support, parent educators must move beyond teaching, demonstrating, and leading group discussion to be successful with this population. It is in the Level 4 setting that parent educators need to use advanced facilitation and intervention skills to guide parents on their journey. Instead of providing an opportunity for parents to enhance skills, these groups address more serious situations that are likely to result in physical or emotional harm to children. This section will address specific intervention skills necessary in working with families with multiple and complex needs, as well as outline a step-by-step process for intervention.

Building on active listening and support skills such as paraphrasing, reflection of feelings, clarification, and summarizing, intervention skills move the interaction to another level. No longer does the parent educator support through listening and guiding the parent in finding his or her own answers. In an interventive approach, the group facilitator plays a more active role in helping the parent gain insight and develop a specific plan. Level 3 active listening skills of the parent educator assist the parent with insight and self-understanding. Level 4 interventive response skills reflect the parent educator's role to understand the parent in order to act in a guiding role. The parent continues to be the decision maker about what strategies he or she is willing to try and what direction he or she will take to make a change. However, the process of intervention signals a shift in the group's dynamics that requires a more directive role from the parent educator.

The term *intervention* may have a confrontational connotation for some who associate it with chemical dependency or other interventions. In the context of the levels of involvement model, this association is not accurate. Intervention, in this sense, is a focused process of assisting a parent in addressing a particularly complex challenge and developing a plan of action for change. Although intervention occurs within the group setting, the focus is typically on one parent's issue.

SPECIFIC INTERVENTION SKILLS

Probing

A parent who is under stress often brings a complex issue to the group but may be unable to present it clearly. The interventive skill of probing can be used by the parent educator in the form of an open or closed question. Probes are used to encourage a parent to

- Elaborate: "Can you tell us more?"
- Obtain more information: "What happens then?"
- Refocus: "Which one of these issues is of most concern?"

Probing questions can be combined with a reflection-of-feelings statement to acknowledge understanding. For example, "You sound pretty overwhelmed right now (reflection). Which challenge would you like to address first?" combines statements that acknowledge, affirm, and help the parent focus on what is most important.

Confrontation

The word *confrontation* tends to have a negative connotation. We can reframe confrontation in a positive way so it becomes a matter of courtesy; it is respectful of group members; it provides an opportunity for excellent modeling; and it maintains group morale (Bowman, 1982). Confrontation need not be negative or aggressive. In fact, confrontation can be done in a very gentle way if an adequate level of trust between the group leader and the parents exists. Parents with multiple and complex needs often have past negative experiences of being corrected. Without a high level of trust and rapport, confrontation may feel punitive.

Two types of situations in which parent educators might use confrontation skills are (a) to address disruptive behavior in the group or (b) to point out a mixed message or discrepancy of a parent's behavior or attitude. The second situation is done on a more limited basis but can be an effective part of intervention.

If disruptive behavior is not confronted in a group, it may be assumed that this behavior is acceptable. Talking about others who are not present, engaging in side conversations, using inappropriate language, monopolizing, or putting other group members down are all examples of disruptive behavior. Although many of these behaviors may be addressed in the forming stages of group development by setting ground rules, parent educators may neglect the enforcement of these rules. Depending on the relationship with the parent and the context of the group, confrontation could occur immediately within the group or individually with the parent later.

Confrontation of a person's behavior or attitude that shows a discrepancy is more difficult to do. Presuming adequate trust and rapport, the parent educator needs to consider whether confrontation could lead to better self-understanding for the parent and, ultimately, to change. Parent educators need to use confrontation sparingly, always in the best interest of the parent, and never to prove a point or vent frustration.

Interpretation

One of the goals of intervention is to provide insight for the parent to enhance self-understanding. It is appropriate, therefore, for the parent educator to interpret or give a possible explanation of a behavior in more depth than paraphrasing. Interpretation should be based on concrete knowledge of child development, family functioning, or parenting skills, rather than on personal biases and experiences. For example, basing an interpretation of a parent's choices that is influenced by the parent educator's values is not appropriate. Encouraging mothers to leave their careers because the parent educator believes that all children must have full-time care by a parent, and because this is the choice he or she made, is not an appropriate interpretation.

Interpretations should also be phrased tentatively. Begin the interpretation with phrases such as "Perhaps . . . ," "I wonder if . . . ," "It's possible that . . . ,"

Box 10.3   Considerations for Confronting

1. Make sure rapport and trust exist before attempting confrontation.
2. Encourage the parent to focus on his or her behavior, not defend his or her actions.
3. Be aware of your own motives in confronting.
4. Consider the timing of confrontation and allow enough time for a response.
5. Choose an appropriate setting, whether private or within the group.
6. Structure the confrontation statement to avoid the word *but*. Use "and yet . . ." instead. (For example: "You say your first priority is your child, *and yet* you admit that you spend very little of your free time with him.")

---

or "It appears as though . . . ," or universalizing by saying, "One of the things we know about families is . . . ," helps to avoid defensiveness and resistance from the parent.

Finally, parent educators can assess the accuracy of their interpretation by asking if it "fits." This demonstrates an openness to the possibility that the interpretation is not accurate and allows the parent to clarify its relevance.

Immediacy

To focus the individual parent or the entire group on the here and now, the skill of immediacy is used. Immediacy is a description of something as it occurs within a group, either while it is occurring or immediately after. Forming statements of immediacy follows a few common rules (Cormier & Cormier, 1998):

- Describe it as it is happening or immediately after.
- Use present tense.
- Use "I" statements when referring to your own feelings or observations.
- Consider the timing and trust level of the group—too soon may be too much.

There are several purposes of immediacy:

- To bring out in the open something that hasn't been stated directly ("I'm feeling like this is a pretty serious issue for you.")
- To generate discussion or provide feedback about some aspect of the group ("I'm feeling uncomfortable when people are discussed who aren't here.")

- To maintain a focus on the "work" of the group ("It feels like there is a lot of support for each other here today.")
- To regroup, focus, and move in another direction ("I'm noticing we are really getting stuck. Let's move on.")

Statements of immediacy are often used to begin the process of a brief focused intervention. The parent educator states what he or she is feeling or observing and asks the parent if he or she is interested in spending some time within the group with this issue in more depth.

PROCESS OF INTERVENTION

Doherty (1995) believes that a Level 4 intervention is appropriate only for more complex parenting issues and those that are particularly problematic to the healthy functioning of the family system. The same interventive skills could, however, be used in a similar process of identifying an issue and working together on a plan of action. The intervention process can be broken down into a step-by-step process.

1. *Begin with immediacy.* "I'm hearing lots of frustration from you. It sounds like you are wanting to spend some time really working on this issue. Is that right?" This statement focuses the parent away from remaining stuck and offers the opportunity to work constructively.

2. *Ask for the group's permission.* "What I would suggest is that either we can look at this as a group and spend some time on it here or Sue and I can talk about it more privately at another time and we can continue with tonight's topic. Either way would be fine." Check in with both the parent and the group, and if both agree, continue the process.

3. *Ask a series of questions that probe and clarify.*

"Tell us what happened."

"What happened then?"

"How did you respond?"

"So what do you mean when you say. . . ?"

These questions give a clearer picture of the issue to the parent educator, to the group, and to the parent.

4. *Use a short interpretation of what the problem is.* "Something you may know about families is that. . . . Does this sound like what happens for you?" This summarizes what is happening without judgment, interprets behavior,

universalizes the issue, if appropriate, and offers an opportunity to either acknowledge or deny the "fit."

5. *Develop a plan of action with the parent.*
    a) Imaging: "How would you like to be when you're with your child?" Concentrate on the parent's behavior and desire for change; avoid focusing on what the child should be like.
    b) Get a commitment. "Would you be willing to try a few things this week?"
    c) Facilitate a plan of alternative action to address the issue with the parent playing an active part.
    d) Identify obstacles and resources. "What would make it difficult for you to do this? What would you need to help you?"
    e) Ask for group input. "What would anyone else like to add?"
    f) Summarize with a time frame. "So this week what you're willing to try is . . . and next week would it be okay if we take just a few minutes to see how things went?"
    g) Restate commitment. "Are you willing to give this a try?"
    h) Empower and support the parent. "I hope some of this will work for you. Feel free to try the parts that feel most comfortable. Good luck with it!"

Interventions need to be brief in order to respect all group members. Spending too much time with one parent ignores the needs of others. It is also important to be selective in deciding to intervene. Level 4 interventions are not a strategy that would typically be used in each session. Watching for the cues of the parent that indicate a higher emotional level regarding a more complex issue, along with the willingness of the group to allocate time for one member, will assist the parent educator in deciding whether to initiate an intervention. Parent educators lead groups following a continuum of education to support to intervention. The needs of the group will dictate which skills are most appropriate for the parent educator to utilize. Interventive skills allow parent educators to move beyond teaching to assisting parents in developing a plan for change regarding significantly complex issues in their roles as parents.

Summary

Group parent education for special populations with complex needs provides many challenges for group facilitators. Collaborative relationships with other helping professionals, deeper understanding of behavior and family dynamics, and specialized intervention skills are all necessary in this role. Although not every group parent education setting needs this high level of intervention, parent educators should be prepared with the knowledge and skills to respond appropriately.

Discussion Questions

1. Of the common parenting issues described by Kristensen, which do you identify with most from your own family of origin? Which do you feel would be most difficult to deal with from a parent in a group? Why?

2. How might behaviors and attitudes influenced by culture and ethnicity be misinterpreted by a parent educator? How can parent educators minimize this possibility?

11

Professional Growth and Development for Parent Educators

"This [parent education] is a lot more complicated than I thought. There is so much to learn and keep track of."

"It looked so easy from my perspective as a parent. I thought it would be fun and easy to facilitate a parent group. I never realized what goes on beneath the surface."

These quotes represent common responses from parents who have entered the parent education licensure program during the past 10 to 15 years in Minnesota. The skillful parent educator can make parent group facilitation look easy. As parents enter our program at St. Cloud State University (MN) as students of parent education, they realize that the role of parent educator is both complex and demanding. However, research on parent education has focused exclusively on curriculum, ignoring the more complex role of the parent educator in high-quality programming. Studies often include a small sample of parents and measure parenting knowledge and skills using a pre- and posttest design (Todres & Bunston, 1993). In more rigorous studies, a control group and random assignment to a group are used. This type of program research examines connections between a parent education curriculum and parent acquisition of new knowledge, attitudes, or skills. The competence of the parent educator who implements or teaches a curriculum is a salient variable that has been ignored in this type of parent education research. Educator competence is a highly complex variable to assess and study. However, it is, perhaps, the most important variable of all. Kumpfer and Alvarado (1998), after reviewing many parent education programs for program efficacy, estimated that 50% to 80% of the quality of a program is related to the trainer. Validated parenting programs or curriculum packages are important tools for parent education, but focused professional preparation and ongoing professional development are needed to improve the quality and effectiveness of parent education. We believe that competent parent educators are the heart of an effective parent and family education program. Curriculum materials are important tools that can add to program effectiveness, but they are *not* the program. They don't function like a software program that can be loaded onto multiple computers and operate in the same way. Curricula are most effective when they are implemented by a competent, caring parent educator who has developed the knowledge, technical skills, and artistry necessary for effective parent education. A skilled professional parent educator has the ability to individualize and structure curriculum to meet the needs of a particular group; to respond to unexpected questions and concerns of parents; and to support parents by addressing and processing feelings and emotions in the group setting. He or she facilitates a group process that is fluid and as unique as the personal makeup of each parent group. The skills involved in this role are highly sophisticated and differ from the minimal skill levels expected to present a preplanned curriculum on specific parenting topics.

The focus of this book thus far has been on the knowledge, dispositions, and facilitation skills that individuals need to be competent and effective parent educators in group parent education contexts. This final chapter will examine the topic of professional growth and development in parent educators. This growth process will be described from a developmental perspective that outlines different stages of professional development for parent educators from beginners/novices to master teachers. The key to supporting professional development in parent educators is the application of reflective practice principles to group parent education. Reflective practice in parent education includes a thoughtful exploration of practice with general goals of improving the effectiveness of practice and promoting ethical practice. Assessment in parent education is one practical aspect of reflective practice that will also be explored in this chapter. Support for professional development in parent education has been limited by the embeddedness of the parent educator role described in Chapter 2. Professionals in related fields tend to view parent education as only a part of their larger role and may find limited opportunities for professional development around specific parent education competencies. Because of the embeddedness of parent education, there has been a tendency to discount the role of parent educator, and the lack of research on characteristics and preparation of parent educators has limited the understanding of the professional development of master parent educators. In this final chapter, we borrow insights about reflective practice from education and related fields. We also draw upon our own clinical experiences as teacher educators, supervisors of parent educators, and program evaluators to outline a model of professional growth and development for parent education.

Developmental Stages of Parent Educators

The development of professionals often follows some specific pathways toward greater competency, comfort, and effectiveness. There has been no research focused on parent educators and their professional development over time. Both authors have had the unique opportunity to observe the development of parent educators in the Early Childhood Family Education (ECFE) programs in Minnesota, which started in the mid-1970s (Kurz-Riemer, 2001). Our own professional development as parent educators and our roles as teacher educators have given us a unique vantage point to observe typical patterns of growth and development in parent educators. Professional development opportunities for ECFE teachers have been provided through statewide in-service workshops twice a year as well as conferences and workshops offered by related professional organizations. All licensed parent educators in Minnesota have to complete 125 hours of approved continuing education every 5 years to maintain their licensure. This environment has nurtured professional growth in licensed parent educators.

Table 11.1 outlines three general stages of growth and development for parent educators in five different areas of development: content knowledge, facilitation skills, teaching skills, self-awareness, and understanding diversity. The potential knowledge bases for parent educators to incorporate into practice are extensive, including interdisciplinary knowledge of child development, child-rearing strategies, family dynamics and development, and awareness of related parenting and family resources.

The novice is often overwhelmed by the breadth of child development and family dynamics content. Beginning parent educators often feel anxious or inadequate when a parent asks a question that is beyond their current knowledge base. For example, a beginning parent educator has designed a parenting session on nutrition for toddlers and has prepared a lesson plan based on what types of food to eat and how much food is necessary for the typical toddler. A parent then asks how long she should expect her toddler to sit down with the family for dinner. Although this is a common concern of parents, it is new to the parent educator and outside the topic information that she has prepared.

Table 11.1   Levels of Professional Development for Parent Educators

Novice Level	Intermediate Level	Master Teaching Level
Knowledge		
Aware of basic child development and parenting information. Some apprehension about being able to answer parents' questions.	Possesses broader knowledge base. Aware of a variety of resources on development and parenting issues.	Confident about being able to answer questions and/or able to find resources. Realization of being well versed.
Aware of basic stages and theories of family dynamics and development.	Able to identify individual families' circumstances in reference to stages and characteristics.	Uses holistic perspective to understand each family's journey. Able to link current challenges and successes to stages and cycles of development. Understands and provides insight into impact of family of origin as well as current family dynamics.
Beginning to understand community resources. Some uncertainty about what is available and how to refer parents to other services.	Aware of basic community services and some comfort with access. Understands referral process.	Able to access information and services easily. Comfortable approaching parents for referrals. Uses a holistic perspective with parents within a collaborative approach.
Group Facilitation Skills		
Understands group process but feels challenged with group leadership role.	Enjoys group leadership. Focuses primarily on content and plan for session.	Confident as a group leader. Able to blend support and possible intervention with content. Understands behavior and can utilize skills to respond.
Understands dynamics of conflict and behaviors. Uncomfortable with dealing with difficult group/individual dynamics.	Has some skills to address challenging behaviors, mostly to defuse them and refocus group.	Is comfortable with addressing challenging or difficult group dynamics. Recognizes and uses "teachable moments." Takes responsibility for healthy group process and development.

Novice Level	Intermediate Level	Master Teaching Level
Teaching Skills		
Understands adult learning styles.	Plans and executes sessions with a variety of teaching methods but uses discussion as a primary method.	Able to assess parents' needs and styles and match methods accordingly. Shows insight in planning and leading to meet diverse needs of parents.
Able to develop and implement an appropriate parent education session plan.	Able to tailor a plan to an individual group. Able to access ongoing needs of group and modify plan, as needed.	Uses creative and varying strategies for group education and process. Has clear goals and objectives, yet uses flexibility as needed.
Professional Identity and Boundaries		
Shows basic self-awareness, but limited understanding of impact on relationship with group and role as facilitator.	Has insight into self, family-of-origin experiences, and their impact on the role as a parent educator.	Maturity and life experiences that reflect deeper understanding and self-awareness. Ability to separate biases and strong values from professional role.
Uncertain about skills and abilities as a parent educator	Growing confidence from positive experiences with parents that affirm abilities as a parent educator.	Quiet confidence in abilities. Leadership role within the parent group, as well as within the profession as a mentor and a guide for other professionals.
Understanding Diversity		
Shows basic awareness and sensitivity to importance of diversity issues. Not sure how to integrate into practice.	Growing awareness of family and cultural diversity and the impact on family and parenting issues.	Values family structure and cultural diversity in programs. Willing to learn from parents; comfortable addressing differences and facilitating discussion to address differences respectfully.

Parent educators who are able to use resources to find information to address specific parent questions begin to expand their knowledge base around common parent issues. A parent educator at the master teacher level has learned to listen carefully to parent questions and has built a solid knowledge base around this set of typical parent concerns. He or she is also able to understand individual parent and family needs and match information and resources to these needs on the basis of a more complex and sophisticated understanding of both children and families as well as firsthand knowledge of relevant community resources.

The growth in facilitation skills over time and a growing confidence in those skills prepares parent educators to address difficult situations more directly and effectively. The parent group leader at the master teacher level has the ability to blend support with content and intervention for group members. Teaching skills also evolve from a basic understanding of adult learning and session design to the ability to informally assess parent needs and styles of learning and match appropriate teaching methods to these needs. The master teacher level also includes parent educators who use creative and varied strategies to engage parents and to facilitate their learning. At times experienced parent educators use a very limited repertoire of methods that feel safe and comfortable to them. They design sessions in the same way for every topic. They begin with a short brainstorm of issues, go on to a minilecture with content material, and finally introduce a small-group discussion of three to four important points. The master teacher continues to ask, "How do I improve my session on self-esteem?" and explores new ideas and strategies for teaching parents. He or she also continues to create and evaluate different theoretical models of teaching.

The professional identity and self-awareness of parent educators also change over time in some predictable ways. New parent educators have limited understanding of their impact on parents and are often uncertain about their own skills as parent educators. As their professional identity develops, however, they begin to understand their own values and biases. They are able to set clear boundaries for their practice. They also are able to begin to mentor other professionals and articulate important insights and effective practices. They are more confident about their skills, as well as more aware of their limitations.

The final area of growth and development that is described in Table 11.1 concerns understanding diversity. Diversity issues within parent and family education are essential for parent educators to understand. Novice parent educators start with a basic awareness and sensitivity about diversity. They often don't know how to integrate this understanding into their practice with families. As they work with families, their experience with and understanding of family diversity expands. Parent educators at the master teacher level embrace cultural and family diversity as a rich and powerful asset to a parent

Photo 11.1   Parent education practice is a complex blend of teaching and
facilitation skills.

group. They are able to address family differences respectfully and directly and
draw upon these differences to create a richer learning environment. When
they meet a parent in their group whose culture or family system is different
from that of other group members, they know how to use this as an opportunity to explore different ideas and practices in a respectful manner that can
benefit the whole group.

The growth process outlined in Table 11.1 begins to capture some of the
depth and breadth of knowledge and skills that parent educators are able to
develop over time if they are given the support and resources to continue to
grow and learn. The embeddedness of parent educators within other roles can
slow down the pace and direction of the growth that is described here. For
example, a social worker who facilitates parent education groups may develop
some of the facilitation skills but may not develop a better understanding of
teaching methods or may be limited in understanding child development. A
clear and direct focus on parent education as a primary professional identity
can support professional growth in a more balanced manner. The professional
identity also creates opportunities to develop and articulate artistry in the role
of parent educator.

Reflective Practice in Parent Education

The Alert Novices, the more reflective interns in this study, had a tendency to ask "why" questions—questions directed at the roots of problems and at the meanings of ideas and action.

—V. LaBoskey,
*Development of Reflective Practice:
A Study of Preservice Teachers*

Reflective practice has been a general term used to describe the attitudes and behaviors of practitioners in a variety of fields who continue to improve their own knowledge and skills and seek to understand how effective practice works (Dewey, 1933; Kirby & Paradise, 1992; LaBoskey, 1994; Palm, 1998; Schon, 1983). Reflective practice will be explored as a paradigm that supports professional growth and development in parent education. This section will introduce the various interpretations of reflective practice that have emerged during the last 20 years. Reflective practice has become a central paradigm in education and currently has a strong influence on preservice and in-service programs for early education, educational administration, and elementary and secondary education (LaBoskey, 1994). Reflective practice in parent education has been less visible and has not been discussed very often in professional literature on parent education (Palm, 1998). Auerbach (1968) described the complexity of group parent education and the need for balance of many competing factors and goals such as facts and feelings, individual and group focus, and general and specific information. Her insights into the complexity of parent education demonstrate an understanding of reflective practice and the complexity of the skills and knowledge base necessary for effective parent group facilitation.

The next section will examine the multiple meanings of reflective practice (LaBoskey, 1994). The history of reflective practice from Dewey (1933) to contemporary ideas (Dokecki, 1996; Schon, 1983, 1987) will be traced to describe the evolution of thinking about reflective practice. A definition of reflective practice for parent education will be outlined, and specific ideas for application to group parent education will be presented. Reflective practice is presented as a practical model to support professional development in parent education. The complexity of parent-child relations within diverse family systems makes parent education a good match for applying a reflective practice paradigm.

MULTIPLE MEANINGS OF REFLECTIVE PRACTICE

Reflective practice is a concept with many different dimensions that has been applied in various professional settings (Schon, 1987). The recent applications in the field of education are the most relevant to understanding how it can be applied to parent education. Confusion about reflective practice often stems from the integrative nature of the paradigm. This integration includes knowledge, values, attitudes, skills, and emotions (LaBoskey, 1994). The appeal of reflective practice is that it attempts to include so many different elements in trying to understand and improve practice. It also presents many different interpretations of how it can be implemented. The three elements of teacher competencies all come into play: dispositions/attitudes, knowledge/content, and skills/techniques. A subtle emphasis on one of these areas can change the tone and focus of reflective practice. On another level, LaBoskey (1994) identified three other dimensions of reflective practice: practical/technical, social/political, and moral/ethical. Although there may be wide agreement about the importance of these dimensions and different types of competencies, the application and focus of reflective practice are likely to end up on one area of competency and one dimension of content. For example, the focus on specific teaching skills and best practices as the content area is one combination that appeals to many practitioners. It helps to understand these broad parameters of reflective practice as a starting point for applying this paradigm to parent education.

Reflective practice is often traced back to Dewey (1933), who described it in a general way as a mode of thought that includes skepticism, perplexity, and mental difficulty. Reflective practice is an attempt to reduce the uncertainty and understand ambiguity by conducting a careful inquiry and searching for new understanding that can improve practice. Dewey understood the complexity of educational practice and the necessity of careful and reflective inquiry to address the complexity and manage the accompanying uncertainty. He had faith in the power of logic and the utility of thoughtful inquiry as the path to greater understanding and improved practice. He also described the basic dispositions that have become essential character traits for reflective practice. Dewey presents three basic attitudes that undergird reflective practice: open-mindedness, responsibility, and wholeheartedness.

Open-mindedness is the desire to know why and keep asking questions and looking at different perspectives to gain a deeper understanding. In parent education, this translates to listening to parents, researchers, and peers to gain a more complete understanding about the complexity of parenting and parent education practice. Responsibility is a sense of social commitment to improving the field, family life, and society by understanding the long-term impacts of practice. The final disposition is wholeheartedness, which represents a passion that allows educators to take risks and follow their ideals and ethics in the face of criticism and tradition. Dewey's ideas about reflective practice represent his ideals about education and reflect some of the basic principles of progressive education. They continue to have meaning and relevance to education and can be applied to parent education in a fresh and meaningful way.

The reemergence of reflective practice in the 1980s (Schon, 1983, 1987) was in response to the increasing awareness of complexity and uncertainty in society and in professional practice. Schon questioned scientific research as the only way to inform practice and solve real-world problems and made a strong case for increased understanding of and appreciation for the artistry of practitioners in a variety of professional fields. The gap between research, theory, and practice has been traced back to professionalization in the beginning of the twentieth century (Schon, 1987). Schon described the real world of the late twentieth century as a "swampland" with messy and confusing problems that were a poor match with the traditional approaches of academic research and theory, which tended to outline clear-cut rational-technical solutions. In addressing problems in real society and real families, practitioners face complexity, change, and value conflicts. Family life in the late twentieth and early twenty-first centuries seems to reflect the characteristics of Schon's swampland: increasing diversity, complexity, and fragility. Schon's focus on trying to understand the artistry of the practitioner who faces the "swampland" problems and makes progress is also relevant to the field of parent education. Our increasing research knowledge base regarding child development and family dynamics has not always informed the practice of parent education or interfaced with the real problems that parent educators face in working with complex and fragile family systems. At the same time that Schon (1987) acknowledged the artistry and intuitive understanding of practitioners, he supported the reconnection of academic research and practice in a spirit of mutual respect and collaboration (Palm, 1998).

Dokecki (1996) explored reflective practice within human service professions and added some important ideas to our understanding. He introduced the term *ethical reflective generative practice*. In his model, all practice in human services is grounded in the ethical principle of promoting the common good. Dokecki also connected his idea of reflective practice to generative theory, "where the practitioner is an inquirer who pursues the development of theory to improve the human condition according to rationally chosen values" (Palm, 1998, p. 9). Dokecki's contribution to reflective practice includes (a) the clear focus on the ethical nature of practice; (b) the connection to generative developmental theory with a clear sense of long-term outcomes; and (c) the emphasis on practitioner-client relationship as a collaborative partnership in solving problems. This model also can be applied to parent education practice and provides both clarity and specific direction for reflective practice.

Palm (1998) applied a number of important ideas from reflective practice to parenting programs for fathers. These ideas can also be applied to the broader field of parent education. The specific characteristics can be adapted for parent educators.

Photo 11.2   Parent educators engage in reflective practice as they meet regarding challenges of group facilitation.

1. The reflective practitioner recognizes the ethical nature of working with parents and families.

2. The reflective practitioner maintains a clear focus on the goal of enhancing human growth and development in both parents and children.

3. The reflective practitioner takes responsibility for establishing collaborative relationships with parents and researchers to improve practice.

4. The reflective practitioner takes responsibility for continuing to develop technical expertise based on theory, research, and practice.

5. The reflective practitioner understands the critical role of artistry/intuition in parent education practice and works to articulate and enhance this artistry. (Adapted from Palm, 1998)

This description serves as both an operational definition and as a model for reflective practice in parent education. The next step is to describe what reflective practice looks like in action in parent education.

REFLECTIVE PRACTICE IN ACTION

Reflective practice provides many opportunities to enhance professional growth and development in parent education. A basic theme or thread that runs through the descriptions of reflective practice is assessment, which includes self-assessment, group process assessment, and outcome assessment. Assessment as a theme includes creative/intuitive thinking, technical skills, and ethical dimensions of practice and professional development in parent education.

Self-Assessment

Self-assessment is a starting place, especially for the beginning parent educator. Self-assessment can help the beginning parent educator focus on his or her own knowledge, dispositions, and skills. The checklist introduced in Appendix A is an example of a self-assessment tool that can be used to identify technical skills and help a parent educator identify specific group facilitation skills to practice and refine. Reflective practice for beginning parent educators includes a number of possible methods to assist with self-assessment. A parent session can be videotaped to provide a detailed record of group facilitation skills for critical analysis. This analysis should be guided by focusing on a limited number of specific technical skills. For example, the parent educator may want to focus on listening and attending skills. The videotape of the session can capture both verbal and nonverbal behaviors that demonstrate different listening and attending skills. A video analysis is one assignment that student teachers in parent education classes complete that includes a written report focusing on specific skills and how they were demonstrated in a parent education session.

Self-assessment can also include peer or supervisory observations. These can address technical skills around teaching and group facilitation, as well as ethical issues. A careful observation by another parent educator can help to affirm skills and offer insights and another perspective of parent–parent educator interactions within a specific session. Peer observation as a means of self-assessment can also focus on more advanced skill sets as parent educators move beyond the beginning levels of competence and start to integrate more advanced skills. It is most helpful to focus on specific skills or issues when an observation by a peer or supervisor is planned. This focus provides more direct and specific feedback. It also requires the parent educator to carefully define and focus on his or her own skills and areas of concern.

Another form of self-assessment can include parent group feedback on the class. The more specific and focused the questions that are posed to the parents, the more useful their responses will be. Student teachers working in parent education often create a short questionnaire to give to a group of parents at the end of their student teaching experience. This helps the students get direct feedback from the parents about their developing skills. It provides affirmation of their strengths and possible areas to focus on for further development.

Keeping a journal is another common form of self-assessment. Student teachers are often asked to keep a journal of their experiences and observations. Journal writing should also be focused not only on descriptions but also on analysis of difficult moments. Journals are an effective form of self-reflection and can provide some insight into our own feelings and reactions as well as stimulating new ideas to try as we address some specific concerns. A journal can be used by the experienced parent educator to focus on a specific group that may be more challenging. It allows the parent educator to reflect on the group dynamics more carefully and systematically. This may help the parent educator to more carefully assess different strategies and how parents respond.

Self-assessment is important for both beginning and master-level parent educators. There are several ways to assess practice skills. Most parent educators tend to work alone with parent groups or individual parents. Parent satisfaction surveys that include specific questions about practice skills can provide useful feedback. For example, a question like "How did the parent educator show sensitivity to your needs?" can elicit the parents' perceptions about parent educator sensitivity as a specific skill area. Parent educators also benefit from supervisor and/or peer observation and debriefing of a parenting session. The motivation for self-assessment comes from a strong desire to understand and improve practice through fine-tuning or developing new group process skills.

Assessment of Group Dynamics and Parent Learning Styles

A second area of assessment focuses on the parent group and on examining group dynamics in systematic ways. One simple measure of group dynamics is an observation of frequency of participation by different group members. This type of assessment can be completed by asking a supervisor or peer to observe the class and record the number of times each person in the group talks. Parent educators usually know which parents are most and least involved in discussion but may gain a more objective perspective on how a group is functioning by this simple type of group assessment. At another level of sophistication is the observation of specific task and maintenance functions that each group member fulfills during a specific session. This may be done by audio- or video-taping a session and analyzing the interactions by reviewing the tape. It also can be done by a peer or supervisor who comes to observe the class. This can provide more information about specific parents and point out some of the group's strengths and some potential problems. The assessment of parent learning styles through a parent group activity is described in Chapter 6. The awareness of different styles through an informal assessment process with parents provides a topic to increase parent awareness of different styles as well as greater self-understanding. The benefit for the parent educator is having a clearer picture of learning styles in a group and specific ideas for methods to use to engage the different learners in the group.

A final assessment of group process can come from a midterm evaluation of the class with some specific questions that focus on group dynamics and individual parents' perceptions of their own engagement in the group process. Ongoing observation of group dynamics is an essential part of facilitating parent groups. The assessment ideas outlined here can provide some additional information for monitoring and intervening as necessary in group process.

ACTION RESEARCH: ASSESSMENT OF PROGRAM OUTCOMES

Action research in this context refers to parent educators defining important questions about practice that they want to address more systematically. For example, Van Nostrand (1993) raised some interesting issues about gender and group interaction patterns. In the context of parent education groups, do men tend to display patterns of either dominance or withdrawing from and discounting of the group? Most parent groups are predominantly mothers, but as more fathers participate, different patterns of group dynamics will occur. Will men and women in the context of group parent education display more collaborative relationships, or will more traditional gendered group dynamics characterize parent groups? A research project could evolve from these questions that leads a group of parent educators to decide to observe a number of classes and record patterns of interaction that they see occurring in mixed-gender groups versus father-only or mother-only groups. They could then work with a researcher to develop a coding system for recording group interactions. Such action research may help illuminate group dynamics and improve practice in this area.

Collaborative action research may also focus on parent and child outcomes. Parent educators have been uncertain about how to approach the assessment of changes in parenting skills and attitudes. Measuring parent education program efficacy is neither simple nor easy. Our concerns with diverse values and beliefs about parenting practices create a complex situation for both researchers and parent education practitioners. The pressure from funding sources to provide empirical evidence of success or change is moving parent educators to look more carefully at outcome questions. This is an ideal opportunity for researchers and practitioners to cooperate in defining realistic goals and indicators of progress. One of the authors has been involved in developing a staff observation measure of adult growth and development in family literacy programs. The measure was developed by asking experienced staff to describe growth trajectories that they have observed in parents who have been in their programs for extended periods of time (some up to 3 years). The

Box 11.1   Parent Education and Reflective Practice

1. Self-Reflection
   a. Keeping a journal about a specific class
   b. Videotape analysis of a specific session
   c. Curriculum writing as a way to share ideas
   d. Self-assessment checklist

2. Parent Perspectives
   a. End-of-the-year evaluations: parent satisfaction with program components.
   b. Parent self-assessments of changes
   c. Parent responses to parenting situations/critical incidents
   d. Parent journals: experiences with application of new ideas

3. Peer Perspectives
   a. Critical conversations with peers about group process issues
   b. Peer observations: focus on specific issue or skill to observe
   c. Guided discussions about ethical issues
   d. Observations of other programs and parent groups

4. Research Perspectives
   a. Teachers as researchers: define projects to address important practice issues
   b. Evaluation research: participate in defining and assessing parent and child outcomes
   c. Reading about theory and application to a specific group
   d. Review literature on a specific topic to integrate recent findings in an area.

measure examines a general set of parenting skills that includes nurturing, setting limits, and parent-child play interactions. In each of these areas, staff described four to five developmental steps that they had observed in parents who started with low parenting skills and improved these skills as they moved through the program. This measure has been adopted by a number of programs to be used as an observation tool for staff to assess progress in parents.

Box 11.1 summarizes a variety of ways for parent educators to be engaged in reflective practice. The different perspectives allow parent educators to collaborate with peers, parents, and researchers in a variety of activities to both examine and improve practice. These different ideas provide opportunities for both individual professional growth and development and advancement of the field of parent education. This is not meant as an exhaustive list but as a list that is suggestive of the wide variety of activities that can be included in reflective practice. Parent educators can reflect on practice individually through self-assessment and also collaboratively with peers, parents, and researchers, as indicated in Box 11.1.

REFLECTIVE PRACTICE AND ETHICAL ISSUES

The final area of reflective practice that we will explore is the development of ethical thinking and practice in parent education. Dokecki (1996) included ethical awareness as part of reflective practice. Increase in family diversity and greater sensitivity to cultural diversity create a social context where parent educators are more likely than ever to face ethical dilemmas in their day-to-day practice. The following situations are examples of these dilemmas:

• A mother in a parent group of middle-class mothers shares her new discipline tip of using liquid soap in her 4-year-old's mouth as a way to punish her for using bad words. The other parents respond positively.

• A group of Mexican American fathers have recently moved from another state. They are attending a family literacy program and begin to complain about the child abuse laws as unfair because they feel that these laws restrict their right to use physical punishment with their school-aged children when the children are misbehaving and really need to have strict discipline.

• A parent educator conducts a home visit with a family with a 9-month-old child who has been identified as a child with special needs based on delayed physical development. The parents are both deaf and want to raise this child as part of the deaf culture even though the child is not deaf. They are requesting that early intervention teachers and therapists limit their verbal interaction with the child so that she can be socialized into the deaf culture.

These situations provide some insight into possible ethical dilemmas that parent educators may face on a regular basis. The typical parent educator would want to resolve these dilemmas through good practice. A true ethical dilemma is a situation where there is conflict between two or more important principles or values that the profession embraces. For example, in the case of the deaf parent family, parent educators believe in the principles of respecting cultural beliefs and values, respecting parents' rights to practice alternative parenting practices and do no harm to children. This situation clearly points out the conflict between parent values and child well-being. There is no easy answer to this situation if the practitioner wants to equally honor all of the principles in which he or she believes.

Parent educators in Minnesota have developed a practical approach to ethical issues through the work of the Ethics Committee of the Minnesota Council on Family Relations (MCFR). This group has designed an approach to ethics that integrates three different ethical frameworks: (a) a principles approach that articulates important principles to guide interaction with parents and other groups; (b) a relational ethics approach that incorporates the understanding of relationships as the context for making ethical decisions; and (c) virtues ethics, which focuses on the moral character of the parent educator. These three approaches form the basis of a case study process for exploring difficult ethical situations in a group setting. MCFR (2000) has published a small booklet that carefully outlines this approach with examples of case studies. The process is outlined in Box 11.2.

Artistry and Intuition in Parent Education

We want to end the book with a model of the parent educator as artist. The notion of artistry seems to best capture the spirit and capability of master teachers in parent education. The parent educator as artist is involved in the creative process of combining group facilitation and educational skills. He or she relies on both the development of excellent technical skills and the use of creative intuition to guide parent groups in learning from and with each other. The parent educator as artist is able to flow with the group while managing the progress and direction of the group. Skilled practitioners (artists) in parent education make this work look easy. Parents are aware of the power of the group and also experience the wisdom of the parent educator, who models respect, care, humility, humor, and curiosity. We believe that reflective practice as described in this final chapter can help to support artistry in parent education. It should, in addition, be used to explore artistry in parent education to more clearly describe and map out the dimensions of excellence in practice. We are only beginning to understand and appreciate the value of genius in parent education.

Summary

The basic knowledge, skills, and dispositions of the beginning parent group leader are essential as a starting place for understanding professional development. We have seen many licensed parent educators move through predictable

---

Box 11.2   Ethics Case Study Process

This process is one way to examine a difficult ethical situation to help identify the potential ethical dilemmas and to generate possible ethical actions.

1. *Identification of Relationships:* Identify important relationships in the situation, using the program practitioner role as the focus point.

What is the relational field? What are the important relationships to consider in this case?

What is the primary relationship for the practitioner to address?

What do we know about this relationship—length, strength, etc.?

2. *Application of Principles:* Look over the list of principles that apply to the relationship. Decide which principles may be relevant to guiding behavior in this situation.

Which are the three or four most relevant principles? Why?

3. *Identification of Contradictions:*

What are the potential/actual contradictions among the relevant principles?

4. *Application of Virtues:* Consider the virtues of caring, prudence, and hope/optimism.

Which is most relevant? Why?

Are all virtues relevant to some degree?

5. *Consideration of Possible Actions:* Brainstorm possible action by parent and family educator, keeping in mind the relationship, the relevant principles, and the virtues.

6. *Selection of Action(s):* Select one action or combination of actions to act upon.

---

stages of growth and development. The professional development of parent educators as described in this chapter has three distinct stages. These stages begin to map out more specific areas of growth that have been observed in long-term parent educators.

Reflective practice, a pathway to individual professional growth and development in a variety of fields, can be usefully applied to parent education. Several activities described in this chapter can be used by parent educators as reflective strategies. Reflective practice can assist the parent educator in improving technical skills, creating a better understanding of the complex nature of parent group dynamics, and more thoughtfully addressing ethical dilemmas.

The model of "parent educator as artist" offers a new way of thinking about and valuing the individual parent educator. Artistry in combining technical knowledge with facilitative and intuitive skills can be supported by reflective practice.

The field of parent education has grown and developed over the past 100 years, as described in this text. We believe that it has evolved into a unique profession that requires specific training from a variety of disciplines. As representatives from the field, we believe that parent education needs to continue its evolution and be recognized for the complex and technical profession that it has become.

Under ideal circumstances, it would not be acceptable to continue adding parent education to the job descriptions of other professionals. Although nurses, psychologists, social workers, teachers, and others bring valuable information and skills to the field, their primary focus is on the physical or mental health of adults, education of children, or assistance for families in accessing resources. Parent educators should be trained specifically with an interdisciplinary understanding of child development, parenting strategies, family systems, adult education, and group facilitation.

In reality, parent education is practiced by a variety of professionals in diverse settings. Many of these professionals have training and backgrounds of enough depth to successfully facilitate parent education and support groups. The contributions of these professionals to the field of parent education should not be minimized. However, to move the profession beyond a focus on either support or education, we need to promote programs that provide extensive training and preservice learning opportunities that blend the skills and expertise of both approaches. Professionally trained parent educators need to learn about working with parents in groups that are educational and supportive. Teaching skills as well as helping skills should be combined so that parent educators can move from presenting information to meeting the diverse needs of groups of parents. It is no longer sufficient to offer parents learning opportunities that provide primarily support or education. It is no longer acceptable to present parent education experiences that do not adhere to the high standards mandated by other professions.

We believe the information in this text will be valuable to any professional who works with parents in groups. Additionally, it will provide insight and strategies for those without specific training in group parent education. It is our hope that for anyone who works with parents in groups, the information will substantiate our view that parent education is a viable profession of worth and merit. We hope that this perspective will challenge other helping professionals, as well as those with limited training, to continue to explore the field and grow in their professional development and practice of group parent education.

Discussion Questions

1. Use Table 11.1 to assess your current level of expertise in parent education. What are areas of strength, and what are some areas that are still under development?

2. Describe the advantages of applying reflective practice to the field of parent education.

3. Outline a possible research question that would be an important action research project for group parent education.

Appendix A

Parent Group Leader Competencies:
A Self-Assessment Checklist

Instructions: Review each item in each of the three major areas and rate yourself from 1 (Not developed) to 5 (Exemplary).

Knowledge: This area outlines knowledge that is specifically related to understanding group dynamics and facilitating parent learning in a group context

_____ 1. Understanding the developmental stages of group process as this applies to parent groups.

_____ 2. Understanding different theories of group dynamics and their applications to parent groups.

_____ 3. Understanding the roles and boundaries of the parent group leader.

_____ 4. Understanding the emotional nature of parenting issues and how this influences parent group learning.

_____ 5. Understanding different leadership styles and their effects on parent group behavior.

_____ 6. Understanding multiple ways to assess parent and family strengths and limitations in the context of parent groups.

_____ 7. Understanding a variety of active learning methods to assist parents in solving problems and making decisions.

_____ 8. Understanding and being aware of various community resources for parents and families and how to connect parents to these resources.

_____ 9. Understanding family and community diversity and how diverse values and beliefs influence parenting behavior as well as parent group dynamics.

Dispositions: This category of competencies refers to character traits and emotional attitudes that have been identified as important for parent educators

(Auerbach, 1968; Braun et al., 1984; Clarke, 1984). These are different from general personality traits or types such as introvert and extrovert. Each individual will have his or her own unique blend of these dispositions.

_____ 1. *Maturity:* Parent group leader is clear about his or her own identity and able to clearly focus on the needs and issues of parents in the group.

_____ 2. *Caring:* Parent group leader is able to focus on the needs of parents and demonstrate understanding, compassion, and support for parents.

_____ 3. *Nonjudgmentalness:* Parent group leader appreciates the complexities of parenting and accepts parents without blaming them for their problems or mistakes. The focus is on helping parents and understanding that there are no easy answers.

_____ 4. *Sensitivity:* Parent group leader is able to perceive and respond to individual parents' needs and feelings.

_____ 5. *Organization:* Parent group leader is able to express goals clearly and provide direction toward parent learning.

_____ 6. *Flexibility:* Parent group leader is able to change direction as needed and balance between individual and group needs of parents.

_____ 7. *Creativity:* Parent group leader is able to design interesting and engaging parent sessions.

_____ 8. *Enthusiasm/Optimism:* Parent group leader has a positive attitude about people and the subject matter and is able to excite parents about learning.

_____ 9. *Honesty:* Parent group leader is clear about his or her own knowledge and limitations.

_____ 10. *Genuineness:* Parent group leader is honest and open in his or her relationships with parents.

_____ 11. *Humor:* Parent group leader is able to appreciate and express what is humorous without ridiculing people or their problems.

Skills: These are presented in general areas followed by very specific behavioral indicators of each general skill area.

1. **Creates a warm and welcoming environment.**
    _____ a. Greets each parent or family member in a welcoming manner.
    _____ b. Demonstrates a genuine interest in parent and child well-being.
    _____ c. Uses effective openings for a session—involves parents in an engaging and nonthreatening manner.

2. **Creates a safe environment for parents to share ideas and feelings.**
   _____ a. Helps group establish and implement ground rules.
   _____ b. Elicits a variety of opinions, values, and philosophies from parents.
   _____ c. Affirms parents in a genuine and supportive manner.

3. **Guides a discussion, giving it form and structure.**
   _____ a. Informs parents of agenda and goals for the session.
   _____ b. Helps parents identify needs and concerns.
   _____ c. Keeps the group focused on the group goals and the topic of discussion.
   _____ d. Asks clarifying questions to better understand parent issues.
   _____ e. Restates and clarifies parent ideas/issues.
   _____ f. Summarizes important ideas/issues.

4. **Models acceptance of each individual as someone to be listened to and respected.**
   _____ a. Listens carefully to parents.
   _____ b. Gives nonverbal messages of acceptance.
   _____ c. Accepts and acknowledges negative feelings and distress.
   _____ d. Restates and/or acknowledges parent contributions to the discussion.
   _____ e. Addresses diversity and facilitates discussion around differences in values, culture, and family structure.

5. **Takes responsibility for establishing a positive and supportive learning environment.**
   _____ a. Helps parents to identify and set their own goals.
   _____ b. Invites parent participation using a variety of methods.
   _____ c. Challenges parents to evaluate and reconsider their ideas.
   _____ d. Uses concrete examples to bring abstract concepts to life.
   _____ e. Adapts information to meet different parent capabilities.

6. **Fosters relationships and interaction among group members.**
   _____ a. Encourages participation of all of the group members.
   _____ b. Connects parent comments and experiences to point out common themes.
   _____ c. Engages the group in problem solving for individual group members.
   _____ d. Addresses conflict directly and respectfully.

Appendix B

National Organizations and Web Sites That Support Parent Education

Following is a list of national organizations that support the field of parent education through advocacy and information, along with their Web sites. Although there are many Internet Web sites currently available for parents, we have chosen those linked to well-established organizations and associations that have succeeded in their mission to support families. This is not intended to be a comprehensive and complete list of resources; rather, it is provided as a starting point for students and professionals to access available information.

American Academy of Pediatrics is composed primarily of medical professionals dedicated to the attainment of optimal physical, mental, and social health and well-being for all infants, children, adolescents, and young adults.
   Web Site: www.aap.org

Child and Family Web Guide is designed by faculty at the Eliot-Pearson Department of Child Development at Tufts University for students, practitioners, and parents. It describes and evaluates Web sites that contain research-based information about child development.
   Web Site: www.cfw.tufts.edu

Educational Resource Information Center (ERIC)–Elementary and Early Childhood Education (EECE) provides a clearinghouse of information on elementary and early childhood education for educators, parents, and families interested in the development, education, and care of children from birth through early adolescence.
   Web Site: www.ericeece.org

Families and Work Institute provides data to inform decision making on the changing workplace, changing family, and changing community. Publications on work and family issues are available.
Web Site: www.familiesandwork.org

Family Support America provides family support as the nationally recognized national movement to strengthen and support families. Links and resources for topical family support issues are provided.
Web Site: www.familysupportamerica.org

The Future of Children is sponsored by the David and Lucile Packard Foundation. It provides research and analysis to promote effective policies and programs for children.
Web Site: www.futureofchildren.org

Minnesota Early Learning Design (MELD) works to enhance the capacity of those who parent to raise nurtured, competent children by providing resource publications and trainings for practitioners.
Web Site: www.meld.org

National Association for the Education of Young Children is dedicated to improving the quality of programs for children from birth through third grade. Brochures for parents and professionals are available; information about policy and legislation, research reports, and critical issues are addressed.
Web Site: www.naeyc.org

National Center for Family Literacy provides training for educators, information on research-based effective practice, and literacy research and raises awareness of the educational needs of both children and parents.
Web Site: www.famlit.org

National Council on Family Relations provides a forum for family researchers, educators, and practitioners to share in the development and dissemination of knowledge about families and family relationships, establishes professional standards, and works to promote family well-being.
Web Site: www.ncfr.org

National Parent Information Network: The mission of this organization is to provide access to research-based information about the process of parenting and about family involvement in education. It is a project of the ERIC system.
Web Site: www.npin.org

National Parenting Education Network is committed to advancing the field of parent education by facilitating linkages among practitioners, knowledge development in the field, and professional growth and leadership.
Web Site: www.npen.org

Zero To Three supports parents and professionals in a multidisciplinary focus on infant and family professionals, medicine, mental health, research, science, child development, and education related to the first few years of life.
Web Site: www.zerotothree.org

References

Anderson, J. (1930). *Parent education: The first yearbook.* Washington, DC: National Congress of Parents and Teachers.

Arlitt, A. (1932). Parent education in the National Congress of Parents and Teachers. In National Congress of Parents and Teachers (Ed.), *Parent education: The second yearbook* (pp. 1–9). Washington, DC: National Congress of Parents and Teachers.

Auerbach, A. (1968). *Parents learn through discussion: Principles and practices of parent group education.* New York: John Wiley.

Bavelok, S. (Ed.). (1997). *Multicultural parenting.* Park City, UT: Family Development Resources.

Bavelok, S., & Bavelok, J. (1988). *Nurturing program for parents and children birth to five years: Parent handbook.* Eau Claire, WI: Family Development Resources.

Bennett, J., & Grimley, L. K. (2001). Parenting in the global community: A cross-cultural/international perspective. In M. J. Fine & S. W. Lee (Eds.), *Handbook of diversity in parent education* (pp. 97–132). San Diego, CA: Academic Press.

Berger, E. (2000). *Parent as partners in education* (5th ed.). Upper Saddle River, NJ: Merrill.

Blume, E. S. (1989). *Secret survivors: Uncovering incest and its aftereffects in women.* New York: Ballantine.

Bowman, T. (1982). Daring to confront . . . with care. *Vocational Parent and Family Newsletter,* no. 13, p. 2.

Bowman, T. (1987). Musings about group leadership: The quiet member. *FRC Report,* no. 2, pp. 16–17.

Bowman, T. (1994, February). Loss of dreams: A special kind of grief. In J. K. Comeau (Ed.), *Family Information Services professional resource materials.* Minneapolis, MN: Family Information Services.

Braun, L., Coplon, J., & Sonnenschein, P. (1984). *Helping parents in groups.* Boston: Resource Communications.

Brim, O. (1959). *Education for child rearing.* New York: Russell Sage Foundation.

Brizius, J., & Foster, S. (1993). *Generation to generation: Realizing the promise of family literacy.* Ypsilanti, MI: High Scope.

Brock, G. (1989, November). *Parenting program with parent-child interaction.* Paper presented at the annual meeting of the National Council on Family Relations, New Orleans, LA.

Broderick, C. B. (1993). *Understanding family process.* Thousand Oaks, CA: Sage.

Bronfenbrenner, U. (1978). Who needs parent education? *Teachers College Record, 4,* 767–787.

Bronfenbrenner, U. (1979). *The ecology of human development.* Cambridge, MA: Harvard University Press.

Campbell, D., Kristensen, N., & Scott, M. (1997). *Manual for implementing Levels 3 and 4 family involvement in early childhood family education.* Roseville: Minnesota Department of Children, Families, and Learning.

Canning, S., & Fantuzzo, J. (2000). Competent families, collaborative professionals: Empowered parent education for low-income African American families. In J. Gillespie & J. Primavera (Eds.), *Diverse families, competent families* (pp. 179–197). Binghamton, NY: Haworth.

Carter, N. (1996). *See how they grow: A report on the status of parenting education in the U.S.* Philadelphia: Pew Charitable Trusts.

Cheng Gorman, J., & Balter, L. (1997). Culturally sensitive parent education: A critical review of quantitative research. *Review of Educational Research, 67,* 339–369.

Clarke, J. I. (1984). *Who, me lead a group?* San Francisco: Harper & Row.

Cooke, B. (1992). *Changing times, changing families: Minnesota Early Childhood Family Education Parent Outcome Interview Study.* St. Paul: Minnesota Department of Education.

Corey, G. (2000). *Theory and practice of group counseling* (5th ed.) Pacific Grove, CA: Brooks/Cole.

Cormier, W. H., & Cormier, S. (1998). *Interviewing strategies for helpers.* Monterey, CA: Brooks/Cole.

Cowan, C. P., & Cowan, P. A. (1988). Who does what when parents become partners: Implications for men, women, and marriage. *Marriage and Family Review, 13,* 105–132.

Cowan, P. A., Powell, D., & Cowan, C. P. (1998). Parenting interventions: A family systems perspective. In I. E. Sigel & K. A. Renninger (Eds.), *Handbook of child psychology: Vol. 4. Child psychology in practice* (pp. 3–72). New York: John Wiley.

Crary, E. (1993). *Without spanking or spoiling.* Seattle, WA: Parenting Press.

Curran, D. (1983). *Traits of a healthy family.* Minneapolis, MN: Winston.

Curran, D. (1989). *Working with parents.* Circle Pines, MN: American Guidance Service.

Darling, S., & Hayes, A. (1989). *Breaking the cycle of illiteracy: The Kenan Family Literacy Program.* Louisville, KY: William Kenan Jr. Charitable Trust Family Literacy Project.

Dembo, M., Sweitzer, M., & Lauritzen, P. (1985). An evaluation of group parent education: Behavioral, PET, and Adlerian programs. *Review of Educational Research, 55,* 155–200.

Demo, D., Allen, K., & Fine, M. (2000). *Handbook of family diversity.* New York: Oxford University Press.

Dewey, J. (1933). *How we think.* New York: D. C. Heath.

Dinkmeyer, D., McKay, G., & Dinkmeyer, M. (1989). *Early Childhood STEP.* Circle Pines, MN: American Guidance Service.

Dokecki, P. (1996). *The tragic-comic professional: Basic considerations for ethical reflective-generative practice.* Pittsburgh, PA: Duquesne University Press.

Doherty, W. J. (1995). Boundaries between parent and family education and family therapy. *Family Relations, 44,* 353–358.

Dunst, C., Trivette, C., & Deal, A. (1988). *Enabling and empowering families.* Cambridge, MA: Brookline.

Egan, G. (1994). *Exercises in helping skills.* Pacific Grove, CA: Brooks/Cole.

Ellison, J. (1997, Spring). Parent education: Models of inclusion. *Views,* pp. 14–15, 22.

Epstein, J. (1995, May). School/family/community partnerships: Caring for the children we share. *Phi Delta Kappan,* pp. 701–712.

Erickson, M. F., & Kurz-Riemer, K. (1999). *Infants, toddlers, and families: A framework for support and intervention.* New York: Guilford.

Family Resource Coalition. (1996). *Guidelines for family support practice.* Chicago: Author.

Fine, M., & Lee, S. D. (2000). *Handbook of diversity in parent education: The changing faces of parenting and parent education.* New York: Academic Press.

Forward, S. (1989). *Toxic parents.* New York: Bantam.

Gadsden, V., & Hall, M. (1995). *Intergenerational learning: A review of the literature.* Philadelphia: National Center on Fathers and Families, University of Pennsylvania.

Galinsky, E. (1987). *The six stages of parenthood.* Reading, MA: Addison-Wesley.

Goldenberg, I., & Goldenberg, H. (2000). *Family therapy: An overview.* Pacific Grove, CA: Brooks/Cole.

Hamner, T., & Turner, P. (1996). *Parenting in contemporary society.* Needham Heights, MA: Allyn & Bacon.

Hildebrand, V., Phenice, L., Gray, M, & Hines, R. (2000). *Knowing and serving diverse families.* Upper Saddle River, NJ: Prentice-Hall.

Hills, M., & Knowles, D. (1987). Providing for personal meaning in parent education programs. *Family Relations, 36,* 158–162.

Independent School District 742 Parent-Child Program. (1993). *PAT educator's manual.* St. Cloud, MN: Independent School District 742 Community Schools.

Johnson, D., & Johnson, F. (1975). *Joining together: Group theory and group skills.* Englewood Cliffs, NJ: Prentice Hall.

Johnson, L., & Palm, G. (1992). *Working with fathers: Methods and perspectives.* Stillwater, MN: nu ink.

Karen, R. (1998). *Becoming attached.* New York: Oxford University Press.

Kirby, P., & Paradise, L. (1992). Reflective practice and effectiveness of teachers. *Psychological Reports, 70,* 1057–1058.

Klinman, D., & Kohl, R. (1984). *Fatherhood USA.* New York: Garland.

Konen, D. (1992). Women facilitators. In L. Johnson & G. Palm (Eds.), *Working with fathers: Methods and perspectives* (pp. 113–128). Stillwater, MN: nu ink.

Kristensen, N. (1984). *A guide for developing early childhood and family education programs.* White Bear Lake, MN: Minnesota Curriculum Services Center.

Kristensen, N. (1990, January). Parenting in the dark. In J. K. Comeau (Ed.), *Family Information Services professional resource materials.* Minneapolis, MN: Family Information Services.

Kristensen, N. (1991). *A sampling of parenting issues that affect adult children of dysfunctional families.* Unpublished paper.

Kumpfer, K., & Alvarado, R. (1998, November). Effective family strengthening interventions. *Juvenile Justice Bulletin,* pp. 1–15.

Kurcinka, M. S. (1989*). Raising your spirited child.* New York: Harper Perennial.

Kurz-Riemer, K. (Ed.). (2001). *A guide for implementing early childhood education programs.* Roseville: Minnesota Department of Children, Families and Learning.

LaBoskey, V. (1994). *Development of reflective practice: A study of preservice teachers.* New York: Teachers College Press.

Levine, J., & Pitt, E. (1995). *New expectations: Community strategies for responsible fatherhood.* New York: Families and Work Institute.

Long, N. (1997). Parent education/training in the USA: Current status and future trends. *Clinical Child Psychology and Psychiatry, 2,* 501–515.

McBride, A. B. (1973). *The growth and development of mothers.* New York: Barnes & Noble.

McBride, B. (1989). Stress and fathers' parental competence: Implications for family life and parent educators. *Family Relations, 38,* 385–389.

McBride, B. A. (1990). The effects of a parent education play group program on father involvement in childrearing. *Family Relations, 39,* 250–256.

McBride, B. A. (1991). Parental support and parental stress: An exploratory study. *Early Childhood Research Quarterly, 6,* 137–149.

McGillicuddy-DeLisi, A. V. (1990). Parental beliefs within the family context: Development of a research program. In I. E. Sigel & G. H. Brody (Eds.), *Methods of family research: Biographies of research projects: Vol. 1. Normal families* (pp. 53–85). Hillsdale, NJ: Lawrence Erlbaum.

McGuire, S. (1994). *Professional boundaries: Keeping clients' needs first.* Center City, MN: Hazelden.

McKenry, P., Clarke, K., & Stone, G. (1999). Evaluation of a parent education program for divorcing parents. *Family Relations, 48*(2), 129–137.

Medway, F. (1989). Measuring the effectiveness of parent education. In M. Fine (Ed.), *The second handbook on parent education* (pp. 237–256). San Diego, CA: Academic Press.

Minnesota Council on Family Relations. (2000). *Ethical thinking and practice for parent and family educators.* St. Paul, MN: Author

Minnesota Department of Education. (1995). *Level Three skills and common mistakes: A training tape for parent and family educators* [Video]. Crystal, MN: Robbinsdale Early Childhood Family Education.

Minnesota Early Learning Design. (2002). Who do MELD programs serve and how do they work? Retrieved January 8, 2003, from www.meld.org/program.cfm?Page ID = 1700.

Moore, A. R., & Clement, M. J. (1998). Effects of parenting training for incarcerated mothers. *Journal of Offender Rehabilitation 27*(1/2), 57–72.

Mueller, M. R. (2000, June 28). *Insights from Minnesota's early childhood community: Summary report of group interviews about program and service integration.* Roseville, MN: Minnesota Department of Children, Families, and Learning.

National Center on Fathers and Families, University of Pennsylvania. (1995). *Core learnings.* Philadelphia: Author.

National Parenting Education Network. (1999). About NPEN. Retrieved January 8, 2003, from www.ces.ncsu.edu/depts/fcs/npen/aboutnpen.html.

Newman, P. R., & Newman, B. M. (1988). Parenthood and adult development. In R. Palkovitz & M. Sussman (Eds.), *Transitions to parenthood* (pp. 313–338). New York: Haworth.

Olson, D. H., & DeFrain, J. (2000). *Marriage and the family.* Mountain View, CA: Mayfield.

Palkovitz, R., & Palm, G. (1998). Fatherhood and faith in formation: The developmental effects of fathering on religiosity, morals and values. *Journal of Men's Studies, 7*(1), 33–52.

Palm, G. (1992). Building intimacy and parenting skills through father-child activity time. In L. Johnson & G. Palm (Eds.), *Working with fathers: Methods and perspectives* (pp.79–100). Stillwater, MN: nu ink.

Palm, G. (1993). Involved fatherhood: A second chance. *Journal of Men's Studies, 2*(2), 139–155.

Palm, G. (1997). Promoting generative fathering through parent and family education. In A. J. Hawkins & D. C. Dollahite (Eds.), *Generative fathering: Beyond deficit perspectives* (pp. 167–182). Thousand Oaks, CA: Sage.

Palm, G. (1998). *Developing a model of reflective practice for improving fathering programs.* Philadelphia: National Center for Fathers and Families.

Palm, G. (2001). Parent education for incarcerated fathers. In J. Fagan & A. Hawkins (Eds.), *Clinical and educational interventions with fathers* (pp. 117–141). New York: Haworth.

Palm, G., & Palkovitz, R. (1988). The challenge of working with new fathers: Implications for support providers. In R. Palkovitz & M. Sussman (Eds.), *Transitions to parenthood* (pp. 357–376). New York: Haworth.

Payne, R. K. (1998). *A framework for understanding poverty.* Highlands, TX: RFT.

Peterson, M. R. (1992). *At personal risk: Boundary violations in professional client relationships.* New York: Norton.

Pfannenstiel, J., Lambson, T., & Yarnell, V. (1996). *The Parents as Teachers Program: Longitudinal follow-up second wave study.* Overland Park, KS: Research and Training Associates.

Powell, D. (1986). Matching parents and programs. In J. Parsons, T. Bowman, J. Comeau, R. Pitzer, & G. S. Schmitt (Eds.), *Parent education: State of the art* (pp. 1–11) White Bear Lake: Minnesota Curriculum Services Center.

Powell, L., & Cassidy, D. (2001). *Family life education: An introduction.* Mountain View, CA: Mayfield.

Rothenberg, A. (1992). *Parentmaking educator training program.* Menlo Park, CA: Banster.

St. Pierre, R., Layzer, J., & Barnes, H. (1995). Two generation programs: Design, cost and short term effectiveness. *The Future of Children: Long-Term Outcomes of Early Childhood Programs, 5*(3), 76-93.

St. Pierre, R. G., Swartz, J. P., Gamse, B., Murray, S., Deck, D., & Nickel, P. (1995). *National evaluation of Even Start Family Literacy Program: Final Report.* Cambridge, MA: Abt Associates.

Satir, V. (1972). *Peoplemaking.* Palo Alto, CA: Science and Behavior Books.

Schon, D. (1983). *The reflective practitioner: How professionals think in action.* New York: Basic Books.

Schon, D. (1987). *Educating the reflective practitioner.* San Francisco: Jossey-Bass.

Simpson, R. (1997). *The role of the mass media in parenting education.* Boston: Center for Health Communication, Harvard School of Public Health.

Smith, C. A., Cudaback, D., Goddard, H. W., & Myers-Walls, J. (1994). *National Extension parent education model.* Manhattan: Kansas Cooperative Extension Services.

Snarey, J. (1993). *How fathers care for the next generation: A four-decade study.* Cambridge, MA: Harvard University Press.

Sunley, R. (1955). Early nineteenth-century American literature on child rearing. In M. Mead & M. Wolfenstein (Eds.), *Childhood in contemporary cultures* (pp. 150–163). Chicago: University of Chicago Press.

Tannen, D. (1990). *You just don't understand.* New York: Ballantine.

Thomas, R. (1996). Reflective dialogue parent education design: Focus on parent development. *Family Relations, 45,* 189–200.

Thomas, R., & Cooke, B. (1986). Summary of profile of parent education study. In J. Parsons, T. Bowman, J. Comeau, & R. Pitzer (Eds.), *Parent education: State of the art* (pp. 19–26). White Bear Lake: Minnesota Curriculum Services Center.

Todres, R., & Bunston, T. (1993). Parent education program evaluation: A review of the literature. *Canadian Journal of Community Mental Health, 12*(1), 225–257.

Van Nostrand, C. (1993). *Gender-responsible leadership.* Newbury Park, CA: Sage.

Walsh, D. (2001). *Dr. Dave's cyberhood.* New York: Fireside.

Webster-Stratton, C. (2000, June). *The Incredible Years* training series. *Juvenile Justice Bulletin,* pp. 1–23.

Name Index

Subject Index

About the Authors

Deborah Campbell holds an M.S. degree in Parent Education and Counseling from St. Cloud (MN) State University. She has been a licensed parent educator for nearly 20 years and has facilitated a variety of parent education groups, including those with teen parents and others with complex issues. She is currently the Director of Early Childhood Family (ECFE) Programs for the Sauk Rapids–Rice (MN) school district. In this role she supervises and mentors licensed parent educators, as well as developing and overseeing educational programs that serve families with young children. She also teaches as an adjunct faculty member in the Child and Family Studies Department at St. Cloud State (MN) University, where she focuses on classes addressing group process and advanced facilitation skills in parent education. She works extensively with other parent education and support programs by providing staff training and consultation on professional boundaries, levels of involvement with families, collaboration, and other related topics for helping professions. She is a regular presenter at local and state conferences and trainings dealing with parent education issues. Additionally, she has coauthored a training manual on the levels of involvement and has written training curriculum for Minnesota's Department of Children, Families and Learning on team building, family literacy, and collaboration. She is the mother of two adult children, Ben and Elizabeth, who have provided her with many life lessons on parenting that inspired her interest and commitment to parent education. She lives with her husband, Larry, in St. Cloud, Minnesota.

Glen Palm has an M.S. degree in human development and family studies from the University of Connecticut and a Ph.D. in social and educational futures from the University of Minnesota. He has been a licensed parent educator for 25 years and also is a Certified Family Life Educator (CFLE). He is a Professor of Child and Family Studies at St. Cloud State University in St. Cloud, Minnesota. He teaches courses in child development, parent education, and parent involvement in early education and has supervised student teachers in the parent education licensure program for the past 15 years. In addition, he is a part-time parent educator and coordinates the Dads' Project in District 742 in St. Cloud. His major research and practice interest has been parent education with fathers. He has written extensively in this area as a coeditor of *Working With Fathers: Methods and Perspectives,* as a regular contributor to Family Information Services on fathers, and as an author of a number of chapters and articles on fathers. He also has worked with the Ethics Committee of the Minnesota Council on Family Relations to develop a set of guidelines for ethical thinking and practice for parent and family educators. He has served as an outside evaluator for Even Start Family Literacy and Early Head Start Programs in Minnesota since 1990. During the summer of 1996, he was a Visiting Scholar at the National Center for Fathers and Families. He has been a frequent presenter on fathering and parent education issues at the state and national levels for the past 10 years. He has held leadership positions with the Minnesota Council on Family Relations and the National Council on Family Relations. He has been a Board Member of the National Practitioners Network for Fathers and Families since 1998 and was a council member of the National Parenting Education Network. Currently, he is a member of the Minnesota Fathers and Families Leadership Network. He is also the father of three children, Marisha, Noah, and Allison. They have grounded him in the joys and challenges of daily life as a parent. In addition, Jane Ellison, his partner of 25 years, has been a colleague in parent education and a constant source of support, insight, and inspiration.